DATE DUE

THE SMART WOMAN'S
GUIDE TO
HEART
HEALTH

THE SMART WOMAN'S GUIDE TO

HEART HEALTH

DR. SARAH'S SEVEN STEPS
TO A HEART-LOVING LIFESTYLE

A Cardiologist's Holistic
Prescription for
Health, Energy, and Happiness

Sarah Samaan, M.D.

THE SMART WOMAN'S GUIDE TO HEART HEALTH
Dr. Sarah's Seven Steps to a Heart-Loving Lifestyle

To preserve patient confidentiality, patients' names and identifying characteristics have been changed. Any resemblance to actual persons is coincidental. The information in this book is not intended to take the place of medical advice from the reader's personal physician. Please consult with your physician or other health care professional before beginning any diet or health program. The author and publisher expressly disclaim responsibility for any adverse effects arising from the use or application of the information presented in this book.

Manufactured in the United States of America.

For information, please contact:
Brown Books Publishing Group
16200 North Dallas Parkway, Suite 170
Dallas, Texas 75248
www.brownbooks.com
972-381-0009

A New Era in Publishing™

Hardbound ISBN-13: 978-1-934812-13-6
Hardbound ISBN-10: 1-934812-13-7
Paperback ISBN-13: 978-1-934812-14-3
Paperback ISBN-10: 1-934812-14-5

LCCN: 2008936626
1 2 3 4 5 6 7 8 9 10

Dedicated with love and gratitude to my mother,

Dr. Jean Moffatt Samaan.

And to the memory of my father,

Dr. Naguib Samaan.

ACKNOWLEDGMENTS

When I first sat down to write this book, I had no idea what lay ahead of me. I have learned so much from the people who have encouraged and supported me along my way. I will be forever grateful to Dedie Leahy for seeing a spark of life in my first stilted manuscript. I am thankful she introduced me to Helen Bond, who helped me to find my voice as a writer. The entire staff at Brown Books has been incredibly supportive, especially Milli Brown, Kathryn Grant, Cindy Birne, and Cathy Williams. Thanks also to the terrific editorial staff, who helped to turn an overgrown manuscript into a full-fledged book.

In my practice of cardiology, I am fortunate to work with the fantastic physicians, nurses, and staff at Legacy Heart Center, my home away from home, and with my patients, who inspire me to learn something new every day.

And finally, my deepest thanks and love to Gary Cooper. Without your encouragement, patience, and confidence in me, I could never have made this book a reality.

CONTENTS

INTRODUCTION

A HEALTHY HEART BEGINS AT HOME

We women are smart people, whether we know it or not. We are nurturing and resilient to most anything that life throws our way. We multitask like mad, we love passionately, and we care and provide for our family and friends. We are also dying needlessly of heart disease, in numbers of epidemic proportion. It is time for us to take control and to recognize the power we have, as women, to prevent this devastating disease.

Thanks to modern medical research, we can identify the major factors that contribute to heart disease—high blood pressure, diabetes, high cholesterol, smoking, sedentary lifestyle, obesity, and genetics. But knowing our risk is not enough. Preventing heart disease must become a way of life—a commitment to an active lifestyle, an investment in a healthy diet, and a resolution to live mindfully, aware that all of our choices carry consequences.

Prevention is every bit as important for people who have never had heart problems as it is for those who have already suffered heart attacks and heart failure. We are all at risk for heart disease. And since heart disease often begins silently in our teen years, learning how to prevent it is essential for all of us—no matter our age.

As a cardiologist, I consider the prevention of heart disease to be my most important and most difficult duty. During a heart attack, when the heart muscle is abruptly cut off from vital blood flow and oxygen, my responsibility is clear and well defined: restore blood flow to preserve life. If you're my patient, your role in this situation is essentially passive. Usually, your only voice in the matter is to give me consent to treat your condition. While a heart attack may get my adrenaline flowing as I hop out of bed at three a.m. for another run to the hospital, I know that with appropriate and timely care, my medical teammates and I can usually quickly and effectively care for the problem. Prevention, however, takes much more dedication and hard work—and it must come from you.

DEALING WITH GENETICS

Ultimately, you are responsible for your own health. But when it comes to genetics and good old-fashioned luck, some of us are more fortunate than others. For our own sakes, and for those we love, we must play the best game we can with the cards that we are dealt.

My father, a physician, was an important inspiration for this book. His mother died at age 48 of a heart attack. She was obese and no doubt suffered from associated health problems, most of which would have gone unrecognized and untreated in her time. When she died, she left behind eight children.

While my spry and lean grandfather lived to the ripe old age of 90, it appeared my father would inherit my grandmother's genes, despite his relatively healthy lifestyle. As a child, I dreaded the sporadic, emotionally charged long-distance phone calls from my father's family as heart disease picked off his siblings one by one. A favorite uncle died on the way to my sister's wedding. A devastating heart attack took the life of another uncle, a heart surgeon, shortly after he left the hospital against his cardiologist's advice. All told, six out of eight beloved aunts and uncles have died—most before the age of 60. Most were obese. All but my father chose to live a sedentary lifestyle, scoffing at the idea of exercise.

My father was 64 when he suffered a stroke. He had high blood pressure, but would never take medicine for more than a few months or go for checkups. He believed he had everything under control. The stroke was debilitating, and he never found much joy in life afterwards. With his stroke came a diagnosis of diabetes, a condition that had probably gone undetected for years. He lived a sad and frustrating life for seven more years before succumbing to heart and kidney failure.

THE ROLE OF PREVENTIVE MEDICINE

My dad was not significantly overweight; he ate fairly well, and he was always physically active. That's probably why he had more time before his stroke. In his case, preventive medicine would have made an enormous difference. He would have been able to enjoy the retirement he worked so hard for, share his children's achievements, and revel in knowing his grandchildren. As a doctor, he knew better, but as a human being, he did not want to admit to being anything less than invincible. His death was a natural event, but one that I wish could have happened many years later. My dad's case is particularly poignant to me because so much of what happened to him was preventable and treatable.

My father became ill and died during my medical training. The sad progression of his illness gave me a deep appreciation of the power of prevention and of the terrible consequences we may pay for not acknowledging the vulnerabilities of our own bodies.

LESSONS FROM A VERY SMART WOMAN

I would be remiss if I did not mention my mother and her powerful influence upon my life choices. She is a British woman, now in her 70s, who grew up in a time when education was considered a luxury for a girl and not worth the expense.

Although her father, my grandfather, was considered the head of the household, he was an alcoholic and a small-time gambler. My grandmother ran the thriving family business, a restaurant and small hotel near the seashore. Of her five children, my mother was the only daughter; my grandmother, a very smart woman, was determined that she would have the independence and opportunities that her own life had not afforded.

To my grandmother, freedom meant an education. As fate would have it, my mother was an avid reader and was greatly influenced by what she read of physician, medical missionary, and musical scholar, Albert Schweitzer, the recipient of the Nobel Peace Prize in 1952. Her father and his cronies teased and ridiculed my mother, but she persevered and became the first in her family to attend a university. She graduated from medical school in 1957, intent on heading off to Africa to follow in Dr. Schweitzer's footsteps as a medical missionary. Somewhere along the way, she met my father, a darkly handsome and brilliant, but decidedly foreign, physician. Their mixed marriage alienated her family for years, but she was in love and determined to make it work.

One thing led to another, as it so often does, and before she knew it, she was a mother of five, living in Houston and practicing family medicine. Although our family was highly unconventional, the responsibility for child rearing still fell squarely on my mother's shoulders. It is a tribute to her love, devotion, and high expectations that we, her children, have all had the opportunity to pursue our own dreams in our own unique ways.

MY MOTHER'S WISDOM

During my father's long illness, my mom continued to work, but devoted the remaining time in her day to his care and comfort. After his death, she moved out to the country to live on a ranch that they had purchased together years before.

She now lives with a menagerie of ponies, donkeys, cows, dogs, cats, chickens, peacocks, and any other creatures who decide to call her place home. Even in retirement, she volunteers at a medical clinic for the homeless and underserved, teaching her brand of care and compassion to newly minted medical doctors-in-training.

I am profoundly grateful for the lessons taught me by my parents. While my father, like many doctors of his generation, never chose to accept the frailties of his own body until it was too late, he treated his patients with great care and respect. Years after his death, I am still deeply touched by the remembrances of his former patients.

My mother is truly a healer; she has touched thousands of lives and continues to make a difference for people who might otherwise go unnoticed. From both my parents, I have learned that there is much we can do as individuals to enrich our lives with good health. We must live life with love and zest and take care of the bodies that carry us through this ever-changing and often unpredictable world.

HONORING THE GIFT OF LIFE
BY LEARNING TO CARE FOR OURSELVES

An important part of caring for our bodies includes enlisting a supportive and skillful physician as a partner in health, to treat conditions that we can't control with healthy living alone and to assure that our efforts to achieve good health are successful.

Caring for ourselves also means listening closely to the messages our bodies give us. Outside of medicine, my passion is horses. We can take a cue from these strong and noble animals who, for all their beauty and strength, depend utterly on humans for their comfort and health. They must trust that their owners will make the right choices for them. When horse owners lack the appropriate knowledge to provide well for their animals, the outcome can be tragic.

We must learn to listen, to pay attention to our own complex and wonderful bodies, just as we would to such a magnificent creature entrusted to our care. That's how we honor the remarkable gift of life. It is not enough to make promises to do better. Caring for ourselves requires conscious action and daily commitment.

To begin the journey toward heart health, we must first equip ourselves with the proper tools, both mental and physical, and the knowledge to use them well.

My goal is to give you these tools and the know-how you need to be heart savvy. *The Smart Woman's Guide to Heart Health: Dr. Sarah's Seven Steps to a Heart-Loving Lifestyle* grew from my desire to teach my patients more than I could in the context of our office visits. I also approached this book as a tremendous opportunity to learn. Many of the sections within these pages came directly from questions patients posed to me. I began to look for a resource that addressed the issues of diet, exercise, vitamins, supplements, alternative treatments, traditional medicine, and other preventive measures in a scientifically rigorous, yet easily accessible fashion. When I didn't find it, I decided to take matters into my own hands. This book is the result.

The process of researching and writing this book has had a profound effect on my practice of cardiology. I have, in a sense, opened my own eyes. While I have always preached the mantra of "diet and exercise," I had not realized just how deeply our small habits and daily choices are connected to our health and to our well-being. I know that writing this book for you has made me a better doctor.

I often say that no one will ever call me to give thanks for not having the heart attack that fate might have given them, but preventing heart attacks in partnership with my patients is the most gratifying part of my job. It is my wish that *The Smart Woman's Guide to Heart Health* will create this same partnership with you for a healthy heart all life long.

STEP ONE

SMART WOMEN TAKE CHARGE OF THEIR NUMBERS

There is no such thing as a typical woman. We come in an endless variety of shapes, sizes, and colors, each of us with our own rich spectrum of passions, obsessions, and talents. But one thing we all share is a dependence on our marvelous bodies to take us through this life in good health.

The first step to a heart-loving lifestyle is to get a handle on some very personal statistics—body size, waist circumference, cholesterol, triglycerides, and other important measurements of heart health. These are numbers that can add or subtract years from your well-being. Take them personally.

1

Heart Disease and Women: The Road to a Healthy Heart Begins Here

Twenty-four hours a day, seven days a week, each minute in the United States, a woman dies of cardiovascular disease—the number one killer and the most important health risk that women face today.

Women fear breast cancer, and rightly so, but the fact is that more women die of heart disease and disease of the cardiovascular system than from all forms of cancer combined. Cardiovascular disease (CVD)—which includes heart attacks, high blood pressure, abnormal heart rhythms, stroke, atherosclerosis (cholesterol buildup in the blood vessels), and congestive heart failure—kills more than 480,000 women each year. That's more than ten times the number of women who die from breast cancer. For simplicity's sake, the terms "CVD" and "heart disease" will be used interchangeably throughout this book.

Thanks to massive public awareness campaigns, most women now know that heart disease is deadly, yet only 13% of us consider it our greatest personal health threat. We are simply not taking this message to heart. It is time we did.

Here's the Great News

Eighty-five percent of heart disease is preventable. You have the power to make the difference in your own life and in the lives of those you love. It is the choices you make and the chances you take each day that give you the power to live a longer, stronger, healthier, and happier life.

Clearing the Way:
Exposing the Dangerous Myths of Heart Disease

Smart women want the facts. So our road to heart power begins with blowing the roof off some of the most common heart disease myths, half-truths, and fallacies.

Myth No. 1: Heart disease is a man's problem.

Fact: Heart disease is far and away the leading cause of death of American women. Although we tend to develop it about ten years later in life than men, two out of every five women will die of disease of the cardiovascular system. Too many others will suffer serious disability or a lower quality of life.

Myth No. 2: Heart disease is for old people.

Fact: Heart disease is not an old-age malady. Fully half of all women's heart attacks occur before the age of 70, and each year, more than 8,000 American women under the age of 45 will suffer a heart attack. Tragically, younger women are more likely to ignore their heart attack symptoms and are more likely to die as a result.

Myth No. 3: Heart disease symptoms are the same for women and men.

In the movies, a man in the throes of a heart attack clutches his chest and collapses to the floor—his symptoms are dramatic and unequivocal. In real life, it may not be so clear-cut. In fact, heart disease often plays out differently for women.

Fact: Women's symptoms may be very different. When a heart attack strikes, women younger than 50 are more than twice as likely to die as men of the same age, in large part because they ignore their symptoms until it's too late.

The classic, textbook warning signs of heart disease can occur in both men and women: chest pain that sometimes radiates to the left arm or neck, clamminess, nausea, and shortness of breath. Usually the pain is brought on by exertion or stress. Only about 30% of women will experience chest pain symptoms, a typical red flag, in the month leading up to a heart attack, while more than 70% will suffer from unusual fatigue.

It is the more subtle signs that women are used to living with—tired, anyone?—that have us confused about heart disease symptoms and worried that we'll just end up looking silly if we go to the emergency room with our concerns.

Compared to men, women are more likely to have nausea, fatigue, neck and jaw pain, shoulder pain, and back pain and are less likely to break out in a cold sweat during a heart attack. Unexplained insomnia is another early symptom that is more common in women than in men.

In the throes of a heart attack itself, more than 40% of women will suffer no chest pain—although many will feel a sudden onset of shortness of breath or overwhelming weakness. These are not complicated differences, but women and their doctors can't ignore these symptoms just because they are not what we might consider typical.

Myth No. 4: Heart disease is usually inherited.

It's easy to blame our parents for our health woes, but the truth is only about 15% of heart disease can be blamed on genetics alone. We might inherit high blood pressure or high cholesterol, or a susceptibility to diabetes, but those are problems that can be managed with a combination of a healthy diet, regular exercise, and, when needed, medication.

Fact: Up to 85% of heart attacks are preventable. Obesity, smoking, lack of exercise, poor eating habits, and other unhealthy choices are major, but preventable, risk factors.

WOMEN'S ARTERIES MAY BE DIFFERENT

Women with heart disease are more likely than men to have arteries that appear "normal" when evaluated by cardiac catheterization. In that procedure, a thin plastic tube, or catheter, is inserted directly into the heart arteries and an iodine-based dye injected that can be seen on an X-ray movie or angiogram. Although apparently normal arteries are usually just that—normal—some women have such diffuse, evenly deposited cholesterol coating their arteries that the vessels appear smooth when they are actually loaded with cholesterol. These arteries might look ordinary, but they react abnormally to stress and are much more likely to close abruptly, causing a heart attack.

Although this uncommon pattern may also be seen in men, it is probably at least twice as likely to occur in women. The problem is that important heart disease may be missed in women, and so may the chance to prevent a life-threatening or life-altering heart attack.

Newer technology, including CT scans and MRIs, may be the key to detecting this type of heart disease in its earliest stages.

PREVENTION: IT'S A PERSONAL THING

Imagine a revolutionary medical breakthrough. Imagine a drug that could reduce the chances of having a heart attack by 60 to 75%.

This new therapy would boost your mood, make you appear more attractive, help you lose weight, liven up your sex life, lower your chances of developing other diseases, such as diabetes and certain forms of cancer, and reduce the risk of dementia and stroke. Moreover, it's all natural, nearly 100% safe, and basically free.

Who would refuse such an amazing treatment that would transform health care and save billions of dollars every year? The answer: most people in this country and maybe even you.

I'm not talking about complicated laboratory science or another fruitless search for the fabled fountain of youth. The key to combating heart disease is available right now. It's called prevention, and the key is lifestyle.

Cardiovascular disease starts its silent assault on the arteries of the heart and other organs decades before it shows up as a heart attack or stroke. Atherosclerosis, or buildup of cholesterol plaques in the arteries, begins as early as childhood. Small cholesterol plaques in the coronary arteries, which feed the heart its vital blood supply, can be found in more than 15% of "normal" American teenagers and in 85% of people over the age of 50.

A heart attack occurs when one or more of these arteries get blocked and blood can't reach the heart muscle. The blockage is usually due to an unstable cholesterol plaque within a heart artery that ruptures or cracks. The body treats this as an injury and tries to repair the disrupted cholesterol plaque. This process results in a blood clot forming inside the artery, abruptly blocking blood flow. Without blood and oxygen, the heart tissue literally begins to die and can no longer function as it did before the injury.

A heart attack generally occurs in a segment of the heart artery that is already damaged by years of slow, progressive cholesterol buildup. In most cases, a heart attack does not just "happen" at age 45, 60, or 75. It is a process, and it has been building for many years.

CALCULATING THE ROLE AND RISKS OF LIFESTYLE

A healthy lifestyle, including a heart-friendly diet, daily exercise, not smoking, and maintaining an optimum weight, will reduce cardiac risk by more than 60%.

Still, less than one in six women chooses to practice a healthful way of life. Close to 20% of women in this country use tobacco, dramatically increasing their chances of heart disease, stroke, cancer, and a myriad of other miseries. Younger women and teens continue to smoke at ever-higher rates.

Most women in this country are overweight, and the problem continues to grow as we sacrifice our health for fast food and sedentary entertainment. As a major contributor to high blood pressure, high cholesterol, and diabetes, weight is far more than a cosmetic issue.

Of course, serious medical conditions can develop under even the best of circumstances, thanks to our genetics. But the heartening news is that by working together with your doctor, you can often prevent and manage high cholesterol, diabetes, and high blood pressure. Live a healthy lifestyle, maintain a normal blood pressure, optimize cholesterol, and use medications when necessary, and you may reduce your cardiovascular risk by as much as 85%.

INHERITED RISK

Many of the risk factors that lead to heart disease are impacted by inherited conditions. I have learned in my practice as a cardiologist that bad luck is an unfortunate fact of life, and high cholesterol, high blood pressure, diabetes, and other serious health problems can develop in people who are absolutely committed to a healthy life style. However, a healthy diet and regular exercise, while perhaps not curative, can nearly always reduce the severity of the inheritable risk factors.

THE LIFESAVING MEDICINES

Many lifesaving medications are available to help treat these conditions and prevent heart disease and other long-term complications, such as kidney failure and stroke. Most have few serious side effects, although careful monitoring and regular follow-up are important. Yet, it is always preferable to avoid the need for medications whenever possible, or to take the least amount necessary to achieve the desired results. A healthy lifestyle combined with the appropriate medications when needed will dramatically improve your chances of living a longer, healthier, more fulfilling, and productive life.

A DAY IN THE LIFE OF HEART DISEASE

As a cardiologist, I see the results of an unhealthy lifestyle and untreated risk factors each day. We are fortunate to live in an era of sophisticated cardiac interventions and surgeries, but despite all our modern technology and lifesaving skills, we cannot cure the disease once it has started—we can only treat it. While your doctor can be a powerful ally, ultimately, the responsibility for prevention is yours.

To illustrate how prevention can save your life and the path that poor lifestyle habits can take you down, let me share with you a typical day in my life as a cardiologist.

At 7:15 a.m. I begin my rounds with 57-year-old Jim, who was hospitalized the night before with a severe heart attack in progress. Fortunately, Jim got to the hospital on time, and my on-call partner opened up a critical blockage in one of his major coronary arteries before any permanent damage was done. Jim smokes two packs of cigarettes a day, admits to drinking two gallons of coffee daily, doesn't exercise, and could stand to lose about 30 pounds.

Jim's father died of a heart attack at the age of 58, but Jim never thought it could happen to him. What he doesn't yet realize is that the process of atherosclerosis has been underway for the last thirty-five years, churning along as a consequence of innumerable unhealthy daily choices, combined with his unfortunate genetic makeup.

My next patient is a 48-year-old woman whose weathered face betrays her years of smoking. Sherry rides her bike regularly with her boyfriend, but recently noticed more shortness of breath and a strange ache in her back and arms. She tried not to worry, but when her symptoms got worse, she headed to the hospital for a checkup. Unfortunately, Sherry has already suffered a heart attack, probably a few days before she came to the hospital. Her heart muscle is working at about half its normal capacity. She swears to me that she will never smoke again. That's good, because another heart attack would probably kill her. She will need open-heart surgery before she leaves the hospital.

Later in the day, I see a 39-year-old woman who weighs more than 300 pounds. Sue is diabetic, has high blood pressure and high cholesterol, and worries about the chest pain she feels when she climbs the stairs to her third-floor apartment. We will schedule a stress test and hope that the results are good. However, I fear that Sue is already well on her way to developing heart disease. Even if the stress test is normal, I will urge her to work on prevention, and she will certainly need medication. Her high blood pressure, high cholesterol, and diabetes—a major risk factor for heart disease—may even resolve if she loses weight and exercises regularly.

In the office, Hank, one of my favorite patients, arrives for a routine visit. He is a charming 85-year-old gentleman who has endured two bypass operations and the loss of his beloved wife. With the help of a careful selection of medications and an active and optimistic outlook, he lives life to its fullest. In fact, his exercise stress test time is better than those of many seemingly healthy people half his age.

Carmella comes to see me about her blood pressure. She is 35 years old, pregnant with her third child, and never lost the 60 pounds she gained with her first two pregnancies. We have worked hard to control her hypertension, but she needs two drugs to keep it down and is seeing a high risk obstetric specialist to help her and her baby get through the pregnancy safely.

Tina, 66, is here at the urging of her family doctor. She has noted some breathlessness lately, but attributes it to her weight and lack of exercise. She was reluctant to take time off work for the appointment. I'm glad she did. Her electrocardiogram is troublesome, and she will need urgent evaluation with a cardiac catheterization.

The last patient of the day is 29-year-old Kendra, who has seen the ravages of heart disease in her own family. She started working out this year and has already lost 30 pounds. Her cholesterol was dangerously high—too high to treat with diet and exercise alone. She has responded beautifully to a low dose of cholesterol-lowering medicine, although she knows that when it comes time to start a family, the cholesterol medication must be put on hold because it can harm an unborn child.

Just one day brings a wide array of opportunities for prevention to make a tangible difference in so many lives.

HOW WE LEARNED THAT WOMEN ARE DIFFERENT

We owe a great deal of our understanding of heart disease, its causes, its effects, and its manifestations in women to the Nurses' Health Study. This long-term gold mine of research into women's health involves 121,700 female nurses who were 30 to 55 years old in 1976, when the study began. Harvard Medical School researchers have closely followed these women's health histories, with detailed lifestyle and dietary information.

The work continues to provide a wealth of information on heart disease and many other health issues pertaining to women. It was the Nurses' Health Study, for example, that reported that we could attribute the majority of heart attacks in women directly to lifestyle factors such as obesity, smoking, lack of exercise, and poor diet.

We are also indebted to numerous other groups, including the Iowa Women's Health Study of more than 30,000 women, the Women's Heath Initiative investigation of hormone therapies, and the Framingham Study, a fifty-year-and-counting project involving most of the residents of a small Massachusetts town. Volunteers in these studies have helped to advance our understanding of heart disease and women immeasurably.

WE'RE DOING SOMETHING ABOUT IT

Along with recent campaigns like National Wear Red Day, promoting awareness of heart disease prevention among women, the medical community is also stepping up its role to educate physicians, health care providers, and the public about women's specific heart-health concerns.

In 2004, the American Heart Association (AHA), with the participation of numerous other health care organizations, published its "Evidence-Based Guidelines for Cardiovascular Disease Prevention in Women," a true landmark document.

This publication, updated in 2007, emphasizes the importance of viewing heart disease as a process, or a continuum. The guidelines are based on the input of thirty-three highly respected cardiologists, cardiothoracic surgeons, nurses, and medical researchers. They address the needs of women in risk groups ranging from the very lowest to the highest risk for heart disease, including those who have already had heart attacks and strokes.

These guidelines take a personal approach to preventing cardiovascular disease in women based on each individual's heart health. It's a heart-smart way for smart women to take charge.

PUTTING THE GUIDELINES TO WORK

The AHA guidelines help physicians make appropriate recommendations for every woman, regardless of age or risk profile. You will learn about the ways that these principles can transform your life for the better in later chapters of this book, and I will explain what these terms mean in language that you can understand. To get a jump start, here are the basics:

- Get thirty minutes of exercise most days of the week.
- Limit dietary saturated fat to less than 10% of daily calories.
- Limit trans fats to less than 1% of total calories.
- Consume less than 300 mg of cholesterol daily.
- Increase omega-3 fatty acids, especially for high risk women.
- Follow a heart-healthy diet high in fruits, vegetables, grains, low fat dairy, fish, and legumes.
- Maintain body mass index between 18.5 and 24.9.
- Keep a waist circumference less than 35 inches.
- Strive for a blood pressure of less than 120/80.
- Set a goal of LDL cholesterol less than 100, and HDL greater than 50.
- Do not smoke or use any form of tobacco, and avoid secondhand smoke.

These straightforward guidelines will help you understand the profound effects of the many simple choices you make every day. Understanding is the first step to achieving balance and control of your own health and well-being. The more you know, the more power you hold in your own hands. Through *The Smart Woman's Guide to Heart Health*, you will discover the tools of prevention and learn how you can alter the course of your own life, regardless of where you stand on the heart disease continuum.

2

OVERWEIGHT? WHAT'S THE BIG DEAL?

How people become overweight is no great mystery. If your dietary intake and your energy output are not in balance, you will gain weight—it's as simple as that. Diet and exercise are the keys to your heart, your mind, and your well-being. While it is possible to be overweight and fit, there is no question that excessive weight will literally drag you down, affecting your health, your job, and your relationships.

Like many people, you may notice your scale creeping up a pound or two every few months. Perhaps you shrug it off, hoping the weight will leave as mysteriously as it came. Unfortunately, time has a way of growing those few unwanted extra pounds into a serious health problem.

Five pounds of weight gain a year may hardly seem worth worrying about, but fast-forward five years, and now you're stuck with twenty-five pounds of unwanted and unhealthy fat and a closet full of clothes that don't fit.

THE STATS ON FAT

If you're overweight, you're not alone. A full 66% of the American adult population is overweight, and about a third meet the criterion for obesity, meaning at least 20% above the recommended weight for height. Seven percent of women over the age of 20 are considered morbidly obese, meaning more than 100 pounds overweight. All told, that translates to 65 million obese Americans, and the number continues to grow.

WHY IS OBESITY SUCH A BIG DEAL?

If you carry some extra weight, as most people do, it might come as a surprise to learn that not only are you overweight, you may actually be obese by medical standards. The body-mass index (BMI), which is now considered a vital sign on par with blood pressure and pulse, uses height and weight measurements to calculate where your weight falls on the healthy-weight continuum. See "Obese or Overweight: How to Find Out" on page 21 or turn to the appendix and learn to calculate your body-mass index.

Why does it matter? Obese girls are less likely to attend college than girls of normal weight, limiting their social and financial opportunities. Studies on the subject have found that people who are obese tend to be socioeconomically disadvantaged, poorly treated by supervisors and coworkers, and more likely to be passed over for a promotion. They are often viewed as less successful, less energetic, and less in control.

However, the problems go much deeper than that. Being overweight is associated with a higher risk of diabetes, high blood pressure, elevated cholesterol, and depression—all of which significantly increase the risk of cardiovascular disease. In fact, even without those particular health complications, the risk of a heart attack is at least doubled in an obese person as compared to a person of appropriate weight.

People who carry most of the fat in their abdominal area (known as "abdominal adiposity," or visceral fat) have an even higher risk for heart disease and other health problems. (Sometimes this shape is referred to as an "apple," while people who carry most of their weight in their hips and thighs are known as "pears.") Although the American Heart Association guidelines recommend that women maintain a waist size of no more than 35 inches, the risk of heart disease actually begins to rise when the belly bulges beyond 35 inches; for men, 35 inches appears to be the safe upper limit.

Fat that collects around the waist can churn out a toxic mix of hormones and inflammatory substances that have been strongly linked to a higher risk of heart attacks, blood clots, and other health problems.

Not only does obesity expose the heart and other organs to these dangerous chemicals, it also requires the heart to work overtime, pumping blood through miles of extra capillaries, and may result in measurable changes in the heart's ability to do its work efficiently. The heart may become thicker and less elastic. These two factors have been associated with congestive heart failure, a condition that is twice as common in obese individuals as in those of normal weight.

While most commonly associated with older folks, heart abnormalities of this type can occur in obese women as young as 20 years old. Since congestive heart failure causes fluid retention and shortness of breath, it has a major impact on quality of life and mortality.

People who suffer from obesity are also more likely to develop serious heart rhythm disturbances such as atrial fibrillation, a rapid and irregular heart rhythm that increases the risk for stroke by 50%.

Obesity intensifies your risk of a frightening range of diseases and ailments. Most people don't realize it, but obesity increases the probability of developing many different types of cancers, including breast, colon, esophageal, uterine, pancreatic, liver, and prostate cancers. It has been estimated that one in seven cancer deaths in men and one of every five in women can be directly attributed to obesity. And there is a host of other health problems, including gallstones, sleep apnea, gastric reflux, Alzheimer's dementia, stroke, blood clots in the legs and lungs, and arthritis, that can be directly attributed to obesity. Obesity even raises the risk of miscarriage.

People who are obese have a death rate twice that of their slim counterparts. On average, obesity will shorten life span by ten to twenty years, thanks to the diseases and disorders it spawns. It also strikes the pocketbook. People who are obese spend 36% more on health care and 77% more on medications than the general population. It should come as no surprise that health care costs for obesity-related problems have now surpassed those for tobacco-related illness—a cost that we all bear.

How Did We Get This Way?

The easy explanation for these alarming statistics is that we are eating more and exercising less. Our average daily calorie consumption has increased by 200 calories per day during the past twenty years. How this has come to be is more complicated.

The Rise of Fast Food

Although many people become overweight without the assistance of fast food, the explosion of fast food restaurants tempting us with high fat, super fast, and super-sized meals is doubtless an important piece of the puzzle. Most of my patients with weight problems will admit to eating fast food at least four days a week—and that may be an underestimation. In fact, the National Restaurant Association reported that as far back as 1997 nearly half the adults in the United States ate a meal in a restaurant on a typical day. As our national spending on restaurant meals increased by nearly 50% between 2000 and 2008, that number has surely risen. What's worse, one in three kids now eats fast food every day.

People who eat fast food at least twice a week are more than 50% more likely to become obese than those who eat their meals at home.

We are a nation of overachievers when it comes to eating. A recent study from the University of North Carolina found a dramatic increase in portion sizes over the past twenty years, not only in fast food restaurants, but also in meals eaten at home. Researchers at New York University found that portion sizes at most restaurants are at least two times that of a "standard" serving, and often as much as eight. Furthermore, studies have shown that both children and adults will eat more when offered more and that many of us underestimate the amount of food we eat. The wider the selection of foods we have access to, the more likely we are to overeat.

SNACKING

Absentminded between-meal and late-night snacking, often on highly processed junk food, is a major source of gratuitous calories. Many of my patients own up to having a mid-morning, mid-afternoon, early evening, and late night snack every day. Giving in to those daily snack-attacks will boost our daily calorie count by an average of 30% per day, and often substantially more. Although snack calories carry every bit as much weight as meal calories, most snackers adhere to the "out of sight, out of mind" philosophy and forget to take these extra calories into account at mealtime.

TV: THE COUCH MAGNET

While we can and do snack anytime, anywhere, snacking while planted in front of the television is practically an American institution. Not only does watching the tube encourage us to feed our growing waistlines, it also prevents us from getting up and working it.

Numerous studies have found that the more TV you watch, the more likely you are to become obese, diabetic, or both. Someone who watches TV just one or two hours daily is 60% more likely to be obese than the next door neighbor who watches less than an hour a day. Watch even more, and the numbers get worse.

KEEPING TRACK WITH A FOOD DIARY

A food diary is a powerful tool that will force you to be honest with yourself about the food you eat. To start, weigh and measure your food, including all snacks and nibbles, for a week. Estimate your calories with a calorie counter (try the USDA Nutrient Database at www.nal. usda.gov/fnic/foodcomp/search). You can also track your workouts with one of the free databases widely available on the Web.

CAN IT BE IN THE GENES?

I often hear the excuse that "my fat is genetic" or "my metabolism is slow." Before falling back on old defenses, take a step back and critically evaluate your eating habits. Studies have shown that up to half of all women underestimate the amount of food that they eat, generally on the order of 20%. Ironically, women who are trying to lose weight tend to underestimate even more substantially than women who are not on a weight-loss program.

At the same time, we are inclined to overestimate the number of calories we burn. A study from the University of Texas found that the more overweight a woman is, the more likely she is to overrate her physical exertion. Most overweight people simply eat more, yet may honestly believe that they are eating less.

To be fair, there do appear to be genetic and hormonal factors that predispose to obesity and binge eating. To help regulate appetite and feeding, the body manufactures a cornucopia of hormones that have powerful effects on the feeding centers of the brain. Perhaps 5% of obese people have a true chemical imbalance of these hormones. A British report of a discovery of a "fat gene" found that the gene accounted for only about seven extra pounds of body weight in people unlucky enough to carry it.

What about metabolism? Well, slimmer people tend to keep moving (you might call it fidgeting!) even when they are doing sedentary tasks, and this may well explain some of the apparent differences in metabolism. A Mayo Clinic study suggested that fidgeters may burn upwards of 350 extra calories a day. Even more telling, people who are obese sit an average of two hours more per day than people who are lean.

OBESE OR OVERWEIGHT? HOW TO FIND OUT

There are several techniques available that can determine scientifically whether your weight is above the medically safe range. The most commonly used one is the body-mass index (BMI). Use the quick and easy table I've provided to help you see where you fall on the healthy weight continuum. You can use the Appendix to get your exact number, or you can calculate your BMI yourself by dividing your weight in kilograms by the square of your height in meters.

ARE YOU OVERWEIGHT?									
Height		Weight (pounds)							
(feet)	(inch)	Healthy			Overweight			Obese	
4	10	88	to	118	119	to	143	over	143
4	11	91	to	123	124	to	148	over	148
5	0	95	to	127	128	to	153	over	153
5	1	98	to	131	132	to	158	over	158
5	2	101	to	135	136	to	163	over	163
5	3	104	to	140	141	to	168	over	168
5	4	108	to	144	145	to	174	over	174
5	5	111	to	149	150	to	179	over	179
5	6	114	to	154	155	to	185	over	185
5	7	118	to	158	159	to	191	over	191
5	8	121	to	163	164	to	196	over	196
5	9	125	to	168	169	to	202	over	202
5	10	129	to	173	174	to	208	over	208
5	11	132	to	178	179	to	214	over	214
6	0	136	to	183	184	to	220	over	220
6	1	140	to	188	189	to	226	over	226
6	2	144	to	193	194	to	232	over	232

A BMI between 18.5 and 24.9 is usually considered healthy while 25–29.9 falls into the "overweight" category. In general, if your BMI is 30 or more, you are considered, for medical purposes, obese. Morbid obesity is defined as a BMI over 40.

Asian people may be healthier with a BMI of 21 or less, since they tend to develop hypertension, elevated blood sugar, and high cholesterol at BMIs above this cut-point. Exceptionally muscular people may be misclassified using this scale, but for most people, the ranges are accurate.

The Skinny on Weight Loss

It is never too soon to tackle a weight problem. Obesity begins in childhood and young adulthood. What you do now bears serious implications for your future health and well-being, and for the health of those you love. Even if you are only mildly to moderately overweight in your early 20s, you carry a high probability of developing obesity by the time you hit the mid 30s, regardless of gender. Furthermore, obese parents are more likely to raise obese children, continuing the cycle of obesity, poor health, and poor quality of life.

The good news is that you do not need to attain an "ideal" weight in order to begin to reap the benefits of weight loss. People who are already seriously overweight can significantly lower their chances of high blood pressure, diabetes, and elevated cholesterol by losing just 5% to 10% of their body weight. The more weight lost, the greater the rewards.

Fight the Food Triggers

Although we all wish for it, there is no magic to losing weight. You simply must eat less than you burn. But it is critical to identify the triggers and to begin to tame the urges that lead to overeating. For many people, eating while exposed to a simple distraction, such as a TV show or video game, blunts the normal sense of satiety, leading to a sort of oblivious overeating. This mindlessness accounts for the mysteriously empty bag of tortilla chips at the end of Monday Night Football. It also explains why moviegoers can eat massive tubs of popcorn without ever coming up for air.

It takes a good fifteen to twenty minutes for our bodies to register a sense of fullness, but when we gulp down our food, we are finished well before we ever get the signal to stop. So slow down and really experience your food. Enjoy it, and learn to be particular about the choices you make. Take your time to savor it, make every bite count, and you really will eat less.

Food portions are triggers, too, so portion control is critical for both food and drink. The larger the serving, the more you're going to eat or drink. Avoid the super-sized soda, or better yet, simply stay away from sweetened drinks and choose water instead.

BEWARE OF SNACKING

If you are truly hungry, choose a piece of fruit, like an apple. The fiber will help fill you up and quiet your cravings. If you enjoy snacking and choose to indulge, factor it in with your daily calorie allowance, and cut back at mealtime. Choose a protein-rich snack, such as an ounce of low-fat cheese with a couple of whole wheat crackers or a small tub of plain yogurt with a little honey or jam. An ounce or less of nuts is another good choice.

Although there are a few granola bars and protein bars that offer a good dose of energy without excessive fat, most are highly caloric (more than 200 calories) and loaded with sugar and preservatives. Play it smart by keeping your snacks under 150 calories, and limit snacking to no more than twice a day.

SMART TIPS FOR DEALING WITH YOUR PERSONAL FOOD TRIGGERS

Keep an honest food diary. Be aware of what you are eating. Take a walk, brush your teeth, call a friend, or direct your attention to something that takes your mind off eating. A project that requires you to use your hands, such as needlepoint, knitting, beading, or scrapbooking, is a great option.

Stop using food as a reward or a way of dealing with stress. Over time, your cravings will diminish, your sense of accomplishment will surge, and you will glow with good health.

OBESITY AND OVERWEIGHT: WHY WORRY?

- Obesity kills 112,000 people every year.
- Overweight and obesity cost the United States $117 billion annually for health care and lost productivity.
- Obese people spend 36% more on health care and 77% more on medications.
- At least half of the medical costs of overweight and obesity are funded by Medicare and Medicaid.
- 66% of Americans are overweight; by 2015, the number will reach 75% unless we change our lifestyles.
- Approximately 32% of Americans are obese; that number may reach 40% by 2015.
- Childhood obesity has tripled in twenty years.

GET HELP IF YOU NEED IT

If you suffer from uncontrollable binge eating, purging, or anorexic tendencies, by all means, enlist your doctor's help. Find a competent mental health specialist, and get the help you need. It is also important to seek medical attention if you believe your overeating is brought on by serious depression or obsessive behavior. Mental illness can be a powerful impediment to good physical health, and it cannot be overcome by willpower alone.

MEDICAL AND SURGICAL OPTIONS

If you are morbidly obese or suffering the consequences of obesity, such as diabetes, high blood pressure, and other medical problems, a lap-band or gastric bypass procedure may be something to consider. These operations reduce the amount of food you're able to put into your stomach and thereby increase the sense of satiety. I've seen these surgeries work for some people, although not everyone will achieve dramatic weight loss.

Any surgery carries potential risks. One in a thousand people will die as a result of the lap-band procedure and one in two hundred from gastric bypass. Life-threatening bleeding, infections, and chronic diarrhea are potential complications, particularly with the gastric bypass. Unless you are truly unable to control the urge to overeat any other way, my advice is to steer clear of surgery.

Currently there are no really effective medications available to help you lose weight. Orlistat (marketed as alli) helps prevent the absorption of fat through the intestine, but has the unfortunate side effect of sometimes uncontrollable grease-laden diarrhea, as well as gas with oily spotting. When it was sold only as a prescription medication, I quickly gave up prescribing it because virtually everyone who took the drug had such mortifyingly unpleasant side effects without enough weight loss to justify the humiliation. The average amount of weight lost is typically less than 10 pounds. While the drug probably won't hurt you, I don't advise taking it.

Sibutramine, also known as Meridia, is a prescription-only weight loss drug that suppresses appetite. It can raise blood pressure and cause heart arrhythmias, and there are also reports of psychosis with the drug, especially in people with bipolar disorder. Results are pretty unimpressive, with most people losing less than 10 pounds in one year. I don't prescribe this drug, and I don't recommend it, since I believe the risks outweigh the benefits.

Achieving a healthy weight is part of the process of building a healthy and heart-loving lifestyle—a process that will enrich and sustain your life for years to come. It is not easy, but it is certainly not complicated. It is perhaps the most important opportunity you will ever have to change your life and the lives of those you love.

3

The Good, the Bad, and the Ugly: Understanding Cholesterol and the Lipid Profile

No matter how healthy she thinks she is, every woman should know her lipid profile. A lipid profile is a measurement of total cholesterol, with a calculation of LDL ("bad") and HDL ("good") cholesterol, along with the amount of triglycerides circulating in the bloodstream. The latest national guidelines recommend that all adults should have a full lipid profile every five years. Medical treatment, when needed, is highly effective and generally very safe.

CHOLESTEROL

Cholesterol plays a critical role in heart disease, although blockages may develop even when levels are normal.

Seemingly healthy people die every day from heart attacks brought on by high cholesterol that was undiagnosed, untreated, or both. Diagnosis is easy—all it takes is a simple blood test, usually performed after fasting for at least eight hours.

Measurements of cholesterol levels are expressed as numbers. A number represents the amount of cholesterol present per deciliter of blood. You may see the numbers expressed as "mg/dL."

Cholesterol can be partially controlled by the food we eat, but only partially, so you can't assume that by eating well you are home free. Sometimes our bodies simply make too much of the stuff. Although modifying the diet is the first step for most people, medical treatment is critical for those at high risk for heart disease and stroke.

Cholesterol is often made out to be the bad guy, but it also a plays a major role in maintaining good health. For example, cholesterol contributes to the maintenance of normal cell membranes and is required for the production of some types of hormones. But we only need a little cholesterol to get the job done, and a cholesterol deficiency is virtually unheard of.

Even more important than the total amount of cholesterol circulating in the bloodstream are the levels of LDL and HDL cholesterol.

LOUSY CHOLESTEROL

LDL stands for low-density lipoprotein. I tell my patients that the "L" stands for "lousy." LDL is responsible for ferrying cholesterol from the blood into the arteries. Accordingly, high levels of LDL usually result in a higher risk of cholesterol buildup, also known as atherosclerosis or plaque, in the arteries of the heart, brain, limbs, and other vital organs. Atherosclerosis is sometimes referred to as "hardening of the arteries."

Among American adults, the average LDL cholesterol is 130. For optimal health, it should be closer to 100. More than 40% of women have LDL cholesterol levels over 130, and nearly 20% have dangerously high levels exceeding 160.

If you have been diagnosed with atherosclerosis (which includes heart disease, stroke, or cholesterol buildup in the arteries of the neck, arms, or legs), your LDL cholesterol should run less than 70 mg/dL. At this level, we can actually start to see cholesterol buildup slowly shrinking away.

Diabetic people (whose risk of cardiovascular disease is up to four times that of non-diabetics) and those with multiple risk factors should also aim for an LDL less than 70 mg/dL. For most people, achieving this goal means medical therapy, but dietary changes have the potential to make a significant impact. Even when medicine is required, a healthy lifestyle will limit the dose required to achieve an optimal cholesterol profile and consequently reduce the potential for drug side effects. In chapter 13, you will learn how to work with your doctor to improve your cholesterol levels through diet, exercise, and, when needed, medical therapy.

No known level of LDL is "too low," although your doctor may start backing down on medication when the LDL gets below 50.

If, like many people, you find yourself in a gray area—no heart disease, no diabetes, but at least two risk factors for coronary disease—then national guidelines dictate that your target LDL should be no greater than 130 mg/dL and preferably less than 100 mg/dL. Conventional risk factors in addition to diabetes include high blood pressure, tobacco use, a family history of early heart disease, age, and gender. Being female and at least 55 years old (or male and at least 45 years old) gives you one risk factor to start off with.

Those with one or none of these major risk factors should have an LDL no greater than 160 mg/dL, although many cardiologists, including me, would argue that even this relatively low risk group of people should strive for an LDL cholesterol of 100 mg/dL or less.

OTHER LDL TESTS DIG DEEPER

If your cholesterol level or risk profile is borderline, your doctor may choose to check a more detailed cholesterol profile in which subclasses of LDL cholesterol are measured. While this is not a common test, it can be useful in certain situations. Smaller, denser LDL particles are more damaging than larger, "fluffier" LDL particles, since they can more easily slip into the wall of the arteries and are more susceptible to harmful oxidation reactions that make the particles more dangerous. Thus, all other factors being equal, someone with a borderline normal total LDL cholesterol but a high level of small LDL particles would be at higher risk for heart disease than someone whose LDL particles were large. In this case, we might be more likely to consider drug therapy in addition to diet and exercise to help reduce the chance of cardiovascular disease. A blood test for apoprotein B provides similar information, since higher levels indicate that there are more of these harmful small particles.

Another test your doctor might suggest is a coronary calcium score. This test, done by taking a quick CT scan of the heart arteries, detects calcification in the arteries. Since cholesterol plaques generally become calcified over time, this test tells us whether there is evidence of plaque, and if so, how extensive it might be.

The test does not tell us anything specific about blockages, although people with a very high score (meaning a great deal of calcium in the arteries) are more likely to have significant disease. The presence of any calcification at all tells us that the process of atherosclerosis has already begun and is an indication to get more aggressive with cholesterol lowering. In my practice, I often use this test to help decide whether or not to start medication in someone who is at an intermediate level of risk.

HAPPY CHOLESTEROL

HDL cholesterol helps to take cholesterol out of the arteries and dump it into the liver, where it is processed so that it can be eliminated from the body. (Think of "H" for "happy.") In general, the higher the HDL cholesterol, the less likely it is that atherosclerosis will develop.

There is really no such thing as an HDL that is "too high." In general, HDL should be more than 50 mg/dL. (The goal for men is 45 or greater.)

Just like LDL, HDL subclasses can also be measured. The smaller HDL particles are thought to be less protective because they carry less cholesterol out from the arteries, although there is still debate about this issue.

Regular exercise, moderate alcohol use, and avoidance of tobacco smoke are all great ways to boost HDL cholesterol. Conversely, a diet of high glycemic-index foods like white bread, potatoes, white rice, and pasta will lower HDL cholesterol. (We'll learn more about these foods in chapter 4.) HDL cholesterol is critical to heart health. While every 1 mg/dL reduction of LDL can cut your risk of cardiovascular disease by 2%, each 1 mg/dL increase in HDL will drop the risk by as much as 3%. Do the math, and you'll see that the numbers can add up quickly.

THE LIVER'S ROLE

Your liver is a central player on the cholesterol team. It manufactures cholesterol from the food you eat. It is adept at turning saturated fat and trans fat into cholesterol, but even carbohydrates contribute to cholesterol production. Cutting back on the cholesterol in your daily diet affects cholesterol levels only modestly, but backing away from saturated and trans fats can have a major impact.

Not all livers are alike, and some people are able to gobble up large amounts of fat without it having a huge impact upon their blood cholesterol levels. Other people are genetically burdened with very high cholesterol levels, no matter what they do. My patient Felicia is a perfect example. A slender, vegetarian runner whose diet is beyond reproach, Felicia had an LDL cholesterol level, before medication, of 250 mg/dL—about twice the level considered normal. The only way to get her level down and protect her from heart disease and stroke was with medication, which has worked beautifully. Felicia's case is extreme, but for most of us, limiting saturated fats and trans fats can have a major effect on our LDL cholesterol levels and, thus, on our risk for heart disease and stroke.

GAMING THE NUMBERS—WHAT YOU CAN DO

Smoking can be detrimental to both HDL and LDL, and conversely, exercise and alcohol in moderation promote healthy lipid levels, with HDL cholesterol benefiting the most. A Mediterranean-style diet rich in mono-unsaturated fats (see chapter 7) can help to optimize the LDL particle size and boost HDL cholesterol levels at the same time.

Even when medication is required, improving your diet will limit the amount of medication you need. Popping a pill is easy, but taking medication does not relieve you of the responsibility you have to yourself to follow a healthy diet and lifestyle. Heart disease is much more than a simple set of numbers, and no drug can substitute for healthy living.

WHAT TOTAL CHOLESTEROL TELLS YOU

What about the total cholesterol level? While many people are fond of reciting this number, it is really not very meaningful. Total cholesterol includes measurement of HDL and LDL cholesterol; it also includes VLDL cholesterol, which is made up predominantly of triglycerides (see below) but is also a precursor of LDL cholesterol.

A very high HDL cholesterol could raise the total cholesterol reading to well over 200 mg/dL (formerly considered the cut-off point for a desirable cholesterol level), but the LDL might still be extremely low, netting a heart disease risk well below normal. Treatment of cholesterol should not focus on the total number, but rather on the HDL and LDL levels.

TRIGLYCERIDES

Triglycerides are another important component of the lipid profile. Triglyceride levels greater than 150 mg/dL have been linked to an increased risk of heart disease, particularly in women. In fact, a high triglyceride level is twice as predictive of heart disease for women as it is for men. Although triglycerides are usually measured in the fasting state, high non-fasting levels may be even more predictive of heart disease risk. High triglycerides are often associated with low HDL cholesterol, a feature typical of the metabolic syndrome (see chapter 13). Extremely high triglycerides (usually more than 1000 mg/dL) can increase the risk for pancreatitis, a dangerous inflammation of the pancreas gland, which sits near the stomach.

High triglycerides may be the result of an inherited genetic disorder, but more commonly, the condition is a direct result of diet and lifestyle. The blood level of triglycerides is determined in large part by your intake of simple carbohydrates, such as sugar, white bread, white rice, and white potatoes, and by the amount of saturated fat you eat. Both of these also contribute to diabetes. Adult-onset diabetics tend to have high levels of triglycerides, particularly when the diabetes is poorly controlled. Exercise and weight loss will lower triglycerides substantially.

UP AND DOWN WITH TRIGLYCERIDES

Prescription fish oil (marketed as Lovaza) at doses of 2 to 4 grams daily may lower triglycerides by 25% to 50%; nonpresription fish oil has a more modest effect unless a large number of capsules are taken (see chapter 11 for more about fish oil supplements). Monounsaturated fats like olive oil can have favorable effects as well. Small amounts of alcohol (one or two drinks daily) can lead to very healthy changes in the lipid profile, but more than that will tend to raise the triglycerides.

Triglycerides can be affected by a variety of prescription drugs. Estrogen replacement therapy may elevate triglycerides in susceptible women, as can testosterone. This effect is seen with the pill forms, but usually not with the estrogen patch. Some blood pressure medications, including diuretics and certain beta blockers, may adversely affect triglycerides. An underactive thyroid gland is often associated with high triglycerides; this condition can usually be diagnosed with a simple blood test.

Lp(a)

Lp(a), referred to by those in the know as "el-pee-little-a," is a tiny relative of LDL cholesterol. A routine cholesterol test will not detect this dangerous little particle. A test must be specifically requested by your doctor. Lp(a) is predominantly determined by genetics, and elevated levels (considered to be more than 30 mg/dL) are frequently found in people who have heart attacks early in life (that is, men before the age of 55, women before 65).

High Lp(a) levels are especially harmful in people with high LDL cholesterol. In the Nurses' Health Study, an elevated Lp(a) was associated with double the risk of heart attacks and other heart problems in women. The Women's Health Study found the risk to be especially high at levels above 65 mg/dL.

THE LOW-DOWN ON LP(a)

Unfortunately, while testing for Lp(a) is easy, treatment is not. Although exercise has little bearing on Lp(a), a diet high in trans fats may increase the Lp(a) concentration in the blood by 20% to 70%. A low fat, high carbohydrate diet (including 20% fat and 65% carbohydrate) may also raise Lp(a) levels, which is one reason we can't ignore the "good fats," which we'll learn more about in chapter 4. In fact, fish oil might reduce Lp(a) levels modestly.

Most lipid-lowering drugs such as statins have no significant effect on Lp(a). Pharmaceutical-strength niacin is one drug that can be used to treat this condition, since, when given in adequate prescription-strength doses, it will lower the level an average of about 25%. (I'll tell you more about this important drug in chapter 13.) But unfortunately, research on medical treatment of high Lp(a) still lags far behind that of the better-known cholesterol abnormalities.

HOMOCYSTEINE

Homocysteine is not actually related to cholesterol or to lipids, but since it has been associated with a higher cardiovascular risk and can be readily tested, a test for it is sometimes ordered along with a lipid profile.

Simply put, homocysteine is an amino acid derived from the metabolism of methionine, one of the essential amino acids. Its measurement is expressed as a number followed by "µmol/L."

Extremely high levels of homocysteine are generally the result of a genetic abnormality, while moderately high levels may be the result of a deficiency in vitamins, specifically folic acid, B6, and B12. Dietary and lifestyle habits can impact homocysteine levels substantially. Although "normal" levels have been considered to be as high as 15 µmol/L, levels greater than 9 µmol/L correlate with a higher risk of atherosclerosis. People with very high levels (more than 15.8 µmol/L) may have triple the risk of a heart attack when compared to people with a normal homocysteine.

Although we used to think that it was high homocysteine itself that caused the problem, the most recent research points to homocysteine as a marker for important lifestyle factors rather than being the culprit itself.

A diet high in saturated fat will tend to raise homocysteine levels. People who drink three or more cups of coffee daily are more apt to have high homocysteine levels, as are smokers and heavy alcohol users.

Fish oil intake is associated with lower levels, particularly when B-vitamin intake is high. Exercise may lower homocysteine, and so may the addition of more foods to the diet with high folate content, such as green leafy vegetables, peppers, cruciferous vegetables, and fortified cereal products. Wine, nuts, olive oil, and mushrooms have been linked to lower homocysteine and lower heart disease risk, as have dairy products like milk and yogurt.

For people with elevated levels of homocysteine, some doctors advocate mega-vitamins, but a growing number of research studies published since 2006 have shown that, while homocysteine levels can be lowered substantially with such supplements, there is no benefit to heart health.

One important study of nearly 4,000 heart attack survivors found that although high-dose vitamins lowered homocysteine levels substantially, their use was actually associated with a slightly higher risk of heart disease and a trend towards a greater incidence of cancer.

C-REACTIVE PROTEIN

High-sensitivity C-reactive protein (hs-CRP) is a protein that increases in the body in response to inflammation. It is clearly associated with heart disease risk, but exactly how information about it should be used remains the subject of much ongoing debate in the medical community.

WHAT HIGH CRP LEVELS MEAN

The Women's Health Study found a high hs-CRP to be even more strongly predictive of a future heart attack than a high level of LDL cholesterol. Studies of people tested just once and then followed for up to twenty years have shown a very high correlation between high CRP and subsequent heart attacks and strokes.

Measurement of CRP is a way to evaluate the likelihood of significant inflammation. From the standpoint of the heart arteries, inflammation is thought to be the trigger that causes many heart attacks.

A cholesterol-laden plaque in a heart artery may be present for years and may not be large enough to cause any symptoms whatsoever until inflammation within the plaque causes it to become unstable. This is what starts the life-threatening cascade of events we call a heart attack: plaque rupture followed by clot formation within the artery, blocking off vital blood flow and oxygen, causing injury, and eventually death, to the cells of the heart muscle.

In addition to its role in inflammation, CRP appears to increase the risk of blood clots and reduce the ability of the heart arteries to dilate normally in response to stress. People with high CRP are also more likely to develop diabetes and high blood pressure.

SHIFTING THE LEVELS

A number of different factors can affect CRP levels. CRP is made in the liver, and fat tissue itself can produce CRP, particularly the visceral, or deep abdominal, fat. Obesity is the factor most strongly associated with high CRP levels.

Weight loss will lower CRP. Exercise, with or without weight loss, can lower CRP by more than 35%. Alcohol in moderation will lower CRP, while heavy alcohol use will raise it. Not surprisingly, a diet high in saturated and trans fats can lead to inflammation of the heart arteries and high levels of CRP. Reducing harmful dietary fats will lower CRP, as will a high fiber diet.

Estrogen replacement therapy and oral contraceptives have been found to increase CRP, a finding that may account for their potentially harmful effects. Smoking will also raise CRP levels. Infections and severe stress may raise CRP, although generally the elevation is self-limited and will drop back to normal once the problem is gone.

Since inflammation related to an infection or injury can temporarily raise CRP, a finding of an elevated level should be followed up with another confirmatory blood test at least two weeks later. Values greater than 3 mg/L are considered elevated and are associated with a heart attack risk of at least one and a half times normal; values less than 1 mg/L are considered optimal. If the level is greater than 10 mg/L, chances are that there is some type of infection or an inflammatory process such as arthritis or infection, so further investigation into those issues should be considered first.

REDUCING INFLAMMATION

What do you do if your CRP is elevated and infection and other inflammatory problems have been ruled out? A healthy diet and weight loss, when needed, is always your first line of defense. Keeping stress under control may help as well.

Statin drugs, which are used to treat high cholesterol, have shown promise in reducing inflammation, even though there is no relationship between cholesterol levels and CRP. That is to say, you may have a normal LDL cholesterol level but a high CRP, or vice-versa. This is important because studies in women have found that even if the LDL level is within the recommended range, based on risk profile, a high CRP is associated with a significantly elevated risk for cardiovascular disease. For this reason, high CRP levels are sometimes treated with a statin drug, even though studies evaluating the outcome of this type of treatment have not yet been completed. Aspirin, which is well known to reduce the risk of heart attacks via its effect as a "blood thinner," may also act on the heart arteries by reducing inflammation, since its preventive effects have been found to be more pronounced in those with high CRP.

LIPIDS, HOMOCYSTEINE, AND HS-CRP: THE CHECKLIST

- LDL cholesterol should be less than 130 mg/dL in healthy people; less than 100 mg/dL is optimal.
- If you have heart disease, diabetes, or are at high risk for heart disease, strive for an LDL below 70 mg/dL. This will probably require medication.
- Saturated fats, trans fats, and dietary cholesterol will raise LDL cholesterol. So will smoking.
- HDL should be at least 50 mg/dL, but the higher the better.
- Regular exercise and alcohol in moderation will raise HDL.
- A high glycemic diet loaded with sugars and starches will lower HDL, as will smoking.
- Keep triglycerides below 150 mg/dL. A high glycemic diet, excessive alcohol, and saturated fats will raise levels.
- Exercise and cold-water fish will lower triglycerides.
- Lp(a) is increased by trans fats and simple carbohydrates.
- Homocysteine is a marker of an unhealthy lifestyle.
- Homocysteine is raised by trans fats, saturated fats, smoking, excessive coffee, and excessive alcohol.

- Exercise, cold-water fish, nuts, green leafy vegetables, dairy, and mushrooms will lower homocysteine.
- Hs-CRP is a measure of inflammation. Obesity, overweight, estrogen replacement, oral contraceptives, smoking, saturated fats, and trans fats raise levels.
- Exercise, moderate alcohol, nuts, high fiber foods, green leafy vegetables, and fruits lower hs-CRP.

STEP TWO

SMART WOMEN ARE
HEALTHY EATERS

Eating well should be a pleasure, but sometimes it all seems so darn complicated. The truth is, it just doesn't have to be that way. Understanding some simple notions of the fundamental building blocks of a heart-healthy diet will pave the way for a lifetime of good health and great food. Once you know the basics, separating the wonder foods from the nutritional evildoers will be a snap. What's more, you'll be able to make heads and tails of all those trendy, elaborate, and sometimes downright mystifying diets that seem to sprout up every time swimsuit season rolls around. The ultimate payoff: a healthier heart, increased vitality, and a body that is leaner, fitter, and more ready to take you where you want to go.

4

DIET: WHY YOU REALLY ARE WHAT YOU EAT

Good food is one of life's true pleasures, and that is just as it should be. A heart-healthy diet with an emphasis on fresh, nutrient-rich, vibrant foods is the foundation for a healthy life and a vigorous heart. When you nourish the body that works so hard for you, not only will your physical fitness and endurance grow, so will your mental energy and focus.

Eating well is not complicated and shouldn't make you feel miserable or deprived, although it will require some discipline and tenacity and the strength to say no. Believe in yourself, and know that you can do this.

When you make the choice to eat well and commit to a healthy way of living, you will slowly begin to notice a profound change in your sense of well-being and vitality. It won't happen overnight, but your cravings will gradually diminish, and you will discover that, although you may still enjoy some of the same high caloric foods that were once your downfall, it will take much less to satisfy your hunger. You will find yourself slowing down at the table, becoming more selective, and taking the time to really savor the nuances and flavors of the foods you eat.

Learning how to live a heart-loving lifestyle begins with understanding some important terminology. Words like "calories," "fats," "proteins," and "carbohydrates" are bandied around daily, but what do these terms really mean to your health?

CALORIES REALLY DO COUNT

A calorie is a unit of energy. You take in calories when you eat or drink—be it a carrot stick, potato chip, or cola. Your body burns up calories each time you move, whether you're watching television, gardening, or jogging. If you want to lose weight you must use up more calories than you consume. It is that simple. We make it hard on ourselves when we don't balance out the equation. If we don't burn off what we eat, then our bodies are forced to store it as fat.

Calories are present in virtually everything we eat, be it carbohydrate, protein, or fat. The difference is that all grams (a measurement we use for food) are not created equal. A gram of fat contains nine calories. Carbohydrates and protein each have four calories per gram. So what you eat is just as important as how much you eat. A recently published Institute of Medicine report breaks down our calorie requirements this way:

Percent Daily Calories	Source
20% to 35%	fat
45% to 65%	carbohydrates
10% to 35%	protein

FIGURE OUT HOW MANY YOU NEED

The average person requires somewhere from 1,600 to 2,200 calories each day to maintain a healthy weight. Depending on your activity level, degree of physical fitness, age, and gender, your needs may differ. For example, women typically require fewer calories than men simply because the average woman is smaller and has less muscle mass than the average man.

In order to figure your personal caloric needs, you first calculate your basal metabolic rate (BMR), more commonly known as your "metabolism." This will show you the number of calories your body needs to function properly at rest—that is, before you factor in activity and exercise.

There is more than one way to calculate your BMR, and you can easily find an online BMR calculator to plug your stats into, or you can do the math yourself. To roughly estimate your BMR, multiply your current weight in pounds by 10. If you weigh 150 pounds, for instance, your BMR is roughly 150 X 10, or 1500 calories. A more complicated formula, known as the Harris-Benedict equation (see page 46) takes into account gender, height, and age. This is more accurate, since younger people have a higher BMR, as do taller people and men.

The truth is, none of these formulas are perfect. Many factors affect your BMR. The leaner you are, the higher your BMR, which is a great incentive to exercise; this also accounts for the higher BMR that most men enjoy, since their body composition tends to skew more towards lean. Conversely, the more fat your body carries, the lower your BMR will be.

Children, especially as they go through rapid growth spurts, have a higher metabolism, as do pregnant women, whose bodies must work harder to develop the growing fetus and prepare to nourish the new baby. Stress, some illnesses, and constant exposure to extremes of temperature (think the Arizona desert in the summer or the Alaskan wilderness in deep winter) raise the BMR. Malnutrition and starvation will lower the BMR, which is one of the many reasons why radical diets fail.

THE HARRIS-BENEDICT EQUATION FOR BASAL METABOLIC RATE

The basal metabolic rate (BMR) defines the number of calories your body needs simply to sustain life in a resting state. Although you can get a very good estimation of your basal metabolic rate simply by multiplying your body weight in pounds by 10 (for instance 150 lbs x 10 = 1500 kcals), the Harris-Benedict equation provides a more precise, although still imperfect, approximation.

W = weight in pounds
H = height in inches
A = age in years

For women:
BMR = 655 + (4.35 x W) + (4.7 x H) – (4.7 x A)
For men:
BMR = 66 + (6.23 x W) + (12.7 x H) – (6.8 x A)

For instance, a 45 year old woman who is 5'4" (or 64 inches) and 150 pounds would calculate her BMR this way:
655 + (4.35 x 150) + (4.7 x 64) – (4.7 x 45) = 1396.8 calories daily

For a man of the same age, with the same height and weight, the BMR would calculate to 1507.3 calories, a difference about equal to one small chocolate chip cookie.

Once you calculate your BMR, it's easy to determine how many calories your body needs, based on how much energy you burn. This can be worked out fairly precisely. You can obsessively calculate the exact amount of time and energy spent doing everyday activities such as sleeping, standing, sitting, and exercising. Or, you can simply estimate based upon your average activity level.

To figure out the number of calories you need in order to maintain your current weight, you start with your BMR. If you are inactive, spending most of the day sitting at your desk or at home on the couch, multiply your BMR by 20% (for example, 1500 X 20% = 300). Then, add the number you get from that calculation to your BMR (1500 + 300 = 1800) to get the number of calories you need.

If you engage in light activity, such as walking around at work for several hours over the course of the day, multiply your BMR by 30% (1500 x 30% = 450) and make the addition (1500 + 450 = 1950).

If your fitness level is moderate, say you exercise several times a week or have a physically active job, you multiply your BMR by 40%.

Finally, if you are extremely active at work or get moving at least four hours every day and rarely sit still, multiply by 50%.

Now that you know how many calories you need, calculate the number of calories you actually eat every day. There are a number of good references available for this purpose. (Try www.nal.usda.gov/fnic/foodcomp/search.) The important thing is to be honest.

When it comes to food, size really does matter. A 10-ounce steak is not the same thing as a 6-ounce steak. Two cups of cereal is four times a recommended serving size of half a cup of flakes. This sounds logical, but study after study shows that most people are not aware of their portion sizes and habitually underestimate the amount that they eat.

To get a feel for portion sizes, you have to get a little compulsive. Create a food diary. Invest in a kitchen scale, and weigh and measure your food for a week. Don't forget to include snacks, "tastes," nibbles, and fast food. You'll learn just how many calories you consume, and you're likely to find some simple ways to reduce how much you eat. After a while, you may not need to measure and record, but don't give up until you are confident that you have developed a sense of proportion.

HOW MANY CALORIES DO YOU REALLY NEED EACH DAY?	
If your activity level is:	First calculate your BMR (weight in lbs x 10) Then multiply your BMR by this percentage. Next, add the two numbers together.
Sedentary	20%
Mild	30%
Moderate	40%
Heavy	50%

LOSE A POUND A WEEK

Since one pound of body fat equals 3,500 calories, cutting out just 500 calories daily will help you lose one pound a week. Even cutting back by 250 calories each day will earn you a two-pound weight loss by month's end. Add exercise to the plan and the pounds will peel off faster and more efficiently.

HOW FAST CAN CALORIES ADD UP?

Let's look in on Kate—a 150-pound, self-described couch-potato mom of two teens, who works as an office administrator. Kate usually skips breakfast because her mornings at home are rushed and chaotic. It's a chore just to get the kids dressed and off to school, and she barely has time to check that her shoes match. To jump-start her morning commute, she stops by her local coffee bar to grab a large cappuccino (270 calories).

At the office, donuts seem to magically appear in the break room. Grateful, Kate grabs two chewy morsels (420 calories) to eat at her desk. She barely tastes them as she digs into the pile of paperwork leaning precariously off the edge of her desk.

By the lunch hour, Kate is starving, but crunched for time. A quick bite with friends at a nearby fast-food joint includes a cheeseburger (530 calories), large fries (320 calories), and a soft drink (150 calories). At 3 p.m., a coworker offers to swing by the convenience store, and Kate puts in her order for a chocolate candy bar (250 calories) and a cola (150 calories). She is exhausted as the afternoon rolls around and is hoping the snack attack will boost her energy so she can get through the day. At home that evening, Kate is too tired to cook. The family is hungry and clamoring for something to eat. A quick call to the pizza parlor, and dinner is taken care of.

Kate eats three slices (750 calories) of a sausage and mushroom pizza, capped off by a dessert consisting of a glass of whole milk (150 calories) and two chocolate chip cookies (250 calories). Then she settles in for a couple of hours of television before bedtime. Still hungry, she snacks absentmindedly on a bag of pretzels (150 calories).

By day's end, Kate's calorie count is 3,390 calories and she's only burned off 1,800 of them for a net positive caloric balance of 1,590 calories. At this rate, she could easily gain more than 10 pounds a month. Put another way, she is eating enough to maintain a weight of 270 pounds, using our BMR calculations. If she only eats this way twice a week, she is still going to gain more than 3 pounds in a month or nearly 40 pounds a year.

Even worse, her diet is heavily loaded with fat and severely deficient in fruits, vegetables, and whole grains, which are critical for a healthy heart, mind, and body. Although she blows two hours in front of the TV, she makes no time in her day to exercise and feels unmotivated to do so. It is no wonder she is exhausted!

Kate's story is no exaggeration. Could it be yours?

It's never too late to take action. The body has a tremendous capacity to heal and to compensate for injury that it has already endured. Learn what, and how much, you are eating. You have the smarts, and you have the power. It really is up to you.

CALORIES COUNT

- Food supplies calories, exercise burns them up. It's that simple.
- Portion size matters. Don't just guess. Know how much you're eating.
- Most people need 1,600–2,200 calories daily, but most of us underestimate our caloric intake by 300–500 calories.
- One pound equals 3,500 calories. Cut out 500 calories each day, and in a week you've lost a pound.

CARBOHYDRATES

Lettuce, cookies, apples, pasta, whole wheat bread, doughnuts. What do these foods have in common? Although their nutritional values differ tremendously, they are all rich in carbohydrates—nutrients vital to the body and the brain that provide both immediate energy and long-term energy reserves.

Carbohydrates are an integral part of a healthy diet, but thanks to a resurgence of trendy low carb diets, they took a bad rap in the early 2000s and have never quite recovered.

The problem is that many people don't understand exactly what constitutes a carbohydrate. While we've been conditioned to think of them as starchy, sugary junk foods, carbohydrates are also a critical energy source, and many carbohydrate-rich foods are high in important nutrients and fiber.

Carbohydrates can be divided into three major groups: sugars, starches, and non-starch polysaccharides (commonly known as "fiber"). We often hear the words "simple" and "complex" applied to carbohydrates. Although these are poorly defined terms, in general, a simple carbohydrate is a sugar.

THE SUGARS—SIMPLE

Sugar is more than just the old familiar white stuff. Monosaccharides, such as glucose, fructose, and galactose, are found in most foods, including fruit, honey, and milk. The disaccharides, such as sucrose, lactose, and maltose, include the sugar we consider "table sugar," as well as sugars found in fruits, vegetables, milk, and even beer.

No one type of sugar is particularly better or worse than any other. The amount we consume is what's important. There are only 16 calories in a teaspoon of sugar, but up to 25% of the total calories of the typical U.S. diet come from sugars. Although sweetened beverages, such as soft drinks and juice-flavored drinks, are obvious culprits, sugar is also found in many breakfast cereals, baked goods, and even prepared pasta sauces. It has been estimated that the average American eats and drinks nearly half a pound of sugar daily.

THE STARCHES—A LITTLE MORE COMPLEX

Starches are more complex. Essentially long strings of glucose, they are bound together in various forms and fashions so that they require more work for the body to break down. They are commonly found in legumes, onions, potatoes, bananas, rice, and grains.

FIBER

Fiber is more resistant to digestion. Fibrous foods include whole grains, most fruits, and green leafy vegetables.

THE GLYCEMIC INDEX

More important than the distinction between "simple" and "complex" carbohydrates is something called the "glycemic index." It measures how fast a carbohydrate-based food is likely to raise your blood glucose (sugar) levels. The higher the number, the greater the blood sugar response and the more potentially harmful to your health.

Foods we digest quickly and absorb more rapidly tend to have a higher glycemic index. Foods rated high on the index typically contain more sugar or are considered more "starchy," such as white bread, bakery goods, pasta, and potatoes.

Foods high in fiber, such as most fruits, non-starchy vegetables, and whole grains have low glycemic indexes because they do not produce such a rapid rise in blood sugar.

The more high glycemic carbohydrates you eat, the higher the blood sugar level will soar. That is why the concept of "glycemic load" is so important. The term "glycemic load" refers to both the glycemic index and the typical amount of food per serving. This is important, because the tables used to determine the glycemic index, which are widely available online, do not compare foods based on the serving size, but rather relate them carbohydrate-gram to carbohydrate-gram. Since not all foods contain the same amount of carbohydrate grams, direct comparisons can be difficult.

For example, the glycemic indexes of potatoes and carrots are similar, yet the glycemic load of a baked potato is more than four times that of a half cup serving of carrots. This difference is because the total carbohydrate content of a serving of potatoes is four times higher than that of carrots. The glycemic indexes of wild rice and white rice are nearly identical, but since the carbohydrate content of white rice is twice that of wild rice, the glycemic load of white rice is also two times higher. On the other hand, the glycemic load of orange juice is very similar to that of a regular cola.

As a rule, snack foods and "white" foods, such as white bread, white pasta, white rice, and white potatoes tend to have a high glycemic load, while more complex foods such as whole grains, sweet potatoes, nuts, and seeds have a lower glycemic load. This is because our digestive systems break down the complex foods slower, releasing glucose into the bloodstream at a gradual rate.

Although I don't expect you to track your daily glycemic load, understanding it will give you a context that will help you judge the value of the food you eat. You can easily track down detailed tables of the glycemic load of a variety of foods by searching online.

WHAT THE GLYCEMIC LOAD TELLS US

Why should we care about a numerical index that ranks our foods by their effects on our blood sugar levels? To put it simply, what goes up must come down. In general, the body releases insulin in response to high blood sugar levels in order to process the sugar and make it available for energy storage. More sugar in the blood means the body must release more insulin, which is especially dangerous in people with diabetes, but can have harmful consequences in non-diabetics as well.

Not surprisingly, a high glycemic load raises the likelihood of developing diabetes. For instance, the risk of developing diabetes in women who have the highest glycemic load and lowest fiber intake is about two and a half times that of women who consume a diet with a lower glycemic load and more fiber.

It also turns out that the higher the daily dietary glycemic load, the greater the heart disease risk. The Harvard-based Nurses' Health Study found that women who consumed the highest glycemic load were nearly two times more likely to suffer heart attacks and coronary heart disease than those whose intake of these foods was very low. The heart disease risk was greatest in overweight women.

Other studies have found an association between a high glycemic load and high blood pressure, high LDL (bad) cholesterol, and reduced levels of HDL (good) cholesterol.

Women who eat a diet with a high glycemic load are also more likely to have higher levels of hs-CRP, a substance in the blood linked to inflammation of the heart arteries and a higher risk for heart disease and heart attacks.

A high glycemic diet has even been associated with early age-related macular degeneration, a condition of the retina associated with blindness.

Even if you're not diabetic or pre-diabetic, a high glycemic diet will sap your strength, leaving you feeling weak and grouchy. The rapid rise in blood sugar is typically associated with a rapid fall, and this is one reason that you may feel tired and unmotivated after eating high glycemic foods. You may also crave more food to help bring the blood sugar up and give you back your sugar buzz.

This rise and fall of blood sugar can create a vicious cycle of hunger, brief spurts of energy, and rapid fatigue. In turn, that will goad you into eating more in order to recapture that fleeting sense of sugar-induced euphoria. Some people, including kids, truly become carbohydrate addicts, craving the highs and dreading the lows. Ultimately, the result will be all too familiar: weight gain, sluggishness, and diminished productivity.

Think about Kate and her fast-food lunch. When the sugar lows hit, she reaches for her afternoon candy bar and soda, and the cycle begins again. It is easy to understand why Kate goes home exhausted and too tired to exercise. It's a safe bet that she is not nearly as satisfied or happy with her life as she should be.

The food we choose can grant us power or take it away. The effect on your pants size notwithstanding, very simple changes in your diet will have deep, powerful, and lasting effects on your quality of life, and the lives of those around you.

SUGAR, SUGAR

- One teaspoon of table sugar is 16 calories.
- Up to 25% of our daily calories come from sugar; this equals about a half pound per person per day.
- Typical high glycemic foods are the white foods such as white bread, white rice, white pasta, and white potatoes.
- The body quickly breaks down high glycemic foods into glucose, or sugar.
- A high glycemic diet increases the risk for diabetes, heart disease, and high cholesterol.

FRUITS AND VEGETABLES

Fruits and vegetables are the underdogs of the food world. They are absolutely critical for good health, yet far too often they are treated as an afterthought, served "on the side," or as a sad, wilted garnish. Many people have grown up in homes in which mass-produced convenience snacks are the norm, so they were never taught the pleasures of biting into a juicy, crisp apple, whipping up a vibrant, multi-colored salad, or brewing a spicy ratatouille, but it's never too late to learn.

ARE THEY REALLY VEGGIES?

The most commonly eaten "produce" items in this country are (in order) french fries, other forms of potatoes, and iceberg lettuce. A full 25% of all the "vegetables" we consume are french fries, which are laden with an enormous amount of fat and very few nutrients. In truth, they hardly deserve to be called vegetables.

HOW MUCH IS ENOUGH?

Current U.S. dietary guidelines recommend five to seven servings of fruits or vegetables daily. More recent medical research has suggested that eight to ten servings are probably optimal. While this might sound a little intimidating, it is as easy as a sprinkle of fruit on your breakfast cereal, a big green salad for lunch, a couple of helpings of veggies at dinner, and some fruit for dessert. A serving is generally considered one piece of fruit, a cup of raw leafy vegetables, a quarter cup of dried fruit, or half a cup of other fruits or vegetables.

While three quarters of a cup of juice is sometimes considered a serving of fruit or vegetable, it does not appear to offer the same protection. This is because the juice is only a fraction of the fruit, and the health benefits come from the full symphony of nutrients and antioxidants working together.

Numerous scientific studies have critically reviewed fruit and vegetable consumption and correlated it with overall risk of heart disease. People who report the greatest number of servings of fruits and vegetables are 20% less likely to die of heart disease or suffer a heart attack when compared to those who eat the least, even taking into account such variables as smoking, dietary fat, and body weight. Each serving of fruits or vegetables above five per day confers a 4% lower risk for heart disease. Those who choose eight or more servings a day, especially green leafy vegetables and vitamin-C rich fruits and veggies, reap the greatest health rewards. High fiber fruits and vegetables also help to improve the cholesterol profile by lowering LDL cholesterol.

HOW TO CHOOSE THE BEST

Which fruits and vegetables are best? Truthfully, they are all worthy of a place at the table, as long as we keep margarine, butter, cheese, and other unhealthy additives to a bare minimum. However, the more colorful a fruit or vegetable is, the more nutrients it is likely to offer. Dark green, leafy vegetables, bright red tomatoes, and rich golden-orange nectarines and peaches are especially good choices. Berries also possess wonderful heart-protective properties.

Potatoes do not do much to support good health. Consider substituting sweet potatoes, a fabulous source of beta-carotene and fiber and one of my favorites. Try them baked in foil or roasted in the oven with yummy spices and a pinch of salt.

Have fun and experiment with Mother Nature's bounty. If it is too time-consuming or expensive to buy all the fixings for a salad, check out your grocery store's salad bar, which will allow you to pick and choose just the right amount of fresh ingredients. Keep your plate colorful, and your heart will be happier.

FRUITS AND VEGGIES: WHAT YOU NEED TO KNOW

- Fewer than one in four Americans eats five servings of fruits and vegetables each day.
- For optimal health, we should include eight to ten servings daily.
- French fries don't count.
- One serving is a half cup of most fruits or vegetables or a full cup of raw leafy vegetables.
- Choose a variety of brightly colored fruits and veggies to get the widest variety of vitamins and other nutrients.
- A diet high in fruits, vegetables, and low fat dairy products has been proven to lower blood pressure. Veggies can also reduce the likelihood of mental decline as we age.

WHOLE GRAINS

It's hard to imagine life without bread, cereal, and pasta. We humans have depended on grains for nourishment since the beginning of recorded history. For centuries it was women who threshed the wheat, kneaded the dough, and baked the bread that sustained their families. But over the last fifty or so years, refined flours from factory farms have far overtaken whole grains in the Western diet. Only about 20% of bread now sold in the United States is whole grain, and less than 5% of the grains we eat everyday are whole grains.

After all those years of humble, coarse milled flours, people believed lily-white refined flours to be more pure and a mark of true gentility. Now we know that the milling process actually removes the most nutritious (and delicious) part of the grain, leaving behind only the starchy middle layer, or endosperm. This part of the grain is rapidly digested and broken down by the body into sugar, which accounts for white bread's notoriously high glycemic nature.

The bran, or outer layer, and the inner layer known as the germ (or embryo) get lost in the refining process, essentially ending up on the cutting room floor. These important parts of the grain are rich in fiber, B vitamins, vitamin E, minerals, and often omega-3 fatty acids. In fact, refining removes about 70% of the minerals, 80% of the fiber, and 25% of the protein contained in the grain.

Other vital nutrients contained in the germ include phytoestrogens and antioxidants, which may have important protective effects for the heart and other organs. Scientists are still studying these substances, but some of them have been found to lower blood glucose, insulin levels, and cholesterol.

Refined flour is found in most of the breads and baked goods sold in grocery stores. Pasta, muffins, pizza, and even most breakfast cereals are also manufactured using refined flour. In many cases, that flour is enriched with niacin, iron, thiamine, riboflavin, and folic acid. This is a major improvement over the bare stuff, but does not go nearly far enough.

WHAT GRAINS CAN DO FOR YOU

Studies show that eating more whole grains, about two and a half servings daily, is associated with as much as a 30% reduction in heart disease risk when compared to people whose diets include no whole grains at all. A diet high in whole grains is also associated with reduced likelihood of cholesterol plaque buildup in the carotid arteries, which supply blood to the brain. Not surprisingly, whole grains appear to lower the probability of developing diabetes. People who eat more whole grains are less likely to develop colorectal cancer. What's more, whole grains are associated with reduced inflammation and may even lessen your risk of peridontitis, or gum disease.

One serving of whole grain food is equal to a slice of whole grain bread or a standard serving size of cereal that contains at least 25% whole grain or bran by weight. This is a great example of how simple choices can have a substantial impact on your health and the health of your family. Replace white bread with whole grain and chuck a few boxes of whole grain cereal in your shopping cart, and you've done it. Whole grains do require more care than refined flour. For instance, you should store flours in the refrigerator or freezer if the package is open for more than a few days so they don't become stale or rancid.

WHOLE GRAINS, BIG GAINS

- Eighty percent of us eat less than one serving of whole grains daily.
- Just two and a half servings of whole grains each day cuts the risk of heart disease by 30%, helps prevent diabetes, and protects against colorectal cancer.
- One serving is one slice of whole-grain bread or a standard serving of whole grain cereal.

DECODING BREAD LABELS

For the full whole-grain experience, whole-wheat bread is your best bet. That's not to say that other "wheat" breads are unhealthy, but unless they are whole grain, they lack the full kick of nutrients and fiber that whole grains offer. Labels can be confusing. The word "wheat" on a label merely refers to the original source of the flour. Wheat bread is whole grain only if the label states "whole-wheat flour." Wheat flour and unbleached flour are not necessarily whole wheat. Unbleached flour may sound more healthy, but in fact, about 80% of its bran has been removed. On any bread you buy, check the ingredients to be sure that "whole wheat" is first on the list.

We've focused on wheat, but there is a world of whole grains waiting to be discovered. Millet, oats, quinoa, and amaranth are nutritious and tasty and worth exploring. These grains are often sold in the form of flour or incorporated into breakfast cereals. And don't forget brown rice, a much smarter choice than its plain white cousin.

FIBER

Whole grains are a rich source of fiber, but fiber is also an important component of fruits and vegetables. Fiber is defined as the plant materials in the diet that are resistant to digestion. Fiber itself is associated with a lower risk of heart disease and high blood pressure and may even play a key role in maintaining weight. Fiber from grains appears to be the most beneficial.

Women who eat more fiber tend to weigh less and to gain less weight over time. The American Heart Association recommends a fiber intake of 25 to 30 grams daily, including 10 to 25 grams of soluble fiber. The average American consumes only 15 grams of any kind of fiber.

WHAT FIBER CAN DO FOR YOU

Soluble fiber from sources such as oat bran, apples, oranges, prunes, and legumes can help lower your cholesterol, mainly by decreasing the absorption of cholesterol through the gastrointestinal tract. (Psyllium is another type of soluble fiber, but as I'll discuss in more detail in chapter 11, it's used as supplement rather than a food.)

Soluble fiber particles attract water and form a sort of gel in the digestive tract, which traps cholesterol-containing bile acids making their way through the intestines and excretes them in the stool. Thus, they are not reabsorbed into the bloodstream.

The insoluble form of fiber that comes from seeds, whole grains, and brown rice does not appear to have the same cholesterol-lowering effect. That is not to say that whole grain cereal isn't nutritious, but if you want to lower cholesterol, choose soluble fiber first.

A high fiber diet is also associated with lower levels of inflammation, as measured by C-reactive protein. A diet high in fiber will make you feel fuller faster, reducing the chance that you will overeat. My patient Jessica credits her before-meal apples for her 20-pound weight loss this year, a claim backed up by research from Brazil.

Fiber also allows sugar to release more slowly into the bloodstream, avoiding sudden peaks and valleys in blood glucose. As a result, less insulin is needed. And we cannot overlook the fact that fiber is a boon for the digestive system and good insurance against constipation.

If you eat your eight to ten servings of fruits and vegetables and two and a half servings of whole grains daily, it will be nearly impossible not to get enough fiber. If fiber-rich foods are not yet part of your life, you might want to add them in slowly, perhaps over the course of one to two weeks, to give your digestive system a chance to adapt. To put it gently, your colon may be a bit surprised at your sudden change of heart!

FIBER FACTS

- Fiber helps you to feel fuller faster and slows the release of glucose into the bloodstream.
- A high fiber diet reduces the risk of heart disease and high blood pressure and supports bowel health.
- Soluble fiber lowers cholesterol.
- Soluble fiber comes from oat bran, apples, oranges, prunes, and legumes.
- Strive for 25–30 grams of fiber each day, including 10–25 grams of soluble fiber.

PROTEIN

Proteins are made up of any number of 20 building blocks known as amino acids. They are involved in all of your body's most important functions. Growth, reproduction, maintenance, and repair of muscle and body organs—you name it, proteins are there. The adult human body is capable of manufacturing all but eight of the amino acids. These eight, dubbed the essential amino acids, must come from the food you eat; without them, your body simply cannot perform normally.

A food that provides all eight of the essential amino acids in proportion to our needs is known as a "complete" protein. With the exception of soy and some grains, such as quinoa and amaranth, complete proteins are mainly found in foods that are of animal origin—meats (including poultry, beef, pork, and fish), eggs, and dairy products.

A vegan (a vegetarian who eats no foods of animal origin) can easily obtain all the essential amino acids by including foods from a variety of vegetable, bean, and grain sources. Infants and young children, however, require a ninth amino acid, histidine, found in dairy, meat, poultry, and fish.

Not all protein is the same. A diet high in vegetable-based protein is associated with a lower blood pressure, while red meat and processed meat (such as lunch meat) are associated with a greater risk of high blood pressure.

While we know a lot about carbohydrates and fats, the role that dietary protein plays in promoting heart health is not as well understood. There is no question that an extremely low protein diet may severely weaken the heart. This is typical in impoverished Third World countries and may also occur with anorexia nervosa.

How Much Is Enough?

Generally, most people require 0.8 mg of protein per kilogram of body weight daily to maintain good health. To find out how much you need, you multiply your body weight in pounds by 0.37. For example, 150 x 0.37 = 55.5 shows us that a 150-pound person will need about 55 grams of protein each day.

The Institute of Medicine has recommended a safe range of protein intake of 50 to 175 grams daily. Of course, your protein needs may vary depending on your health and activity level. A highly competitive athlete requires substantially more protein than a garden-variety couch potato.

Since the range of acceptable dietary protein is quite broad, it is not critical that you routinely count every gram. However, understanding how much protein is in a typical serving of food will help you recognize that it does not take much to meet your body's requirements. The USDA considers a serving of lean meat, poultry, or fish to be 2 to 3 ounces, and our daily requirement to be two to three servings

Most 3-ounce servings of meat, fish, and chicken contain 15 to 25 protein grams. The leaner the cut, the more grams of protein per ounce it will contain. An ounce of cheese, a cup of milk, and half a cup of beans, or two tablespoons of peanut butter will net you 8 grams of protein; one egg supplies 6 grams of protein. Tofu is a protein powerhouse with 20 grams per half cup and 25% fewer calories than a 3-ounce piece of steak. You also get small amounts of protein from other foods like grains and vegetables, even though we consider those foods to be "carbohydrates."

For most of us, the amount of protein in our daily diet is more than adequate to meet our needs. You can buy a variety of protein supplements, including powdered amino acids, at many self-styled "nutrition" stores, but you really don't need them. Although manufacturers tout their ability to improve strength, muscle mass, and endurance, these claims are not much more than wishful thinking. For a strong, fit, and lean body, you've got to amp up your exercise program. Simply eating large amounts of protein, without a commitment to regular exercise, will not increase your muscle mass—although it may increase your dress size.

Remember that each gram of protein carries four calories. Not only will protein supplements add calories to your diet, in some cases, they may actually be harmful, since excessive amounts of protein can damage the kidneys and the liver in vulnerable individuals.

PROTEIN: WHAT YOU NEED

- To calculate your daily protein requirement, multiply your body weight in pounds by 0.37 (or your weight in kilograms by 0.8).
- Between 50 to 175 daily grams of protein is safe for most people.
- We need about 4 to 9 ounces of animal protein, or its vegetarian equivalent, to meet our daily needs.

THE SKINNY ON FAT

Fat has been greatly maligned and seriously misunderstood by the public and health professionals alike. For years, many of us in the medical profession have badgered our patients to follow the "low fat, low cholesterol" mantra. We have blithely promised a lifetime of good heart health to those who follow an extremely low fat diet without fully understanding the consequences of heeding such advice.

As a result of this fat phobia, low fat snacks, bursting with sugar and simple starches, have crammed store shelves, sabotaging our best intentions.

SIMPLY PUT, FAT IS COMPLICATED.

Certain types of fats are critically important to our health and well-being. Fats are the most concentrated and efficient sources of energy available and are responsible for much of the flavor we associate with good food. Fat will produce a sense of satiety much more quickly than protein or carbohydrates, helping to cut cravings. Most importantly, fats are involved in virtually all the functions of the body, including those of the brain. Some are even vital for maintaining optimal cardiovascular health.

Too little fat can have a negative impact on the lipid profile. People who choose diets that are extremely low in fat and high in carbohydrates may find their lipids turned topsy-turvy, with lower levels of good cholesterol, or HDL, and higher levels of blood fats, or triglycerides.

How Much Is Enough?

A reasonable diet will include 25% to 30% of calories from fat, as long as those fats come from the right sources. For someone who requires 2,000 calories a day, fat intake should run between 55 and 65 grams.

Aren't All Fats Alike?

Like carbohydrates, not all fats are created equal. There are three major types of fat: saturated, unsaturated, and trans fat. While all fat carries the same number of calories per gram, it is the type of fat you eat, even more than the amount, that impacts your cardiovascular risk.

Fat is made up of fatty acids, essentially long chains of carbon atoms. Whether a fatty acid is saturated or unsaturated depends upon its chemical structure. If each one of the carbon atoms has a hydrogen atom attached, we call it saturated. Conversely, if even one carbon atom is missing a hydrogen atom, then it is unsaturated. When unsaturated fats are treated by a process called "hydrogenation," it changes their chemical structure in a fundamental way. These modified fats are called trans fats. They reach our grocery shelves and restaurants as partially hydrogenated oils or vegetable shortening.

Unsaturated Fat

Let's start with the good fats. Unsaturated fats are a vital part of good nutrition. The best sources are vegetable oils, olive oil, nuts, grains, and fish. Poultry, beef, and pork also provide modest amounts of unsaturated fats mixed in with the saturated fats. Unsaturated fats are usually liquid at room temperature.

Monounsaturated fats (sometimes referred to as omega-9 fatty acids) have only one unsaturated carbon. They are found in abundance in olive oil, canola oil, nuts, and avocados. This heart-friendly type of fat has beneficial effects on the cholesterol profile and may also improve the ability of the heart arteries to respond to stress. A number of studies have found that people who eat more monounsaturated fats significantly lower their risk of developing heart disease.

Monounsaturated fat may even favorably affect the body's response to insulin and help to lower blood pressure, as long as it is used in moderation. Too much of any type of fat in the diet will tend to raise blood pressure.

Substitute olive oil for butter, or eat a diet higher in nuts than meat, and your bad cholesterol (LDL) can be reduced by as much as 15%, while HDL, or good cholesterol, could rise by about 4%.

In fact, one Spanish study reported that people who consumed about four tablespoons of olive oil daily had an 82% lower risk of heart disease than those whose diet included little or no olive oil. We can attribute this in large part to the monounsaturated fat oleic acid, which makes up 55% to 85% of olive oil. Olive oil's other components, including antioxidant vitamins, polyphenols, and other polyunsaturated fats, are probably also heart protective.

"Extra Virgin" and "Virgin" olive oils contain more naturally occurring nutrients and anti-oxidants than regular olive oil and have a more favorable effect on HDL cholesterol, making them the best choice.

Polyunsaturated fats, found in cold-water fish, nuts, grains, and vegetable oils, are essential for good health. This type of fat has a powerful impact on the cholesterol profile. People who choose a diet high in polyunsaturated fats tend to have lower cholesterol levels and a lower risk of heart disease than those whose diets are low in fat but high in carbohydrates. This is why your doctor's time-honored advice to follow a low fat diet is misinformed to some extent, and one reason that the grocery aisles full of low fat but high carb treats have done nothing to improve our health.

Polyunsaturated fats include two types of essential fatty acids—omega-3 and omega-6—that the human body cannot manufacture on its own and which we must obtain from the foods we eat. Omega-3 fatty acids are found in walnuts, soybeans, flaxseed oil, and cold-water fish. Vegetable, seed, nut, and olive oils are sources of the most common omega-6 fatty acid.

Both omega-3 and omega-6 fatty acids are vital for the healthy function of all our cells, our hormone-producing glands, our immune systems, our cholesterol transport systems, and our brains. Omega-3 fatty acids have been associated with a lower risk of blood clots, heart attacks, dementia, strokes, and a decreased likelihood of potentially fatal heart rhythms. Omega-6 fatty acids may help the body ward off diabetes when included in a well-balanced diet.

Omega-3 and omega-6 fatty acids compete in the body for enzymes that break the fatty acids down and allow them to perform their important functions, so it is important to maintain a healthy balance in order for our bodies to put these fats to work. A typical American diet includes somewhere between fourteen and twenty times as much omega-6 fatty acid as omega-3.

Most of us are significantly lacking in the omega-3 fatty acids, which is much to our detriment. The optimal ratio of omega-6 to omega-3 should be approximately 5:1 or less. That means that we should boost our omega-3 intake by adding more fish and nuts to our diets and drastically reduce our use of most vegetable oils. Doing so will not only improve our cardiovascular health, but it may have other important effects. For example, a higher omega-3 to omega-6 ratio is associated with a lower risk of breast cancer in premenopausal women, while excessive levels of omega-6 fatty acids may contribute to inflammation of the blood vessels, raising the risk of cardiovascular disease. You'll learn more about omega-3 fats in chapters 5 and 11.

SATURATED FAT

There is no doubt that saturated fat is a major contributor to heart disease. This is the primary form of fat found in meat, poultry, and dairy products. Coconut and palm kernel oils, commonly used in processed snack foods, are the main plant sources of this type of fat. Saturated fats are usually unappealingly solid and greasy at room temperature, but melt at cooking temperatures, providing the yummy mouth-feel that we associate with high fat foods.

A study conducted by the Los Angeles Veterans Hospital found that people who substituted unsaturated fat for saturated fat in their everyday diet reduced their risk for coronary heart disease by 31%. Similarly, the Nurses' Health Study reported in 1997 that replacing calories from saturated fats with an equivalent amount of unsaturated fat calories would reduce the risk of heart disease by 42%, and comparable results were also found in a 2005 study from Finland.

Saturated fat raises the LDL blood cholesterol ("bad" cholesterol) more than any other fat besides trans fats. Even a single meal high in saturated fat can be harmful. As they stream though your arteries, saturated fats can hinder the normal function of your arteries, decreasing the blood vessels' ability to respond normally to stress and increasing the likelihood of developing potentially fatal blood clots. While most studies on the subject have been done with animal fats, this effect has also been seen with coconut oil, putting a hole in the popular theory that plant-based saturated fats are more healthful.

A meal high in saturated fat may also trigger an abrupt rise in inflammatory C-reactive protein (see chapter 3) and other inflammatory substances, and at the same time inhibit HDL cholesterol, making our arteries more vulnerable to injury.

Unless you're a vegan, it's hard to avoid saturated fat altogether, but it makes sense that it should account for less than 7% of your total caloric intake. As a rule, keep saturated fat to no more than 20 grams daily; you'll do even better if you strive for a daily limit of 15 grams of saturated fat.

Cutting Out Saturated Fat

Cut back on red meat. Even if you chop off all visible fat, fat is marbled within the muscle fibers and is difficult to avoid completely. Poultry contains less saturated fat if you cut off the skin, but is still a significant source.

Although seafood also contains small amounts of saturated fats, many varieties of fish are rich in heart-healthy polyunsaturated omega-3 fats. To keep the saturated fats at bay, think of poultry and meat as side dishes, keeping portions small, and give vegetables and grains the starring role at mealtime.

Since dairy products are also chock-full of saturated fats, be aware of the amount of cheese and butter you eat, including cheese in pizza, sandwiches, and salads, and butter smeared on steaks and fish. A large slice of cheese pizza serves up as much as 55 grams of saturated fat.

Low fat and non-fat dairy foods are a great option for people who want a high quality source of calcium and protein without all the saturated fat. Choose skim milk on your breakfast cereal, or better yet, switch to soy milk, which is great for your heart and has additional health benefits that I'll tell you about in chapter 5.

Snack foods are often landmines of palm and coconut oils. The good news is that the nutrition information is readily available on the package—just don't forget to read it. You'll find that even some brands of protein bars contain substantial amounts of saturated fat.

TRANS FATS

Trans fats are "transformed" polyunsaturated fats that lurk just about everywhere mass-produced food is found. Vegetable shortening, hard margarines, crackers, popcorn, candies, baked goods, cookies, snack foods, fried foods, and salad dressings all are likely to be harboring these bad guys. Trans fats begin life as relatively inoffensive polyunsaturated fats, such as soybean oil or even fish oil. Through a chemical process, more hydrogen atoms are added—this is where we get the term "partially hydrogenated"—to make these oily fats more solid.

When polyunsaturated fats are put through this process, they also become more stable and much less likely to become rancid, which lengthens shelf life and makes food manufacturers and grocery stores happy.

The process, however, creates a type of fat that is chemically and biologically different from its original source. Trans fats occur in miniscule amounts in nature. But the wide acceptance and commercial success of partial hydrogenation, to the tune of $2.4 billion per year, has created an enormous source of trans fats—overloading our systems with far greater amounts than our bodies are designed to handle.

BAD, BAD, BAD

Trans fat is a lipid triple whammy, raising bad cholesterol (LDL), lowering good cholesterol (HDL), and boosting triglyceride levels. Overall, the detrimental effect of trans fats on the cholesterol profile is more than double that of saturated fats.

Trans fats have been linked to an increase in belly fat, which is just the kind of fat we want to avoid because it is more dangerous than body fat stored in other areas.

What's more, trans fats may increase the risk of blood clots in the arteries of the heart and other organs, leading to a higher risk for heart attacks and stroke. They can make our cells more resistant to insulin, making us more susceptible to diabetes and its associated complications. CRP, a measure of inflammation closely tied to cardiovascular disease, is higher in people whose diets include trans fats. What's more, women who breast-feed pass their trans fats along to their infants, exposing them to possible harm during a critical point in development.

Based on an overwhelming body of data showing trans fats to be harmful, manufacturers must now include them on standard nutrition labels. Restaurants and fast food restaurants, some of the worst offenders, are not usually required to provide this information, although many will do so if you ask. With New York City a trail-blazing example, some cities are considering an all-out ban on trans fats, and many restaurant chains, wary of consumer backlash, are searching for healthier alternatives.

HOW HARMFUL CAN THIS BE?

Aren't trans fats better than saturated fats, anyway, and isn't this just another trendy "don't"?

Far from it. The dangerous effects of trans fats have been recognized since 1994, when Harvard researchers estimated that at least 30,000, and perhaps as many as 100,000, deaths per year from heart disease could be directly linked to trans fats. A report published in 1997 from the ongoing Nurses' Health Study suggested that if we were to take the 2% of average daily calories that come from trans fats and replace them with polyunsaturated and monounsaturated fats, we could lower the risk of heart disease by more than 50%. This percentage was even more substantial than the conclusions reported with saturated fats.

Although trans fats have only recently hit the daily news, these findings are more timely now than ever before. Between 1997 and 2007, our average daily trans fat intake increased more than 25%. The average American in 2003 consumed nearly 6 grams of trans fat every day, much of it from cakes, cookies, crackers, and other baked goods.

Studies from around the world have shown that people who eat an average of 6 grams of trans fats daily have a 39% higher risk of dying from heart disease as compared with those who eat about 1 gram daily.

If fast food is part of your diet, your trans fat load is likely to be even higher. A single serving of large fries cooked in partially hydrogenated vegetable oil assaults you with more than 8 grams of trans fats, in addition to nearly the same amount of saturated fat. When deep-fried in trans fat, chicken nuggets and fried fish burgers dish up a good 5 grams or more each. A piece of pie can amount to about 4 grams, while donuts and danishes pile on 3 grams apiece. A typical serving of hard margarine contributes 1 to 2.5 grams of trans fats.

The bottom line: there is really no safe amount of trans fat. Although the American Heart Association recommends limiting trans fats to no more than 2 grams daily, your best bet is to avoid them altogether.

HOW TO AVOID TRANS FATS

Become a label reader—there's no shame in it, and I promise it will make you smarter. Although manufacturers of packaged foods are now required to list trans fat content, if a standard serving size contains less than half a gram, it can claim to be trans fat free. These half-grams can add up quickly, so to be sure, look for "partially hydrogenated oils" in the list of ingredients.

Avoid hard margarine. Softer margarines are less hydrogenated (so they are oilier at room temperature) and are a safer choice, although olive oil is even better.

Curb your sweet tooth for all the reasons we've already discussed, but also because so many pre-packaged and bakery goodies contain margarine or vegetable shortening (another partially hydrogenated product), so are likely to be loaded with these deadly fats. I have found partially hydrogenated soybean oil in a wide variety of seemingly innocent products, including baby crackers, breakfast cereal, whole grain bread, and "nutrition bars."

Do not be fooled by labeling that proclaims "cholesterol free" or "cooked in vegetable oil." Although these statements are truthful, they are misleading and don't mean the product is healthy.

You've got to stay heart smart. Now that trans fats have reached our national consciousness, some companies have made an ironic about-face, substituting lard, a saturated fat, for trans fats, which allows them to promote their products as trans-fat free.

Perhaps even more insidiously, palm oil is increasingly replacing trans fats in a wide range of snack foods, despite the fact that it is dangerously high in saturated fat. While it is promoted as a more natural alternative, the industrial production of palm oil endangers a wide range of indigenous Southeast Asian rain forest vegetation and wildlife, including the Sumatran tiger, orangutans, and native elephants.

Dietary Cholesterol

People whose diets are exceptionally high in cholesterol are more likely to suffer heart disease and strokes, it's true, but in general, there is not a dramatic correlation between cholesterol consumption and heart disease. On average, the body manufactures three times more cholesterol "from scratch" than is found in the typical American diet. Cholesterol plays a critical role in the protection of nerve fibers, supports hormone production, and maintains the integrity of your cell membranes, but most of us get more than we need. The recommended daily intake of cholesterol is 300 mg for most people, although if you have heart disease, the American Heart Association recommends no more than 200 mg each day.

To give some perspective, a meal that includes a quarter-pound burger with cheese and a large order of french fries will supply more than 50 grams of total fat and about 20 grams of "bad" fats (saturated plus trans), but only 95 mg of cholesterol. One egg, on the other hand, contains 190 mg of cholesterol, but only 4.6 grams of fat.

Unless beef, pork, cheese, and eggs are regulars on your menu, the advice your doctor may give you to follow a "low cholesterol diet" may be well-intentioned, but it is unlikely to have a major impact on your cholesterol level.

FATS: FRIEND OR FOE?

- Fats are responsible for much of the flavor in food and help us feel full. Our daily fat intake should be about 25% to 30% of calories consumed, as long as we choose the healthier forms of fat.
- Monounsaturated fats (omega-9s) are found in olive oil and canola oil. They reduce the risk for heart disease and improve the lipid profile.
- Omega-3 fatty acids come from fish, flaxseed oil, and walnuts. Omega-3s reduce the risk for heart attacks, dementia, stroke, and heart rhythm abnormalities.
- Omega-6s come from most vegetable oils. In moderate amounts, they are important for good health, but too much can lead to inflammation.
- Saturated fats are found in meat, poultry, dairy, coconut, and palm kernel oils. Saturated fat raises the risk for heart disease, stroke, and dementia. It is associated with higher LDL, lower HDL, higher CRP, and an increased risk for blood clots. Limit saturated fats to less than 20 grams daily.
- Trans fats are found in hard margarine, vegetable shortening, and in many snack foods. Trans fats are the worst form of fat for heart health—even worse than saturated fats. The FDA allows a label to state "no trans fats" if the amount per serving is less than half a gram. If the phrase "partially hydrogenated oil" appears on the ingredient list, trans fats are there.

5

THE TRUTH ABOUT THE
WONDER FOODS

Not only does the food we eat nourish and sustain us, but some
foods can actually help us to heal, safeguarding our health and
vitality. Medical science is only beginning to unlock the secrets of these
special foods, but the foods I will tell you about have all been studied with a
scientifically impartial and open-minded approach.

Be wary of self-styled experts who attribute fantastical properties to
some "newly discovered" food—particularly if they are selling it. If it sounds
too good to be true, it probably is. My goal is to help you achieve a healthy
heart without the hype and to make it fun and tasty at the same time. While
virtually all foods from nature will promote good health, the "wonder foods,"
salmon, soy, nuts, and berries, have the power to enrich, and maybe even
save, your life.

SALMON AND OTHER SEAFOOD

A delicious and versatile fish rich in heart-protecting omega-3 fatty acids, salmon is a nutritional multitasker. When we add salmon and other fish that are high in omega-3 fatty acids to our plates, not only do our taste buds rejoice, but we are also providing our hearts with hard-core protection, and perhaps our skin and nervous systems, too. Eating fatty fish just once or twice a week appears to cut the risk of death from cardiac disease by about a third and to reduce mortality from any cause by more than 15%.

Although salmon has been the media darling, a number of other cold-water fish, including bluefin tuna, mackerel, herring, and sardines, are also excellent sources of omega-3 fatty acids. And while not considered omega-3 powerhouses, oysters, mussels, rainbow trout, and swordfish do supply moderate amounts of the good stuff.

Most of the leaner and warmer-water fish are fairly meager sources of omega-3s, although they are still excellent choices for healthy protein that is low in saturated fat.

Just in case you're wondering, nope, fried fish won't cut it. Studies have shown no protective advantage, once the fish is fried in a toxic grease bath and slathered with mayonnaise. In fact, some of the fattiest and most caloric fast food sandwiches are those made with fried fish.

YOUR HEART ON OMEGA-3S

There are probably several different ways that the marine omega-3 fatty acids provide heart protection. The theory is that when the heart is under severe stress, such as during a heart attack, the fatty acid is released and helps to stabilize the cell, thereby protecting it from a potentially lethal rhythm abnormality.

This theory is important when you consider that more than 50% of sudden deaths from heart disease (what we doctors call "sudden cardiac deaths") occur in people who have no prior history of heart problems. Fully 300,000 deaths in this country every year can be attributed to sudden cardiac death due to a catastrophic heart rhythm abnormality that affects the ventricles, the lower pumping chambers of the heart. This can occur as a result of a heart attack, a weakened heart muscle, or from an electrical malfunction of the heart. Many survivors of cardiac arrest suffer irreversible brain damage and damage to other vital organs as a result of insufficient oxygen to the brain. Rather than deal with the aftermath, we'd much rather prevent such a catastrophic event, and that's where omega-3s may help.

Omega-3 fatty acids provide other benefits to the heart, including decreased susceptibility to blood clots, lower triglycerides, lower blood pressure, improved blood flow, and reduced inflammation. Less serious, but more common, heart arrhythmias such as atrial fibrillation may also be reduced.

Numerous studies conducted worldwide attest to a protective effect of salmon and other omega-3 rich fish. For instance, a study of American women found that those who ate fish two to four times a week had a 31% lower risk of heart disease than those who ate fish less than once a month, as well as a lower risk of sudden cardiac death and stroke. The more fish the women ate, the greater the reduction in risk. However, eating fish as little as one to three times a month reduced cardiovascular risk by an impressive 21%.

Besides the clear cardiac advantages, there is some evidence that eating fish regularly may reduce the risk of prostate cancer, breast cancer, macular degeneration, and depression, possibly though the effects of omega-3 fatty acids. It may even help to keep your skin supple and healthy.

Omega-3s such as those found in cold-water fish are of critical importance to the developing brain. They are associated with higher levels of fine motor development, verbal intelligence, and social behavior. Sadly, many pregnant and nursing women simply don't get enough of this vital nutrient, but correcting the problem is not that simple.

MERCURY—THE DARK SIDE OF SEAFOOD

As with many good things, there is a dark side. For fish, that means mercury and other pollutants found throughout the waters of the world and, consequently, in the bodies of the fish we eat. Mercury comes primarily from coal-burning power plants; in the United States alone, 48 tons of the toxin is released into the environment each year. When mercury enters our bodies through the fish we eat, it easily crosses into the brain through the bloodstream and may become trapped there. When levels of mercury are high, neurological symptoms such as tremors, numbness, tingling, nervousness, and poor concentration may occur. Although it's not usually necessary, a blood test can readily detect high levels; tests of hair and nails tend to be less accurate.

Fortunately, our adult bodies are very good at ridding themselves of excess mercury, and usually simple avoidance of high mercury foods will bring levels down over a period of months, without the need to resort to other forms of therapy.

PREGNANCY, CHILDREN, AND MERCURY

For infants, children, and the developing fetus, the risk is far greater since high levels of mercury can interfere with normal brain development. Mercury is excreted in the breast milk, making it particularly harmful for nursing infants. The Institute of Medicine recommends that pregnant women, those considering pregnancy, and children eat only 6 to 12 ounces of seafood per week and avoid fish that tend to be especially high in mercury.

The FDA has specifically advised that pregnant women, breast-feeding women, and young children completely avoid these four species: tilefish (also known as golden bass or golden snapper), swordfish, king mackerel, and shark.

The tilefish has one of the highest mean concentrations of mercury (1.45 parts per million, or ppm, as reported by the Food and Drug Administration), and the other three species also carry very high concentrations (0.96-1.00 ppm).

While not as toxic as the four fish named above, Ahi tuna (often used for sushi), white albacore tuna, lobster, and halibut are also quite high in mercury. Pregnant and breast-feeding women and children should eat no more than a total of 6 ounces of canned albacore tuna each week, since this type of tuna, along with tuna steak, has more mercury than canned light tuna. Even fish with relatively low levels of mercury, such as canned chunk-light tuna, mahi mahi, and crab, should not be eaten more than twice a week. Salmon, shrimp, scallops, oysters, farmed catfish, freshwater trout, and flounder typically have the lowest levels of mercury.

MERCURY AND YOUR HEART

Recent studies have focused on the potential effects of mercury on the heart. Mercury may inactivate the antioxidant properties of a number of important factors in the body and may also increase the risk of blood clots. A study from Finland found that men with the highest mercury intake had almost twice the risk of cardiovascular disease as those whose diets included very little.

The people in that study who consumed the greatest amount of omega-3 fatty acids had a 44% lower risk of heart events compared with those who consumed the least. But people with the lowest levels of mercury plus the highest omega-3 consumption lowered their risk by as much as 67%. Similar findings were reported in a study involving men in eight European countries and Israel, although a study of 30,000 men in the United States found no definite correlation between mercury and heart disease.

WILD OR FARM-RAISED?

Fish in the wild produce omega-3 fatty acids from their diet of plankton and algae, delicacies that are not available to farmed fish. This distinction is one important reason that wild salmon is usually more flavorful, rich, and colorful. Farm-raised fish may be relatively deficient in omega-3 fatty acids since they are often fed fish chow that includes less-expensive omega-6 fatty acids. To give it that healthy pink omega-3 glow, farm-raised salmon is typically cosmetically enhanced with food coloring. Farm-raised salmon may also be comparatively deficient in vitamin D.

What's worse, farm-raised salmon is more likely to have high levels of man-made toxins such as dioxin and PCBs (polychlorinated biphenyls), industrial pollutants banned in the 1970s, but still present in the environment. European-raised salmon tends to have higher levels of contaminants than salmon from North and South America. Salmon farming also contributes to the pollution of the world's oceans, due to the wide-spread use of pesticides and antibiotics, as well as waste-products that are released into the surrounding waters.

Your Aunt Betty's fresh catch of the day may not be such a good bet either, since many local waterways are contaminated with PCBs. Overall, experts believe that the health risk from toxins such as these is probably fairly low, but high levels have been linked to cancer in animal studies. Neurological problems such as impaired memory have been reported in adults who regularly eat sport fish from polluted waters.

Developmental delays, learning disabilities, and poor immunity are known to occur in children of women exposed to high levels of PCBs during pregnancy. PCBs are generally found in the fattiest part of the fish, including the skin. To determine your level of exposure, blood testing for PCBs is available, but it costs well over $1000; instead, reduce your exposure to these toxins by limiting your consumption of farm-raised salmon and fish caught in polluted local lakes and waterways. Once PCBs have taken up residence in your body, it may take years to clear them.

WHAT ARE THE ALTERNATIVES?

If fish just doesn't float your boat, jump to this chapter's next section to learn about plant-based omega-3 sources, or turn to chapter 11, where you'll learn about omega-3 fatty acid supplements.

While there are as yet no specific guidelines on fish-oil supplements during pregnancy, many obstetricians recommend them as a safer source for omega-3 fatty acids since the mercury and other toxins are usually filtered out. Of course, if you are pregnant or nursing, be sure to ask your doctor's advice before taking supplements of any kind.

GO FISH

- Salmon is a powerhouse source of omega-3 fatty acids. Many other cold-water fish also supply omega-3 fatty acids.
- Omega-3 fatty acids appear to protect the heart by preventing life-threatening heart rhythm disturbances. They also lower triglyceride levels.
- Eating fish two to four times a week is associated with a 30% to 50% reduction in heart disease risk.
- Mercury is a contaminant found in many fish; it may increase the risk of heart disease. Mercury levels are excessively high in tilefish, swordfish, king mackerel, and shark. Other toxins such as PCBs are found in fish from a variety of sources.
- Pregnant women, nursing women, and children should eat no more than 12 ounces of low-mercury seafood per week in order to limit exposure to toxins.

NUTS—MORE THAN JUST A FUNNY WORD

For years, the well-meaning "low fat brigade" vigorously preached the evils of nuts because of the high fat content of these crunchy little goodies. The irony is that by doing so, they turned many people away from a tremendous source of healthy fats and plant protein. A true wonder food, nuts not only reduce the risk of heart disease, stroke, and diabetes, but they are also a terrific and satisfying snack.

Nuts are indeed high in fat, but it is primarily the heart-healthy monounsaturated variety. Per ounce, they supply 160 to 200 calories, 50% to 75% of which are fat calories. One ounce amounts to about twenty almonds, pecan halves, or cashews, or fourteen walnut halves, or 2 tablespoons of natural (not processed) peanut butter.

Rich with monounsaturated fat, pecans, walnuts, hazelnuts, and almonds are low in naturally occurring saturated fats. Brazil nuts, with more than 25% saturated fat and a high overall fat content, are less heart friendly. Cashews are somewhere in the middle. They are relatively lower in total fat than most nuts, so their overall saturated fat content of about 21% is less troublesome, as long you don't overdo it. Macadamia nuts, which are more than 70% fat by weight, are very caloric, but in small amounts can be a good source of monounsaturated fatty acids.

Walnuts are particularly dear to our hearts, since one ounce supplies about 2500 mg of omega-3 fatty acids, as well as abundant monounsaturated fatty acids. Walnuts provide ten to fifteen times more omega-3 fatty acids than other nuts, making them a smart addition to a healthy diet. They are also high in antioxidants and low in saturated fat.

Nuts provide a variety of other important nutrients, including vitamin E, magnesium, and folic acid. They are a good source of fiber, including heart-healthy soluble fiber, which may help explain why a diet containing liberal amounts of nuts and nut products has been shown to improve the cholesterol profile above and beyond what might be expected based on the fat composition alone.

One of the first studies to look at the heart-protecting effects of nuts found that people who ate nuts more than four times a week had a risk of fatal coronary heart disease nearly 50% lower than those who ate nuts less than once a week. The benefits were similar amongst males and females, elderly and young people, smokers, nonsmokers, and vegetarians. Comparable findings were reported in the Physicians Health Study of more than 21,000 men, followed for seventeen years. Men who ate one ounce of nuts at least twice a week had half the risk of sudden cardiac death as men who rarely ate nuts.

Other research has found that women who regularly eat nuts at least five times a week may reduce their chances of developing diabetes by more than 25%, compared to those who eat no nuts at all. Even eating nuts just one to four times weekly may cut the risk of diabetes by more than 15%.

THE ALL-AMERICAN PEANUT

Peanuts, an American tradition, are technically speaking, not really nuts at all. In fact, they belong to the family of legumes, which are plants with edible seeds that are packaged in pods. Legumes, including soybeans, are terrifically good for you. A large national study reported in 2001 that when legumes were eaten four or more times per week, the risk of coronary heart disease was reduced by 22%. In 2002, the Nurses' Health Study reported that eating peanut butter five or more times a week was associated with a 21% reduction in the risk of developing adult onset diabetes, compared to people who rarely, if ever, touched the stuff.

Peanuts provide considerably more protein than most nuts—about 25% by weight—and they are also higher in fiber. They are a valuable source of monounsaturated fatty acids and do offer a reasonably good amount of polyunsaturated fatty acids, with only a modest helping of saturated fat.

I personally ate a peanut butter and jelly sandwich for lunch every day during my first five years in grade school. (I'm not quite certain what that says about me, but I sure looked forward to lunch every day.) As healthy as peanuts can be, however, peanut butter is not all goodness and light.

Manufacturers typically add partially hydrogenated oils (the dreaded trans fats) or palm kernel oil (saturated fat) to peanut butter to help prolong shelf life. You're much better off choosing the all-natural form of peanut butter. Although it usually has to be stirred before eating, due to separation of the peanut oil, refrigerating after opening and stirring will help prevent this separation.

Before you plunge into the nut bowl, remind yourself that moderation is the key to good health and happiness. It only takes one ounce of nuts five days a week to make a world of difference in your risk of heart disease or diabetes. If you choose to add nuts to your diet—and you should—they should be used in place of something less healthful. For example, a peanut butter sandwich instead of a ham sandwich is a great choice, as long as you go easy on the peanut butter.

Don't sabotage your good intentions by overdoing it.

GO NUTS

- People who eat one ounce of nuts each day may lower their risk of fatal heart disease by 50%, when compared to people who eat no nuts.
- A diet high in nuts and peanuts is associated with a greater than 20% reduction in the risk of diabetes. Nuts may lower LDL and Lp(a) by 10%.
- One ounce of nuts provides 160-200 calories. Peanut butter serves up 100 calories per tablespoon.
- Avoid peanut butter that is manufactured with partially hydrogenated oils and tropical oils.

SOY

In October 1999, after reviewing twenty-seven important clinical research studies, the FDA authorized manufacturers of soy-based foods to provide health claims for soy protein and its role in reducing the risk of coronary heart disease. Soy protein in the range of 25 to 50 grams daily has been associated in some studies with lower LDL cholesterol on the order of 3% to 15% and appears to have the greatest effect in people whose baseline cholesterol levels are elevated. Working this amount of soy protein into your daily fare may also reduce triglycerides by about 10% and cut homocysteine levels.

Soy appears to help lower blood pressure for some people. A Chinese study of people with hypertension found marked reductions in blood pressure in people who ate 40 grams of soy protein every day. In a Boston study of hypertensive postmenopausal women, when 25 mg of daily protein intake from animal sources was replaced with 25 mg of soy protein, there was a significant blood pressure reduction (about 10mm Hg systolic and 7 mm Hg diastolic), which is comparable to the results we usually see with a mild anti-hypertensive medication.

There are numerous other ways in which soy can help keep our bodies healthy and strong. In postmenopausal women with the metabolic syndrome (characterized by obesity, high blood pressure, and high blood sugar levels), soy nuts have been shown to improve blood sugar control when used in place of less healthy foods. Soy-based foods such as soy beans (fresh or roasted), soy milk, tofu, textured soy protein, tempeh, and miso are excellent sources of soy protein, and usually also provide isoflavones, which are substances that might account for soy's remarkable benefits to our health.

While nearly 80% of edible fat consumed in the United States comes from soy oil, this is often in the form of partially hydrogenated oil (that is, the evil trans fats I told you about in chapter 4). Natural soy oil is better, but it provides none of the most important health benefits from soy, including high quality protein, fiber, and other plant-based nutrients.

DO ISOFLAVONES MATTER?

Isoflavones are chemicals that occur naturally in plants and bear certain similarities to our own estrogen. Plants produce isoflavones to protect themselves from harmful microorganisms and stress. They are nutritionally available to us in important amounts in the form of soy. Chickpeas, also known as garbanzo beans, and a major ingredient in hummus, a middle-eastern specialty, are another good source.

The importance of isoflavones and their role in a heart-healthy diet is only just beginning to be understood. A study in primates from 1997 sheds some light on the subject. Monkeys fed soy-based diets both with and without isoflavones were found to have major differences in the amount of atherosclerosis they developed. Although the arteries of both groups looked better than the arteries of those on a regular diet, the isoflavone group came out far ahead.

One theory is that isoflavones may act as antioxidants, preventing damage to the artery walls that may lead to plaque buildup and heart attacks. What's more, isoflavones help to lower LDL cholesterol. They may reduce the growth of cells in the arterial walls that are involved in the development of atherosclerosis, improve the elastic tone of the arteries, and reduce clot formation that is important in the mechanism of a heart attack. There is also a great deal of interest in the possibility that phytoestrogens, including isoflavones, may reduce cancer risk.

The effects of soy isoflavones may be different for women than for men. Most studies have not shown any change in HDL cholesterol in men who increase their soy consumption, but women who eat more than 32 grams of soy protein daily may increase this "good" form of cholesterol by 7%. Lp(a) may also decrease in women who eat soy-based foods, with little or no change reported in most studies in men. Likewise, arterial elasticity may improve more in women than in men. The data is still somewhat sketchy, and a study of postmenopausal women aged 60 and over found no improvement in lipids in this population.

WHERE ISOFLAVONES COME FROM

Soy oil and soy sauce do not contain isoflavones, but soy protein does. However, if the soy protein has been processed with ethanol at the time of manufacturing, the isoflavones are washed away. The closer soy is to its natural state, the more isoflavones it will have. For example, dehulled or defatted soybeans have less isoflavones than a virgin soybean.

The isoflavone content of soy is dependent on the crop and the conditions under which it was grown. The average isoflavone content of soybeans is 1 mg per gram, but the range can be anywhere from 0.4 to 2.4 mg per gram. Therefore, it is difficult for manufacturers to be specific about the isoflavone content of their products, since any given product may include soy from several different sources.

Isoflavones in fermented soy products such as tempeh appear to be easier for the body to utilize than those in other soy products. Our body's ability to put isoflavones to work may be inconsistent. Wheat fiber in the gut may reduce the body's capacity to absorb isoflavones, due to the fiber's binding effect. What's more, an individual's own unique gut "microflora" (or resident beneficial bacteria) may affect the absorption of soy isoflavones.

ARE ISOFLAVONES SAFE?

Since isoflavones are phytoestrogens, structurally very similar to estrogen, this has raised some concerns about their safety. Estrogen, once touted as a "wonder drug" for its heart-saving potential, is now viewed with much concern and distrust, as more recent studies have shown a serious capacity for harm, in terms of both heart disease and cancer risk, in some women. That does not appear to be the case for soy phytoestrogens.

There is no convincing evidence that soy increases the risk of breast cancer or uterine cancer, and some studies do indicate that phytoestrogens may in fact reduce these risks. However, until more is known about cancer and phytoestrogens, caution is definitely advisable, and you should check with your doctor if your risk for these conditions is high.

There has also been concern raised about the effect of soy on the thyroid gland. As long as you are not iodine deficient, this is unlikely to be a major issue. However, if you eat a lot of soy, let your doctor know so that routine blood work can be done if needed.

HOW MUCH IS ENOUGH?

The American Heart Association has specifically advised against isoflavone supplements and other soy-based pills and potions (see chapter 11), but continues to advocate soy in the diet as an excellent source of protein, fiber, and other nutrients. The AHA points out that perhaps the most important role soy can play is as a heart-friendly alternative to saturated fat-laden animal protein.

While the FDA suggests a goal of 25 grams per day of soy protein in order to improve heart health, the isoflavone content of food can vary quite widely, and no definite recommendations have been made regarding isoflavone intake. A typical serving of a soy-based food provides 20-35 mg of isoflavones. The Japanese diet includes, on average, about 50 mg/day of soy isoflavones, while the average soy-deficient American diet contains about one-tenth that amount. Japanese people following a traditional soy-based diet have about half the heart disease risk of Americans. Coincidentally they also have lower risks of breast, prostate, and endometrial cancer—risks that rise in people who move to the United States and take up our "traditional" high saturated fat, low soy American diet.

HOW TO GET MORE SOY INTO YOUR DIET

So how do you go about adding more soy to your diet? A simple first step for the timid is to substitute soy milk for your usual cow's milk in your breakfast cereal and coffee. Don't cringe—soy milk doesn't have to be the watery, grainy liquid you may remember from years ago. There are several terrific brands (Silk, Sun Soy, and Whole Foods house brand, to name a few) that are readily available at the supermarket, in or near the dairy section. These milks can also be used for cooking, and since they tend to be creamier than skim milk (but often just as low in calories), they work well in cream-style soups and other recipes. For variety, you can also buy soy milk in flavors such as vanilla, coffee, chai tea, and chocolate. A typical brand of soy milk provides 6.25 grams of soy protein and roughly 40 mg of isoflavones per 8-ounce serving.

Once you're ready to venture into soy-land, you'll find all kinds of delicious options. Edamame, steamed green soybeans often served warm in Japanese restaurants, are great all by themselves or in a salad; so are crunchy roasted soy nuts, which come in a variety of flavors. Don't overlook the wonderful (and super easy to prepare) soy sausages and soy burgers, which you can usually find in the freezer case at the grocery store, and which can fool even a committed carnivore, including my dog.

Tofu is another way to add some healthy protein to your diet. Since tofu takes on the flavors of the foods it is cooked in, it is a natural in stir-fries and casseroles, and soft tofu can also be used in desserts because of its creamy texture.

Texturized vegetable protein (TVP) is yet another alternative. It often comes in a dry form, but increasingly can be found in the freezer section at the supermarket. When reconstituted and cooked with spaghetti sauce, barbecue sauce, or chili, for example, it is a remarkably good substitute for ground beef. Experiment with tempeh, a fermented form of soy, since it is a potent source of isoflavones. As always, be smart about portion size. Good foods have calories, too.

SUPER SOY

- 25 grams of soy protein per day is recommended; 30 to 50 grams may be even better.
- Soy protein may lower LDL cholesterol and triglycerides modestly; in women, it may raise HDL, although probably not in women over 60.
- Soy protein may help improve the tone of blood vessel walls and reduce the risk of blood clots.
- Soy protein is a heart smart replacement for red meat. Good sources of soy protein include soy milk, edamame, roasted soy nuts, soy burgers, tofu, tempeh, and textured vegetable protein. Soy protein is not found in soy sauce or soybean oil.

BERRIES AND OTHER BRIGHT TREASURES—THE ANTIOXIDANTS

Blueberries, strawberries, raspberries, and cranberries are easy to love. They're beautiful, they taste great, and they are rich in heart-protective antioxidants.

Antioxidants block the action of free radicals, which are highly reactive substances that have at least one unpaired electron. (In the more stable state, negatively charged electrons are paired with positively charged protons, keeping the electrical charge neutral). Free radicals are not all bad; when present in healthy quantities, they help to produce energy and to kill harmful bacteria. They may also protect against cancer by preventing harmful chemical reactions that stimulate the growth of abnormal cells.

But when there is an overabundance, free radicals can cause harmful reactions that lead to serious damage of our cells and arteries. Oxidation of LDL cholesterol by free radicals, for example, is one thing that makes the LDL so dangerous to our arteries.

While most fruits and vegetables are naturally high in antioxidants, berries, in particular, are superb health boosters. Blueberries have substantially greater antioxidant activity than most other fruits and vegetables, and the more we learn about them, the more fascinating they become. While most research to date has been on rodents, blueberries appear to have some very important brain-boosting properties, enhancing learning ability and slowing down age-related decline.

Strawberries and raspberries are also antioxidant powerhouses. Studies of raspberries have shown that the darker the berry, the greater the antioxidant activity. And cranberries aren't just for Thanksgiving anymore. Preliminary research suggests that they may contain substances that aid in relaxation of the arteries and perhaps even help to reduce the chance of blood clots.

Pomegranate juice has impressive antioxidant properties, too, and may limit the ability of LDL cholesterol to be oxidized, thereby reducing the rate of cholesterol buildup in the arteries. A research trial of people with heart disease, funded by the pomegranate industry, reported significant improvement in stress test results in pomegranate drinkers.

The most active component of pomegranate juice appears to be ellagic acid, an antioxidant that is also found in red raspberries, strawberries, cranberries, blueberries, and walnuts.

Another important antioxidant is lycopene, which provides the red pigment to tomatoes, watermelon, and grapefruit. Lycopene has been associated with heart protection and reduced cancer risk.

Oddly enough, lycopene is better absorbed from processed tomato products like spaghetti sauce and tomato paste than from fresh tomatoes.

Tomatoes are also a great source of vitamin A and provide a number of other antioxidant nutrients, fiber, and potassium.

Antioxidants are abundant in nature. Essentially any highly pigmented plant is likely to supply you with these very important plant chemicals (also known as phytochemicals), although berries and tomatoes are especially rich. The wider the variety of pigmented fruits and vegetables you choose, the greater the range of antioxidants.

COMMIT TO COLOR

Add berries to your breakfast cereal and perk up your morning. Ask for mixed berries for dessert when eating out—but remember to hold the whipped cream. Create a riotous salad with a variety of green leafy vegetables, colored peppers, and tomatoes, and forgo the pale iceberg lettuce, which is a relatively meager source of antioxidants. Order a reduced-cheese veggie pizza with tomato sauce on a thin whole wheat crust, and you're good to go. Eat an orange rather than drink it since many of the phytochemicals are contained in the fruit itself. Don't be afraid of spinach, kale, and other gorgeous dark greens. Remember some of the lighter colors, too. Besides adding flavor, onions and garlic, for example, also contain important antioxidants. Experiment with color and your life is sure to be richer for it.

6

THE EVILDOERS:
TRUTH OR FICTION?

D anger is lurking on your dinner plate. The news is blaring from your TV and car radio, jumping off the newspaper headlines, and popping up everywhere you look online. The soccer mom down the street, your mailman, even the guy behind the counter at the convenience store knows all about it. Sometimes it seems like everyone has the scoop on "good" food and "bad" food.

You know there are healthy fats, unhealthy fats, and downright dangerous fats, yet many people still insist that all fat is bad. Eggs, salt, and chocolate are other dietary taboos, but have they really earned their evil reputations?

BUTTER OR MARGARINE: JUST LET IT SLIDE?

For years, doctors and other health professionals urged people to dump the butter in favor of what was thought to be the obvious healthier choice: margarine. Although this butter-impersonator has no cholesterol and little to no saturated fat, many people still haven't got the word that hard margarine, with its abundance of trans fats, may be even more harmful to the arteries than real butter. While the labels proclaiming margarine to be "all vegetable oil," "high in polyunsaturated fat," and "cholesterol free" are true, these claims ignore trans fat, a truly bad actor.

Vegetable shortening, frequently used as a butter substitute in baking, is also loaded with trans fats, although manufacturers are starting to come up with alternatives. Ironically, some of these new and improved products contain lard, the greasy animal fat that shortening was designed to replace.

Butter supplies very little in the way of trans fats and provides a calorie and total fat content similar to margarine, although it is three to six times higher in saturated fat. To avoid saturated fats and minimize your trans fat exposure, choose soft margarine. Per serving, tub margarine contains one-fourth to one-half the amount of trans fats as stick margarine; squeeze margarine is even better.

In an effort to boost the nutritional value of margarine and other spreads, some manufacturers have incorporated plant sterols and their derivatives, plant stanols. These products include Benecol and Take Control margarines. They decrease the amount of cholesterol the intestinal tract can absorb. LDL cholesterol may be lowered by 10% to 20%.

The drawback is that this sort of effect is achieved only when substantial amounts, typically 4 tablespoons or more, of the margarine are consumed on a daily basis. I'll tell you more about these natural cholesterol reducers in chapter 11.

Olive oil is the healthiest alternative to butter and margarine, chock-full of antioxidants and healthy monounsaturated fat. But like all fats, butter and margarine included, the calorie count ranges between 100–120 calories per tablespoon, so it's important to work this into your daily calorie equation. While olive oil cannot be used as an across-the-board substitute, it works beautifully with bread and vegetables and is a perfect complement to salads.

What if, like me, you find the taste of butter irresistible, and don't want to give it up completely? If you choose to indulge in this luxury, make sure you do it in moderation. One teaspoon contains 35 calories and 2.5 grams of saturated fat, or about 15% of your daily allotment. If you bump it up to a tablespoon, suddenly you've reached half of your recommended daily saturated fat intake, and 100 calories. The way I see it, eating well should not be about sacrifice, but about being smart with the choices you make.

EGGS: IS THERE A SUNNY SIDE?

Eggs supply about 30% of the cholesterol in the average American's diet. One egg provides about 5 grams of total fat, only 1.5 grams of saturated fat, and 200 mg of cholesterol. The total recommended daily intake of cholesterol for most of us is 300 mg, although people with heart disease should stick to 200 mg or less. And while it's smart to shy away from high cholesterol foods, for most people, dietary cholesterol plays a relatively minor role in determining the blood cholesterol level. This is because the body manufactures about three times as much cholesterol from other dietary sources such as saturated and trans fats.

When the likelihood of heart attack or stroke was studied in relation to egg consumption, eggs did not appear to contribute much risk, except in people who were diabetic. Although the landmark Framingham study found no clear association between egg consumption and blood cholesterol level, another large study found that people who ate six or more eggs per week had 2.7 times the risk of heart disease as those who ate less than one egg per week.

Eggs are big business, so marketing geniuses have been hard at work, trying to turn them into health food. For instance, eggs that are higher in omega-3 fatty acids are now widely available. You may also find "free-range" eggs at your grocery store. The chickens that lay these eggs do not necessarily produce better eggs unless they are truly well-fed, free wandering birds like the ones you might find on a small family farm.

The bottom line: it appears that eating one or two eggs once or twice a week is not particularly harmful unless you are diabetic. If you choose to eat eggs, cut back on cholesterol elsewhere in your diet.

Several commercial egg substitutes are on the market and work particularly well for baking; tofu and bananas may also be substituted as binders in some recipes.

If you like eggs, you may want to opt for an egg-white omelet instead of a full egg omelet, since the cholesterol is concentrated in the yolk. Eggs are a good source of protein (about 6 grams per egg), a little over half of which is found in the egg white. If you really enjoy the yolks, use one whole egg together with two or three egg whites, and be sure to cook in olive oil or canola oil rather than in bacon grease. Egg-Beaters and other similar products made from egg whites are a simple way to avoid egg yolks without the mess. Add vegetables, including peppers, tomatoes, onions and mushrooms, for flavor and texture, and you'll be surprised at how little you miss the yolks.

SODIUM: SHAKING THE HABIT

High blood pressure, or hypertension, is a problem of epic proportions in the United States, afflicting 50 to 60 million Americans. High blood pressure is a major contributor to more than 1.25 million heart attacks per year and is also the most important and preventable cause of stroke. Each year, up to 2 million people will develop hypertension, yet only two thirds of those who have high blood pressure even know that they have it and only about half are actually treated for the problem. It has been estimated that less than half of those treated are adequately controlled to a blood pressure of less than 140/90.

There are many factors that contribute to high blood pressure (which we'll go over in more detail in chapter 13), but for many people, sodium in the diet is a major troublemaker. The chief source of sodium in our diet is salt, although monosodium glutamate (MSG) may also be an important player, particularly in Asian diets. People with hypertension, especially in the early stages, can often avoid medical treatment simply by cutting back on salt.

Our daily minimum requirement of sodium is a mere 500 mg, or about one-fifth of a teaspoon of salt. Yet the average American consumes on the order of 4000 mg of sodium a day, or nearly two full teaspoons of salt. The recommended maximum daily intake of sodium is 2300 mg for people under 45 and 1500 mg for people 45 and older and for people with high blood pressure.

Who really needs to worry about sodium? People with borderline to high blood pressures stand to benefit the most from reducing sodium intake. African Americans, who tend to be more salt sensitive, should be especially vigilant about sodium. It behooves anyone with heart disease to watch their sodium. Decreasing salt intake by about half can result in significant improvements in blood pressure—improvements that may lead to a measurable reduction in the risk of stroke, heart attack, and congestive heart failure.

SALT AND CONGESTIVE HEART FAILURE

Congestive heart failure is an increasingly common condition that occurs when the heart's ability to pump is not sufficient to meet the body's demands. It is characterized by fluid retention, particularly in the lungs, but also in the soft tissues, most typically the legs. (Don't panic. Not everyone with swollen legs has heart failure, although many people experience swelling in the hands and feet after a salty meal.)

Congestive heart failure may be caused by weakness of the heart muscle, stiffness of the heart muscle, or both. Many factors may contribute to the development of heart failure, but a major player is high blood pressure. People who are afflicted with congestive heart failure are often extremely sensitive to salt. For some of these folks, a pepperoni pizza can mean a trip to the emergency room.

If you are overweight and eat more than the recommended amount of salt, your risk of congestive heart failure is 40% higher than those whose salt intake falls within the recommended levels.

WHO HID THE SALT?

The fact is that most of the salt we eat doesn't come from the salt shaker, but rather from the salt that has been added to our food before it ever makes it onto our plates. Important sources are processed foods such as lunch meats, ham, hot dogs, soups, pizza, pasta sauces, prepared rice, crackers, and cheeses. The following foods contain a full 1/2 teaspoon of salt, or about 1200 mg of sodium, per typical serving: one bouillon cube, two large pickles, eleven pretzels, one cup of canned soup, 3 ounces of bologna, 2 teaspoons of soy sauce.

Fast-food is a sodium landmine. Combine a quarter-pound cheeseburger with large fries and you have not only a day's supply of fat, but also nearly 1,500 mg of sodium. Four slices of sausage pizza or a typical fast-food chicken dinner supplies about 2,300 mg, which is your daily sodium allotment. Other restaurant food tends to be just as bad, even when the dining is upscale. Be particularly wary of Asian-style food, which is often laced with liberal amounts of soy sauce and MSG. If you're not careful, you could easily get up to 15 grams of sodium this way, a staggering 10 times the recommended amount.

Get smart about reading labels. Even if a label proclaims its product offers "reduced sodium," it is not necessarily low in sodium. For a product, such as soy sauce or soup, to be labeled this way, it merely needs to contain at least 25% less sodium than the regular product. "Light in sodium" is better; that product must contain at least 50% less sodium than the regular equivalent. "Low sodium" means 140 mg sodium or less per serving, and "very low" means 35 mg sodium or less. The sodium content is included on the standard nutrition labels on all prepared foods. It's up to you to read it.

Getting used to a reduced salt diet may take a little time, but studies have shown that after two to four months on a low salt diet, your taste buds will adjust. Cut back gradually and you're more likely to be successful.

CHOCOLATE WISHES

Chocolate's scientific name, *Theobroma cacao*, translates literally to "food of the gods," and who can argue with that? A taste of the divine—could it really be so bad? The truth is that it is not so much the chocolate that is at fault, but rather the bad-guy ingredients that it travels with: sugar, butter, and cream. A typical 1.6-ounce milk-chocolate bar contains 225 calories, 26 grams of carbohydrates, and about 13 grams of fat, 8 of which are saturated fat grams. Definitely not a heart-smart choice, no matter how loudly it may call your name.

Cocoa powder (not to be confused with hot chocolate mix) is a very different animal. Per tablespoon, unsweetened cocoa powder provides 12 calories, 2.9 grams of carbohydrates, and only 0.7 grams of fat.

To the great delight of chocolate lovers everywhere, chocolate has been discovered to be a very good source of antioxidants known as flavonoids. While medical data on the effects of cocoa is sparse, scientists have recently discovered some very interesting properties of this magic bean. One study, reported by a group at Pennsylvania State University, involved supplementing the diets of healthy volunteers with cocoa and dark chocolate and comparing them to volunteers who ate a chocolate-free diet.

Keeping all other factors as equal as possible, including fat and carbohydrates, they reported several important findings. First, those who were fed the chocolate diet had a 4% rise in HDL cholesterol—small but significant. In addition, there was a measurable improvement in antioxidant capacity, which reduced the amount of harm that LDL cholesterol was able to inflict on the arteries.

Other studies have found that cocoa inhibits blood platelet function slightly, meaning that it may have the power to lower the risk of dangerous blood clots. Chocolate may also improve the ability of the arteries to respond normally to stress, and it may even help to lower blood pressure. A small study from Italy reported an impressive ten point drop in blood pressure when lucky test subjects were fed a 3.5 ounce bar of flavonoid-rich dark chocolate every day, whereas several other studies have also reported significant, although less impressive, reductions.

The benefit of chocolate appears to be limited to dark chocolate; in fact, combining chocolate with milk, such as in milk chocolate or hot cocoa, dramatically decreases its antioxidant effects. And white chocolate, which contains cocoa butter but not cocoa solids, seems to have no antioxidant effect at all.

Complicating matters further, much of the popular dark chocolate that is widely available is actually low in flavonoids. It is the flavonoids that give dark chocolate its bitter taste. Since many Americans have yet to develop a liking for this bitterness, manufacturers have developed processes to remove the flavonoids from their products. To get your full quotient of antioxidants, look for extra dark chocolate with high cacao levels of 70% or greater.

Healthier ways to enjoy chocolate include cocoa nibs, which are nuggets of coarsely ground cocoa beans, usually with a little sweetener. Also, you can substitute three tablespoons of cocoa plus one tablespoon of oil for an ounce of baking chocolate in recipes, and while this will not save any calories, it will allow you to substitute a healthier polyunsaturated fat for one that is saturated. Personally, I like to splurge on a really high quality chocolate bar and savor a small square or two every day. However you choose to enjoy it, it's good to know that this little taste of heaven is no longer entirely taboo.

THE TRUTH ABOUT THE EVILDOERS

- One teaspoon of butter equals 35 calories, 11 mg cholesterol, 4 g total fat, and 2.5 g saturated fat, or about 15% of your daily saturated fat allotment.
- Hard margarine is high in trans fats, while butter contains virtually no trans fats. Trans fats are more dangerous than saturated fats. The softer the margarine, the less trans fat it has.
- One egg equals 5 g total fat, 1.5 g saturated fat, and 200 mg cholesterol. The total recommended daily intake of cholesterol is 300 mg. Limit whole eggs to four or fewer per week.
- The average American eats 4000 mg of salt each day. Keep sodium to 2300 mg daily if you're under 45; cut back to 1500 mg if you're 45 or older, or have high blood pressure or heart disease.
- At least 75% of the salt we eat is hidden in fast foods and processed foods.
- Dark chocolate (but not milk chocolate) is a very good source of antioxidants, but most chocolate bars are full of saturated fats.
- Dark chocolate might improve lipids, lower blood pressure, and reduce the risk of blood clots.

7

THE BATTLE OF THE DIETS

It's one thing to understand the basic building blocks of a healthy diet. But putting those pieces together can be downright puzzling, especially if you want to lose weight and get healthier at the same time. Popular diets tend to run in cycles, just like hemlines. But what's trendy may not always be what's best for us.

Among the most intriguing popular diets are the high carbohydrate/low fat diet, the high protein/low carb diet, the Mediterranean diet, the Japanese diet, and the vegetarian diet. Each has its own unique appeal.

Only the high carb/low fat and Mediterranean diets have been rigorously studied with respect to their effects on heart health. Both diets came out way ahead when compared to our traditional Western diet.

The high protein/low carb diets have been studied in people without heart disease for up to a year, but their long-term effects on heart health and overall health are not known. We do know, however, that a diet high in saturated fat can have harmful effects on the heart and blood vessels, so there is good reason to be concerned about a regimen that allows unlimited quantities of bacon, beef, and cheese. Remember what your smart mother told you: if it sounds too good to be true, it probably is.

THE HIGH CARBOHYDRATE, LOW FAT DIET

Given what we know about the importance of fruits, vegetables, and whole grains, it is no wonder that many cardiovascular specialists have recommended choosing a diet rich in these high carbohydrate foods. In the 1980s, Dr. Dean Ornish, a cardiologist and research scientist who is a prominent proponent of a high carbohydrate, low fat diet, proposed a radical shift in the way Americans eat and live. He advised that no more than 10% of daily calorie intake should come from fats and that the majority of calories (about 70%) should come from complex carbohydrates. This recommendation is in stark contrast to the typical American diet, which breaks down to about 35% fat, 50% carbohydrate (predominantly simple carbohydrates), and 15% protein. Dr. Ornish's plan also bans cholesterol, whereas the average American diet includes up to 500 mg of cholesterol daily.

The carbohydrates in a diet of this type specifically include whole grains, fruits, vegetables, and legumes and not highly refined carbohydrates such as fat-free sweets, white breads, and white pasta. Limiting these high glycemic foods is crucial, since a diet with a high glycemic load is associated with a greater likelihood of heart attacks, stroke, and diabetes, along with weight gain.

In a study of forty-eight highly motivated people with significant heart disease (thirty-five of whom actually completed the study), Dr. Ornish and his colleagues at California Pacific Medical Center were able to show a modest reversal of cholesterol plaques in the heart arteries after just one year by introducing a whole-foods vegetarian diet, combined with an intensive lifestyle modification, including aerobic exercise, yoga, stress management, group therapy, and smoking cessation. In contrast, those people enrolled in the study who declined to take part in this admittedly rigorous therapy showed measurable worsening of their cholesterol buildup.

At five years the results were even better in the low fat vegetarian group, while people who did not participate had further growth of their cholesterol plaques. What's worse, their blockages were more unstable, putting them at higher risk for a heart attack. In fact, the risk of heart attack or other cardiovascular problems was nearly two-and-a-half times greater in those who did not follow Dr. Ornish's regimen. People who stuck to the program also lost weight (about 24 pounds) and kept about half of that weight off over five years.

No doubt, the intensive life-style modifications made an enormous difference in the lives of the people who followed the program. In truth, we really cannot be certain how much of the improvement to attribute to diet and how much to the dramatic lifestyle changes. In a blow to the theory that it was the diet alone that made the difference, the Women's Health Initiative Dietary Modification study of nearly 60,000 women found no reduction in cardiovascular or cancer risk in postmenopausal women who followed a diet that limited fat to just 20% of daily calories for eight years. Nevertheless, Dr. Ornish has convincing, long-term data, a claim that devotees of most other diets cannot make.

WHY DOESN'T EVERYONE EAT THIS WAY?

What could be wrong with the high carbohydrate, extremely low fat approach? It sure isn't easy. It goes without saying that it is difficult for most people to stay the course with this type of diet. What's more, several decades ago, when the high carbohydrate diet was originally developed, data regarding the importance of healthy fats was just emerging. A diet this restrictive essentially excludes nuts, seeds, and fish, all of which are now known to be associated with a lower risk of heart disease, stroke, and, in the case of nuts, diabetes.

Only small amounts of omega-3 fatty acids are permissible on a very low fat diet. Remember that these "good" fats, as well as monounsaturated fats such as olive oil, benefit cholesterol and other lipid levels.

As it turns out, a diet very high in carbohydrates and very low in fat will lower not only the "bad" LDL cholesterol, but also the "good" HDL cholesterol. HDL cholesterol is known to help slow the development of atherosclerosis, and lower levels of HDL have been associated with a higher risk of heart disease. Proponents of the low fat, high carbohydrate diet counter that the reduction in HDL from this type of diet may not carry the same implications as low HDL due to other dietary and lifestyle conditions, but this argument remains theoretical.

Triglycerides may also increase with a high carb diet, especially one high in simple high glycemic "white" carbs like white pasta, white rice, white bread, and white potatoes. (Of course, these high glycemic foods are not sanctioned by the Ornish proponents.) Finally, in a very low fat diet, vitamin D levels may be inadequate, particularly if the diet includes few or no animal products.

Let me share one example with you of how the best "high carb" intentions can go bad. My patient Sherry, a diabetic, was 58 years old and determined to get back into shape after her office visit revealed high blood pressure and a weight gain of 15 pounds over the past year. She and her husband joined a gym, contracted with a personal trainer, and began working out religiously. When she came back to see me a few months later, her blood pressure was nearly normal, and her weight had dropped a full 10 pounds.

At first, I couldn't explain why, with these stellar improvements, her HDL cholesterol had dropped more than 30%, her triglycerides had doubled, and her blood sugar was elevated, while her LDL remained virtually unchanged. When I quizzed her about her diet, the puzzle was solved.

Sherry's trainer, an enthusiastic guy in his early 20s, had explained that since she was working out harder, she needed to eat more simple carbs like pasta and rice, and Sherry had followed this recommendation with gusto. Unfortunately, this was absolutely terrible advice. Even worse, since Sherry was diabetic, she was highly sensitive to the sugar-raising effects of these simple carbohydrates. The truth is that many trainers are not qualified to give this type of guidance, no matter how well-meaning they may be. Fortunately, we caught the problem early, and Sherry is now back on track.

THE HIGH CARBOHYDRATE, LOW FAT DIET:
REALITY CHECKLIST

- 70% of calories come from carbohydrates, 20% from protein, and 10% from fats, with no cholesterol.
- Highly refined, high glycemic carbohydrates are not part of this plan. Better choices include whole grains, fruits, vegetables, and legumes.
- Combine this diet with intensive lifestyle changes to help reverse heart disease.

DRAWBACKS:
- It can be difficult to stick to because you may not feel full.
- The original diet lacks nuts, seeds, and fatty fish, which means lower omega-3 levels.
- HDL (good) cholesterol may drop and triglycerides may increase.
- Vitamin D levels may fall.

THE HIGH PROTEIN, LOW CARBOHYDRATE DIET

It is hard to imagine that a diet that is diametrically opposed to the low fat, high carbohydrate program could inspire similar weight loss and health claims, but that is exactly what boosters of the high protein, low carbohydrate, high fat diets contend.

This regimen, sometimes referred to as a ketogenic diet, takes many forms, including the Atkins diet, the Stillman diet, the South Beach Diet, and the Zone; versions of it have been around since the 1860s.

In general, a high protein, low carbohydrate diet provides 30% to 60% calories from protein, 5% to 15% from carbohydrates, and up to 55% from fat. Since free access to high protein, high fat foods, such as steak, eggs, and bacon, is a cornerstone of many of these diets, they have been eagerly embraced by those who have found the low fat approach too difficult or unpalatable.

The low carb diets have captured the attention of millions of people, and many people have lost weight using these programs. Whether they've kept it off is another story. Most have not.

Just how does a high protein diet work? It works just like other diets—by reducing calories consumed. While the pounds may seem to melt off very quickly in the beginning, most of this early weight loss turns out to be water loss, or diuresis. Since high carb foods often hold water within the intestines, getting rid of them simply means less water in the body, and a lower number on the bathroom scale.

After one to two weeks, ketosis begins. In ketosis, fat is broken down for use as fuel by the body. This fat breakdown produces substances called "ketone bodies." You can even test your urine with special dipsticks to see if this process is taking place. (This type of ketosis should not be confused with diabetic ketoacidosis, a life-threatening condition that may occur in uncontrolled diabetics, but has been reported on rare occasion in people following an extreme low carb diet.) Although devotees of these diets may claim otherwise, ketosis is not necessary for weight loss, nor is it desirable.

Ketosis is well-described in animals, particularly in dairy cattle following calving. I found this description of ketosis in cattle, published in the Pennsylvania State Extension circular #372: "The animals usually have a gaunt appearance and milk production is decreased. Cows may appear depressed, restricted in their movements, their hair coat may appear rough, and their eyes may be glazed. Their breath may have a characteristic odor of ketones." Happily, "death from ketosis rarely occurs." Not very attractive, is it? In fact, ketosis is well-known to cause halitosis (bad breath or should we call it cow breath?!) and constipation in humans. Ketosis-breath has even been mistaken for alcohol, as one hapless airline pilot discovered when he was detained by airport police.

DOES A LOW CARB DIET WORK?

On the surface, the low carb, high protein, high fat diet appears to be counterintuitive and possibly even harmful. Indeed, it may well be, but there are some interesting research studies that validate some of the many claims made.

For instance, some have found that such diets may contribute to improvements in the lipid profile, weight loss, and reduced body fat when combined with exercise, dietary supplements, and group sessions for six months.

In fact, the high protein, low carb diet comes out a little ahead of the low fat diet in terms of weight loss and lipids, but the fix is not that simple. Overall, it appears that the weight loss achieved on a high protein diet is not due to any magic formula, but simply to reduced calorie intake. It may just be that these diets are easier to stick with than those of the high carb, low fat variety. This was the conclusion of a group from Stanford who painstakingly evaluated 107 articles in the medical literature that reported data on a combined total of 3,268 participants. And there are some potentially harmful side effects of this diet that its proponents do not publicize.

THE PERILS OF THE HIGH PROTEIN–LOW CARB DIET

First, after you eat a meal high in saturated fat (typically from an animal source such as the steak or pork beloved by high protein advocates), a load of these nasty fats is dumped into the bloodstream to circulate. The immediate result is a decrease in what we call arterial compliance. The arteries become stiffer and less pliable, and the effect lasts at least six hours, increasing the vulnerability to heart attacks. Higher-fat diets also are associated with higher levels of fibrinogen in the bloodstream, which is associated with a greater susceptibility to blood clots, strokes, and heart attacks. Saturated fats may also increase blood levels of homocysteine, CRP, and Lp(a) (see chapter 3).

Although it is true that both high fat and low fat diets may improve blood pressure, this appears to be directly related to weight loss. High fat diets in which weight loss does not occur are well known to raise blood pressure, and a richer diet has been known for centuries to raise the risk of gout.

Less well known, but of great importance to women in particular, is the association of a high protein diet with loss of calcium, which may lead to osteoporosis. In fact, the risk of bone fracture is significantly higher in women who eat protein to excess. Because of this calcium loss, which occurs through the urine, the risk of kidney stones is also higher. In people who have kidney disorders—a condition common in diabetics—high protein diets may stress the kidneys beyond what is safe and contribute to the progression of kidney failure. The American Kidney Foundation has advised against extremely high protein diets and has suggested that the maximum safe level of protein intake in healthy people without kidney problems should be considered 2 grams per kg of body weight. For a 150-pound person, this would equal about 140 grams of protein, which is still substantial.

Finally, by avoiding healthy carbohydrates such as fruits, vegetables, and whole grains, and by increasing red meat, the likelihood of developing colon and rectal cancers increases. Women who eat more red meat also appear to be at higher risk for breast cancer, particularly the hormone-receptor positive form of the disease.

THE HIGH PROTEIN, LOW CARBOHYDRATE DIET

- Also known as the ketogenic diet, Atkins Diet, or Stillman Diet. The South Beach Diet is a smarter variation on this theme.
- 30% to 60% of calories come from protein, 5% to 15% from carbohydrates, and up to 55% from fat, including saturated fat.
- Weight loss in the first two weeks is mainly water. After that, the diet works by simply reducing calories consumed.
- The diet may improve lipids and blood sugar.

POTENTIAL RISKS:
- stiffening of the arteries
- increased risk of blood clots
- increase in homocysteine, CRP, and Lp(a)
- osteoporosis
- increased risk of breast cancer and colorectal cancer
- kidney stones
- worsening of kidney function in diabetics and others who have kidney disease

THE MEDITERRANEAN DIET

As a nation, we are unrivaled in our innovation, leadership, and individualism. When it comes to diet, we still have a lot to learn.

In 1970, the landmark Seven Countries Study began to explore heart disease risk factors in seven countries, including five European nations, Japan, and the United States.

Overall, the investigators tracked more than 12,000 men aged 40 to 59 in sixteen different centers. In 1995, twenty-five years later, researchers reported follow-up data on these men, who had by then reached the age range of 65 to 85.

Across the years, clear-cut differences in health and prevalence of disease had emerged, fundamentally transforming our understanding of nutrition and culture. The divergence in mortality rates was stunning. After statistical adjustment to account for the variations in the ages of the men who were studied, the Japanese mortality rate from heart disease was only 3.2% at 25 years; in Mediterranean Southern Europe, 4.7%. The highest mortality from heart disease was found in Northern Europeans, who weighed in at 20.3%, followed by the United States at 16%.

Even more intriguing, at similar cholesterol levels, the Japanese and Southern Mediterraneans had only one-half to one-third the number of heart disease deaths as did citizens in the United States and Northern Europe.

For example, at a total cholesterol level of 210 mg/dL, the twenty-five-year mortality rate from heart disease in Japan and Southern Mediterranean Europe was 4% to 5%, as compared to 10% in Inland Southern Europe, 12% in the United States, and 15% in Northern Europe. It was obvious that there was something that the Mediterranean and Japanese people were doing right that the other countries were doing wrong. That vital factor turned out to be the traditional diets of these regions.

WHAT MAKES THE MEDITERRANEAN DIET SPECIAL?

Although it may sound exotic, the Mediterranean diet is based on whole grains, green vegetables, fruit, olive oil, and fish. These foods are readily available, easy to prepare, and, for the most part, reasonably familiar to our taste buds. Tomatoes, onions, garlic, and herbs are also integral to this cuisine. Wine is part of the culture and typically enjoyed with the evening meal.

The Seven Countries Study focused on the diet of the inhabitants of the Greek island of Crete, an ecosystem that provides an exceptionally rich variety of heart-protecting foods. Traditional inhabitants of Crete consume up to thirty times more fish than a typical North American. And while beef is eaten on occasion, the cattle in Crete are grazing animals, so higher levels of omega-3 fatty acids are found in Mediterranean beef than in typical factory-farm-raised American animals.

Likewise, the chickens are free-roaming, with a substantial portion of their diet coming from local plants including purslane, which is rich in omega-3 fatty acids. These fatty acids are found in abundance in their eggs. In fact, the omega-6 to omega-3 ratio in Cretan eggs is estimated to be 1:3, as compared to the U.S. ratio of 19:4. (See chapter 4 for more about fats.)

Countering the conventional low fat wisdom, the fat content of the Mediterranean diet works out to about 30% to 35% of daily calories. The critical difference is that the artery-clogging saturated fat content is no more than 8%, and there are no trans fats whatsoever.

Daily protein intake is around 15%, and cholesterol is approximately 200 mg daily (about the equivalent of one egg). Although cholesterol levels tend to be lower on this diet than those of the United States and Northern Europe (traditional inhabitants of Mediterranean countries average 200 mg/dl compared to 240–255 mg/dL for the United States and Northern Europe), the risk of heart disease death is lower, even when we compare people with the same levels of cholesterol. This finding is thought to be due to the effect of dietary antioxidants on LDL cholesterol in the bloodstream, preventing the LDL cholesterol from becoming oxidized and thus more harmful to the blood vessel walls.

It doesn't hurt that people who follow a Mediterranean type of diet are 40% less likely to be obese than are those whose diet more closely resembles our typical Western diet.

ADDING YEARS TO A HEALTHY LIFE

Although this healthy way of eating makes sense, some would debate that perhaps it is not the diet at all but something else the Mediterraneans are doing right. Without a doubt, they do have a more active lifestyle and perhaps a lower level of stress as well.

To help shed some light on the matter, in the late 1980s to early 1990s, researchers in Lyons, France, decided to put the diet to the test in heart attack survivors. About 600 patients under the age of 70 who had suffered a heart attack within the past six months were randomly assigned to a Mediterranean diet plan or usual care. The experimental subjects were told to increase green vegetables, root vegetables, breads, and fish and to reduce the amount of red meat in their diet by replacing it with poultry. They also ate fruit every day and replaced their butter with a special canola-oil based margarine and olive oil. Wine with meals was encouraged.

A little more than two years later, sixteen people had died of heart disease in the control group, as compared to only three in the Mediterranean diet group. When adjusted for other variables, the overall risk reduction for cardiovascular death in the Mediterranean group was a stunning 76%, despite the fact that there was no major difference in cholesterol profiles between the two groups.

Four years later, this way of eating provided sustained protection, with a 47% reduction in the combined incidence of heart attack, unstable heart disease, stroke, heart failure, pulmonary emboli (blood clots in the lungs), and blood clots in the legs. This result was despite no major difference in weight, blood pressure, or cholesterol profile between groups, although those with lower cholesterol levels fared even better.

Those whose blood work indicated a high level of dietary omega-3 fatty acids were at a greater advantage, since their risk of heart disease was lower still. Remarkably, the Mediterranean group also benefited from a 61% reduction in the risk of cancer, including breast cancer.

More recently, researchers in Greece followed more than 22,000 apparently healthy adults for nearly four years and reported their findings in 2003. Those who adhered to a more traditional Mediterranean diet had 33% fewer deaths from heart disease and 24% fewer cancer deaths than those who avoided this type of diet. The benefit held true irrespective of gender, smoking status, and physical activity. When the elements of the diet were broken down, there was no one food or component of the diet that appeared to be more important than the others.

In other studies, the Mediterranean-style diet consistently comes out ahead. Blood glucose levels, insulin levels, and blood pressure are lower, and the cholesterol profile improves. One group found that in those who add more olive oil (about a liter a week), CRP also drops significantly. People with the metabolic syndrome (see chapter 13), who are at high risk for diabetes and heart disease, have been able to slow down or even reverse this process by following a Mediterranean-style diet.

Foods of the Mediterranean are easily found at your grocery store and, depending on your taste, can be prepared very simply or with great complexity. The effects can be profound. A 50% to 70% risk reduction is far greater than can be achieved with almost any single drug. These nourishing foods have the potential to add years of good health to our lives.

THE MEDITERRANEAN DIET

- This diet is based on the diet of the Greek isle of Crete, not your favorite Italian restaurant.
- 30% to 35% calories come from from fat (but only 7% to 8% from saturated fat), 15% from protein, and 50% from carbohydrates.
- Fresh vegetables and fruits, nuts, legumes, unrefined cereals, fish, and monounsaturated fats such as olive oil make up this diet. Enjoy alcohol in moderation.
- Are you a vegetarian? This diet adapts easily for you.
- The Mediterranean diet may lower heart disease risk by 33% to 70%, and cut cancer risk by 25% to 60%.

THE JAPANESE DIET

While the Mediterranean diet is easy for our Western palates to love, the Seven Countries study also highlighted the diet and way of life in Okinawa, a string of 161 islands located between Japan and Taiwan. Traditional

Okinawans, whose villages carefully register birth, marriage, and death statistics, enjoy excellent health and remarkable longevity.

Until 1985, when fast food began oozing its way across Japan, the age-adjusted death rate from cardiovascular disease in Okinawa was less than one-fifth that of the United States and 30% to 40% less than Japan's national average.

The traditional Okinawan diet is really very humble. The Japanese sweet potato (*Ipomoea batatas*) takes the place of rice and provides a major source of energy. Austrian researchers have found that an extract from this sweet potato may help to improve diabetes control and possibly even lower cholesterol. Seaweed, soy, herbaceous plants, fish, and jasmine green tea are also important elements. Protein accounts for just 10% to 20% of calories consumed. Fish and soy are the chief sources of protein, with negligible amounts coming from meat, poultry, and eggs. At least 80% of the diet is plant based, and the fat content, at about 30%, is mainly polyunsaturated. The diet is not perfect since Okinawans do eat moderate amounts of miso soup, which has been linked to a higher incidence of cancer.

PUT DOWN THAT FORK

One fascinating aspect of the traditional Okinawan diet is its low caloric content. The people of this culture follow a custom of eating until just about 80% full, a practice which is a far cry from our ever-popular all-you-can-eat food troughs. Not only does this caloric restriction help to keep them lean (the average BMI of Okinawan elders is 18–22), it also may help to explain why they live longer.

This is important because there seems to be a key difference between maintaining weight by burning off more energy than you eat, and simply eating fewer calories.

The major theory that explains this important effect of calorie restriction upon life-span is that of reduced "oxidative stress." What this means is that free radicals, which are generally damaging to the cells of the body and are considered to be responsible in large part for the aging process, are reduced in a chronic calorie-restricted diet. Less food means less of the harmful chemicals that are part and parcel of the food we eat. For traditional Okinawans, daily calorie intake is estimated to be 17% lower in adults and 36% lower in children than the Japanese national average.

Back home in the United States, the Harvard Alumni Health Study and the Nurses' Health Study have both found overall lower mortality in people with a BMI 15% to 20% below average, although there is no way to know if they kept slim by eating less or by exercising more. Most likely, it was a combination of the two.

Perhaps as important as diet is the Okinawan lifestyle; members of this culture tend to be physically and mentally active throughout their entire lives. Moderation is viewed as a virtue, and optimism is rampant. Spirituality is an important part of daily life. Smoking is relatively uncommon amongst the traditional members of this culture. Not surprisingly, the incidence of dementia is low.

Because of the global reach of Western diet and lifestyle, many younger Okinawans have fallen prey to fast food. In fact, Okinawa can now boast the greatest concentration of fast-food restaurants per capita in all of Japan, and Okinawans on average are currently the heaviest people in the country. Longevity has plummeted, especially for men, who seem to be more easily influenced by the abundance of fast food, but younger Okinawan women, and their waistlines, are quickly catching up.

THE JAPANESE DIET

- 20% of calories come from protein, 30% from fat (mostly polyunsaturated), and up to 60% from carbohydrates.
- The principal protein sources are fish and soy. The diet also includes sweet potato, seaweed, herbaceous plants, and green tea.

> - Okinawans stop eating when they are 80% full. Studies show when you restrict calories, you live longer.
> - Okinawan elders have one-fifth the risk of heart disease as Americans, and live healthier and longer lives.

The Vegetarian Diet

The term "vegetarian" is rather vague, and encompasses a diverse group of vegans and lacto-ovo vegetarians, among others. A vegan eats absolutely no animal-derived products and therefore avoids dairy foods and eggs. Lacto-ovo vegetarians include dairy (lacto) and eggs (ovo) in their diets. These distinctions are important, because dairy products and eggs are important sources of protein, but they also supply saturated fats and cholesterol. Vegans generally consume extremely low amounts of saturated fats and no cholesterol.

Because vegetarians are such a varied group, it is difficult to make sweeping generalizations. However, several studies have investigated different types of vegetarians and come up with some interesting observations.

The Oxford Vegetarian Study, based in England, included 6,000 vegetarians and 5,000 non-vegetarians. The meat-eaters were friends and relatives of the vegetarians who were recruited for the study. Detailed information on diet and lifestyle was obtained, and the participants were followed for about twelve years.

Taken as a whole, everyone, vegetarian or not, had a lower death rate than the national average. The investigators speculated that this was because the vegetarians tended to be healthier people in general, and so their non-vegetarian friends and relatives were also more likely to lead a healthy lifestyle.

Despite the overall good health in this study, some very important differences emerged. For instance, after twelve years, the vegetarians had a 20% lower risk of death from all causes and a 27% lower risk of death from heart disease. Among the meat eaters, the risk of heart disease death progressively climbed as animal fat intake rose, such that the top one-third of animal fat consumers had a greater than threefold increased risk of dying from heart disease when compared to their veggie friends.

FINDING BALANCE

Is a vegetarian diet all good? Not necessarily. Vegans, and some lacto-ovo vegetarians, are more likely to be deficient in B12, a condition that can usually be rectified with supplements. We all need B12, but the issue becomes critically important during pregnancy. (I'll discuss the B vitamins more in chapter 10.)

As with any sort of diet, balance is essential. Lacto-ovo vegetarians have it a little easier than vegans since they eat "complete" proteins, which supply all the essential amino acids in the form of dairy products and eggs. (Essential amino acids are those that the body cannot manufacture itself, making the diet the only source of these nutrients.) For vegans, obtaining a sufficient amount of protein may get tricky but is usually not a major problem. For example, soy, unlike most plant products, is a complete and versatile protein. Other vegan protein sources include grains, seeds, nuts, and legumes.

While it is not essential to combine proteins at every meal, incorporating all of the essential amino acids, it is important to get an adequate amount of essential amino acids over the course of the day. This requirement is not complicated. Broadly speaking, a complete protein meal can be achieved by combining legumes with grains, which can be as simple as beans with brown rice or peanut butter on whole wheat bread.

Getting Enough Omega-3s

Although it's easy to get plenty of protein with a vegetarian diet, it can be difficult for vegetarians to include enough of the omega-3 fatty acids that are so important to cardiovascular health.

Flaxseed and walnuts are two common vegetarian sources of omega-3 fatty acids. While walnuts are a much better source of omega-3 than other nuts, the percentage of these fatty acids in walnut oil is low, weighing in at less than 10%. Flaxseed oil is a great supplemental choice for vegetarians, since it contains 57% omega-3 and 17% omega-6 fatty acids. Flaxseed oil must be refrigerated or it quickly goes rancid. And because it should not be exposed to direct heat, flaxseed oil cannot be used in cooking, although it is a smart complement to salads, pasta, and vegetables. Some people even drizzle it on their morning oatmeal.

Whole flaxseeds are not useful since they just pass through the body undigested, so you have to grind or crush them to make them work for you. Ground flaxseeds can be sprinkled on salads and cereal. Flaxseed oil capsules, which I'll tell you more about in chapter 11, are a reasonable alternative.

One caveat: excessive amounts of flaxseed oil can interfere with normal functioning of the thyroid gland by affecting iodine uptake. For this reason, limit flaxseed oil to no more than four tablespoons per day.

Although it is the best vegetarian alternative, flaxseed oil cannot hold a candle to fish oil. While our bodies can put fish oil to work right away, the omega-3 fatty acid that comes from plant sources (known as ALA, or alpha-linolenic acid) must be converted by special enzymes before it can be used effectively. This chemical process is slow and not very efficient, and it can be hindered by saturated fat, trans fat, cholesterol, and alcohol. An extremely low protein diet can also impede this process.

In addition, omega-3 and omega-6 fatty acids compete for the same enzymes. Foods rich in omega-6, including corn oil, sunflower oil, and safflower oil, can interfere with the body's ability to utilize the omega-3 fatty acids. A smarter choice is olive oil, a monounsaturated fat that minds its own business and does not influence this conversion process.

THE VEGETARIAN DIET

- Lacto-ovo vegetarians eat dairy and egg products; vegans allow no animal products whatsoever.
- Protein sources for vegans include soy (a "complete" protein), grains, seeds, and nuts. Lacto-ovo vegetarians also get protein from dairy products and eggs.
- Vegetarians tend to live longer and have less heart disease than non-vegetarians.
- Vegetarians may lack omega-3 fatty acids. However, flaxseed oil and walnuts are reasonably good sources.
- Strict vegans need vitamin B12 supplements to maintain good health.

BATTLE OF THE DIETS: WHO WINS?

When it comes down to it, what we really want to know is: what is the "right way" to eat?

Low Fat: The Ornish Way

The results achieved by Dr. Ornish and others who espouse the low fat approach are impressive, but diet was only part of the program. Lifestyle modification was tremendously important in the studies reported, and the drop-out rate was high.

High Protein: The Atkins Route

If you take the other extreme by following an Atkins-style high protein, low carbohydrate diet, you will lose weight more quickly, but much of that will be an illusion since the initial weight loss is essentially water weight. Longer-term, the weight loss may be somewhat greater than with the low fat approach, but that is due to reduced calorie consumption, not to any magical effect of ketosis.

While the short-term effects of this diet do not appear to be harmful, we do not know as much about the effect this sort of diet may have on the heart.

Since we do know that saturated fats have both immediate and long-term harmful effects on the heart arteries, I can't recommend this type of diet to you, especially if animal fats are the principal fat source.

However, increasing protein to about 30% of calories consumed, while limiting saturated and trans fat, and keeping the glycemic load low may have an important effect on suppressing appetite and contribute substantially to weight loss and overall well-being.

Dining on the Mediterranean

The Mediterranean style of eating makes a great deal of sense and is my diet of choice. Fruits, vegetables, monounsaturated fats, omega-3 fatty acids, and moderate amounts of alcohol are the backbone of the Mediterranean diet. All of these elements are easy to find, taste great, and require as much or as little effort as you are willing to spare. There is enough healthy fat so that you won't feel deprived, and the variety of foods and flavors is broad. This nutritional approach has been studied in non-Mediterranean cultures and even in vegetarians with highly favorable outcomes. Who can find fault with a diet that has the potential to reduce heart disease by 50% or more?

How the Okinawans Do It

Likewise, the diet of the Okinawans gives us plenty of food for thought. We Americans have gotten ourselves into a great deal of trouble by believing that we must continue to eat until our ever-expanding bellies tell us to stop. The importance of finishing a meal before feeling completely full is profound and may be the most important lesson the Okinawans can teach us. While Japanese cuisine may elude you, the key components of the Okinawan diet—fish, soy, brightly-colored vegetables, and green tea—have well-known heart-protective effects and are readily available at virtually any grocery store.

Life among the Veggies

A vegetarian lifestyle makes sense on many levels. The only important drawback from the standpoint of heart health is the absence of cold-water fish, with their rich supply of omega-3 fatty acids. Flaxseed oil is a reasonable alternative, but vegetarians will need to pay close attention to get enough omega-3 fatty acids to achieve heart protection on par with fish eaters. Vegans need to be sure to supplement with vitamin B12.

Just like countless meat-eaters, many vegetarians eat too many simple starches and saturated fats. Grilled cheese on white sandwich bread is not any friendlier to your heart than a box of fried chicken. If, however, elements of the Mediterranean and Okinawan diets are integrated into a vegetarian diet, the food you eat could truly save your life.

8

THE BIG FAKE OUT: THE SKINNY ON SWEETENERS AND OTHER FOOD FAKES

SUGAR: THE REAL THING

We may be smart, but when it comes to sugar, our brains tend to go a little gooey. Sugar is the original sweetener, and the average American shovels in more than 135 pounds of it per year, much of it from sugar-saturated soft drinks; children may put away even more. Our addiction to sugar has fueled the burgeoning rates of diabetes and obesity in adults and kids alike. Pancreatic cancer has also been linked to high levels of sugar consumption. How can something so sweet be so wrong?

Most table sugar, or sucrose, starts out as sugar cane and sugar beets. That sounds simple enough. Your body breaks the sugar molecule down into glucose and fructose, two simpler sugars that are easily absorbed. Fructose, which is also the sugar found in fruit, is taken up by the bloodstream a little slower than glucose, since it has to be converted into glucose by the liver before it can be used.

Despite its bad rep, sugar delivers only 16 calories per teaspoon. So a teaspoon or even two in your tea is really no big deal, unless you're a diabetic. But a soft drink is not such innocent fun. Chug a single can of soda pop, and you've bought yourself the equivalent of a whopping 10 teaspoons of table sugar. Just for kicks, measure out 10 teaspoons of sugar and see what that looks like. Shocking, isn't it? And when taken in quantities that large, sugar, the ultimate simple carbohydrate, provokes wild swings in blood glucose levels, setting you up for the cycle of sugar highs followed by those awful sugar cravings that will inevitably sneak in, fooling you into thinking you're hungry for more.

High Fructose Corn Syrup

Corn syrup is the base for most commercial sugar sweeteners. Corn syrup is processed in such a way that it is higher in fructose, making it more stable. This form of sugar, known as high fructose corn syrup (HFCS), is typically found in soft drinks and snack foods like cookies, cakes, and crackers. Manufacturers prefer HFCS because it is less expensive than sugar, mixes well with other ingredients, and helps to retain product freshness. Thanks to HFCS, commercially baked goods, like breads and cookies, stay soft and chewy.

There is really nothing intrinsically "bad" about high fructose corn sweetener, but the massive quantities that we consume, often without realizing it, are truly alarming and contribute mightily to our growing rates of overweight and obesity. On average, Americans glug and gobble about 63 pounds of high fructose corn syrup each year, about half of our entire sugar consumption and up to 10% of our total calorie intake.

Keeping It Natural

"Raw" sugar, which has a richer flavor than regular sugar, is essentially table sugar with a little molasses; add a bit more molasses, and you have brown sugar. Molasses does provide some important nutrients such as calcium and iron, but the amounts consumed in a typical serving are generally inconsequential. Honey and naturally occurring syrups may be more appealing, but probably offer no major health advantages over sugar. Although they provide some antioxidants and other nutrients, the quantities per teaspoon are not likely to be enough to make much of a difference.

THE SODA TRAP

Sugary soft drinks are an unmitigated health hazard, concealing 150 calories of highly concentrated glucose in one 12-ounce can. They are the greatest single source of sugar in the American diet and one of the easiest ways there is to pack on the weight. Drink twenty-three sodas in a month, less than one a day, and you've just bought yourself one pound. Voila! In a year, you've gained 12 pounds, without even trying. Women who drink at least one soda a day are nearly twice as likely to become diabetic as those who rarely drink these beverages.

Fruit drinks pack a potent slug of sugar, too. These deceptively bright-colored concoctions are often nothing more than artificially flavored and colored water mixed up with high fructose corn syrup. A typical cup of fruit-flavored yogurt is loaded with about seven teaspoons of sugar. Even your pre-sweetened cereal may add three teaspoons of sugar or more to your morning.

SHOULD YOU FAKE IT?

Given this sticky mess, it's no wonder that many people have switched to artificially sweetened sodas and food products. In fact, the artificial sweetener market is now a $1.5 billion-a-year industry, with 70% to 80% of that attributable to soft drinks.

Do artificial sweeteners really help you to lose weight? The reviews are mixed. Some researchers have reported no overall effect on total caloric intake, since the calories saved by swilling artificially sweetened sodas and other foods are often made up by increasing calorie consumption later in the day.

However, an eight-year observational study from the University of Texas, San Antonio found that those who habitually drank diet sodas were even more likely to become obese than people who drank the same amount of regular sodas.

Other studies have found that the risk for heart disease is no lower in those who choose diet sodas, compared with regular soda drinkers. The theory is that by drinking diet sodas, people may believe themselves to be more virtuous, and thus entitled to larger portions of their favorite high caloric foods.

Artificial sweeteners do not retrain our taste buds to appreciate a lower level of sweetness, so they may well be self-defeating. But for those who choose to use them, there are now five FDA-approved artificial sweeteners: saccharin, aspartame, acesulfame-K, sucralose, and neotame. Stevia is a sixth sweetener that is used in many countries but has not been approved for use in the United States. Sugar alcohols are a special type of sweetener used in sweets designed for people with diabetes. Although the sugar alcohols do provide calories, they are handled differently by the body than sugar.

SACCHARIN

Saccharin is 300 to 700 times sweeter than sugar. While high doses of saccharin have been linked to the development of bladder tumors in rats, a human cancer connection has never been proven. The FDA considers saccharin safe for human consumption. (Nevertheless, you might want to avoid feeding it to your pet rat.)

ASPARTAME

Aspartame, a chemical concoction of two amino acids, phenylalanine and aspartic acid, is about 200 times sweeter than sugar. It is used in many commercial foods including cereals, yogurt, ice cream, and, of course, soft drinks and other beverages. The maximal accepted daily dose is 40 mg per kilogram body weight, or about 2800 mg for a 150 lb person. A can of diet soda contains less than 100 mg of aspartame.

A Health Warning: If You Have Phenylketonuria, Avoid Aspartame

Because people with phenylketonuria cannot break down phenylalanine, those with this rare genetic abnormality must steer clear of aspartame. This condition is typically diagnosed at birth with a routine blood test. If a phenylketonuric person is exposed to phenylalanine, she may suffer severe brain damage. This is why standard label warnings are required for packaged products made with the sweetener. Since phenylalanine is also found in common protein sources, artificial protein supplements are required to maintain normal health.

Is It Safe for Others?

Since aspartame's approval by the FDA, many anecdotal reports have suggested neurological dangers including brain tumors, seizures, and headaches. The aspartame brain cancer scare, which arose in 1996, was quickly debunked when it was shown that aspartame could not have contributed to a reported rise in brain cancer, since the cases of brain cancer cited had already begun developing prior to the introduction of aspartame.

A study published in the New England Journal of Medicine in 1995 reported on eighteen people with seizure disorders who claimed that aspartame provoked their seizures. When these people were studied continuously for five days with brain wave monitors and given high doses of aspartame or placebo, there were no seizures observed, effectively disproving the connection.

In other studies, researchers found no effect of aspartame on brain wave activity, mood, psychological function, headaches, or any other measures of neurologic or psychologic function. A 1994 Vanderbilt study reported no effect on cognitive performance or behavior in children, even at high doses. In people with Parkinson's disease, research has likewise shown no evidence of ill effects.

Some People Could Have Problems

Other smaller reports have been less favorable, although less definitive. Some people probably do have an increased susceptibility to headaches with aspartame. Children with certain types of seizures may be more prone to seizure activity if they consume aspartame. A small study in 1993 suggested that people with bipolar depression may become more depressed if they use aspartame.

Aspartame appears to be safe for most of us, but there are some people who are sensitive to it, and those people should avoid using this sweetener. As long as you do not suffer from phenylketonuria, there is no convincing evidence that aspartame use will cause you permanent harm.

ACESULFAME-K

Also known as acesulfame potassium, this artificial sweetener is 200 times sweeter than sugar. It is used in thousands of products around the world. Unlike aspartame, prominent package labeling is not required since this chemical is not known to adversely affect people with phenylketonuria or other specific health problems. In the United States, it is found in soft drinks, chewing gum, dessert and beverage mixes, dairy products, and candy, among other things. Acesulfame-K is sometimes used in conjunction with aspartame. There is no proof that this sweetener is harmful, although concerns regarding a possible cancer risk, at least in animal studies, continue to surface.

SUCRALOSE

Sucralose, derived from sugar, is free of calories and 600 times sweeter than sugar. Sucralose has been studied for about twenty years, and there are no confirmed adverse effects on human health. Animal studies have shown that the majority of sucralose that is consumed is simply excreted by the body and not absorbed.

Neotame

Neotame is 7,000 to 13,000 times sweeter than sugar. Like the other artificial sweeteners, it is used in soft drinks, chewing gum, yogurt, candy, and desserts. Extensive research reviewed by the FDA prior to neotame's approval found no compelling evidence of detrimental health effects.

Stevia

Stevioside is an extract from the leaves of a shrub found in Paraguay and Brazil known as stevia. It is noncaloric and said to be 250 to 300 times sweeter than sugar. It is widely used in South American countries and is also popular in Japan. Although it has not been approved as a food additive in the United States, it can be sold as a supplement. Unfortunately, there is simply not adequate data for the FDA to review to resolve whether this substance is safe for use as an additive. To date, some studies have shown that stevia may have a beneficial effect upon blood pressure, but it might also reduce male fertility by lowering levels of testosterone.

Sugar Alcohols

The sugar alcohols are a class of sweeteners that can occur in nature, so they are not considered artificial. Examples of sugar alcohols include sorbitol, xylitol, mannitol, hydrogenated starch hydrolysates, and maltitol. The sugar alcohols provide 1.5 to 3 calories per gram as compared with sugar, which weighs in at 4 calories per gram. Despite the name, sugar alcohols do not contain ethanol, and they are not exactly sugars. Since they are absorbed very slowly from the gut and require very little insulin to metabolize, sugar alcohols are commonly used by diabetics seeking a sweet treat without the risk of high blood sugar. Dentists like the sugar alcohols because they do not cause tooth decay, another important advantage over regular sugar.

Sugar alcohols are found naturally in many foods, including plums, pineapples, carrots, asparagus, apples, mushrooms, berries, and lettuce. In moderate to large amounts, they may cause intestinal bloating, gas, and diarrhea because they are not completely absorbed from the intestine and may act somewhat like a laxative. Prunes are a great example of a food with high sugar alcohol content and a potent laxative effect.

FAKE FATS

Driven by a desire to eliminate fats from our diet but keep the greasy snacks that we love, we have demanded artificial fat substitutes to go along with our phony sweeteners. These pseudo fats take many forms. You have probably eaten fake fats without even realizing it. Products labeled "light," "reduced fat," "low fat," or "fat-free" are likely to be manufactured with fat substitutes, particularly if they are modified versions of higher-fat foods.

Most fat substitutes are derived in some way from carbohydrates or from egg or milk protein. They help processed foods retain moisture, increase thickness and texture, and provide what is known as a "mouth feel" reminiscent of the real thing. You will find them in low fat salad dressings, low fat dairy products, low fat spreads, and some bakery products.

While these fat substitutes may not completely fool your senses, they are safe and have not been shown to affect overall nutritional status or digestion. The same can probably be said about some unique types of fat known as caprenin and salatrim, which are chemically modified fats that provide 5 calories per gram, as compared to real fat's 9 calories per gram. A more controversial fake fat is a substance known as olestra.

IS OLESTRA DIET MAGIC?

Olestra is a chemical melding of sucrose and fatty acids that is indigestible by the body. Simply put, it passes right through the gastrointestinal tract and is excreted unchanged.

Because it is not really a food, but merely a traveler, many concerns have been raised about olestra's effects on the intestinal system itself. There is no evidence that olestra affects the mucosa, or lining, of the digestive tract, and it is not broken down by the beneficial bacteria that live in the colon. Some reports have made note of increased flatulence and softer stools with the use of olestra.

The Magic Is Up to You

Although olestra appears to be safe, will it really help you drop the pounds? Snacks made with olestra are not calorie-free. Although the fat may be gone, the simple carbohydrates and salt remain. So even though these products are lower-calorie versions of conventional snack food, they are by no means healthy treats, and the calories still count.

THE FAKE-OUT FACTS

- The average American eats 135 pounds of sugar each year. Kids may eat even more.
- One teaspoon of sugar has 16 calories; a can of soda supplies the equivalent of 10 teaspoons.
- Artificial sweeteners may not help you lose weight because the calories saved are often made up for with other high caloric foods.
- When it comes to sugar alcohols like sorbitol and mannitol, "sugar-free" does not mean noncaloric. These lower-calorie sugar substitutes are safe, but may cause gassiness and diarrhea.
- "Fake fats" are probably safe, but may not help in weight loss.

STEP THREE

SMART WOMEN KNOW HOW TO TAKE A BREAK (WITHOUT CHECKING OUT)

Heart-smart women have healthy habits. We may savor a good cup of coffee in the morning and a glass of wine at night, but we know the word "moderation." Smart women don't smoke or use illicit drugs—period. We have too much life to live to waste it on smoky weeds and toxic chemicals.

9

Rituals, Vices, and Addictions, Oh My! The Truth about Caffeine, Alcohol, Tobacco, and Illicit Drugs

Crowded in by our daily responsibilities and obligations, we may find ourselves looking for a way to open a little space in the day, to take time to pause and reflect, and to re-energize. Many of the small rituals we create and embrace over time are harmless and unobtrusive; some may even offer unexpected blessings of good health. A steaming mug of coffee or a bracing cup of tea (a cuppa, as my grandmother was fond of saying) helps ease us into the morning or stretch out our dwindling energy in the afternoon. A glass of wine with friends or family adds dimension and structure to a wonderful meal or an evening of stimulating conversation.

Our rituals can also be terribly destructive. As a smoker lights her first cigarette of the day, she does so knowing full well that this habit is dangerous and addictive. Alcohol in excess contributes to a world of misery for the drinker, for the ones who care about her, and for those who may be harmed by her booze-tainted lapses of judgment. Even caffeine, when taken to extremes, can be detrimental. And while every school child knows to say "no" to illicit drugs, many drug users do not realize the damage they may inflict on their hearts and bodies.

CAFFEINE: PICK YOUR POTION

Anyone who has ever pulled an all-nighter knows that too much caffeine can cause the heart to race, the hands to shake, and the eyes to twitch. As a cardiologist, I frequently meet with patients referred to me for palpitations, or pounding heartbeats. After a complete consultation, evaluation, and round of testing, the culprit often turns out to be none other than an oversized java habit. To put the issue into perspective, check out the caffeine chart below.

Daily doses of more than 300 mg of caffeine daily are considered potentially harmful. Some people are extremely sensitive to caffeine and should avoid it completely. And while you may enjoy your morning coffee buzz, caffeine is active in the bloodstream for up to nine hours, so it is best to switch to unleaded after noon.

BEVERAGE	CAFFEINE CONTENT
Coffee (8oz)	150mg
Decaffeinated coffee (8 oz)	5mg
Black tea (8 oz)	40–60mg
Green tea (8 oz)	15mg
Cola (8 oz)	35-50mg
Energy drinks (size varies)	80-300mg

COFFEE

In countries where coffee is filtered (as it is, for the most part, in the United States), studies have found no significant effect upon the lipid profile. The exception is in smokers who drink coffee, in whom LDL (bad cholesterol) appears to increase disproportionately.

Homocysteine levels tend to rise in heavy coffee drinkers, particularly women, although this effect can probably be blamed on the roasted coffee bean rather than the caffeine.

In fact, there are probably other elements of the magic bean that contribute to the coffee buzz itself. One study measured blood pressure, heart rate, and nervous activity of the muscles before and after giving test subjects a triple espresso, a decaffeinated triple espresso, intravenous caffeine in an amount equivalent to the triple espresso, or intravenous salt water. Half of the study subjects were habitual coffee drinkers and half were not.

The study found that in those who did not usually drink coffee, decaffeinated coffee actually raised muscle nervous system activity similarly to caffeine, suggesting that something other than caffeine was at work. So when you go home with a case of the coffee jitters after ordering a decaf, don't be too quick to blame the waiter for bringing you the wrong brew.

Coffee may do more than just keep you awake. Coffee drinkers appear to be substantially less likely to develop Parkinson's disease than abstainers, and may even have a lower risk of diabetes. The antioxidant properties of coffee are another hot topic of research. Coffee is a major supplier of polyphenols, or plant-based antioxidants. One study reported that women who drank between one and three cups of coffee daily had a reduction in risk of death from cardiovascular and inflammatory disease (including infections, diabetes, and rheumatoid disease) of about 25% when compared to abstainers; there was, however, no effect on cancer deaths. But before you make another lunge for the coffee pot, know that drinking more than three cups of coffee actually diminished the cardiovascular benefit for women in this study. Four or more cups a day may tend to increase feelings of stress and anxiety.

Although coffee may transiently increase the blood pressure, the rise is usually small, short-lived, and unlikely to pose a significant risk to most people who drink three cups or less. However, while the evidence is inconsistent, those who drink five to six cups daily may raise their heart attack risk by 40% while more than ten cups a day appears to increase the risk by 250%.

Decaffeinated coffee does not appear to carry the same threat, although it may cause more gastric upset, and it may even have undesirable effects on blood lipids. However, like regular coffee, it does appear to provide some protection against diabetes.

Keep in mind that one cup is 8 ounces—not a super-duper mega-mug. Too much of a good thing is usually too much. If you suffer from palpitations, you may be better off avoiding coffee altogether since caffeine will often worsen these symptoms. Side effects are not limited to the heart. People with gastrointestinal problems such as esophageal reflux and irritable bowel may find that coffee intensifies these conditions as well.

THE SCOOP ON COFFEE

- One to three 8-ounce cups a day is fine for most people, although some will experience irregular heartbeats and anxiety with any amount of caffeine.
- More than three cups of coffee a day may cause palpitations, raise blood pressure, increase homocysteine levels, and increase the likelihood of a heart attack.
- Although caffeinated coffee is most likely to keep you up at night, even decaf can trigger nervous system activity in the muscle tissue.
- Moderate coffee drinkers might reduce their risk for heart disease, Parkinson's disease, diabetes, and rheumatoid disease.

TEA

Unlike coffee lovers, people who choose tea tend to have slightly lower blood pressures, particularly those who drink green tea. And devout devotees of tea may be a little more serene than the java heads. A study from the University College, London, found that drinking English black tea was associated with lower levels of the stress hormone cortisol and a greater sense of relaxation when compared to a tea-free drink that was spiked with an equivalent amount of caffeine. Blood platelets were also less active in the tea drinkers, indicating a reduced susceptibility to blood clots.

Some 78% of tea consumed in the world is black, 20% is green (including white tea), and less than 2% is oolong. The classifications depend on the stage at which the leaves were harvested and how they were processed. ("Tea" is made from *Camellia sinensis* only. Herbal "teas" do not count as tea; they are more correctly termed tisanes.)

Green, white, and oolong tea provide powerful flavonoid antioxidants known as catechins, while the antioxidants in black tea are somewhat less potent. Many studies have lumped all tea drinkers together; most have shown remarkable benefits of tea-drinking regardless of the choice of brew.

In 1999, Harvard researchers reported a 44% reduction in the risk of heart attacks in American tea drinkers who enjoyed at least one cup of tea daily. A later study, also from Harvard, followed 1,900 patients who had already suffered heart attacks. After less than four years, the tea drinkers were 30% to 40% less likely to have died than the non-tea drinkers, with those drinking at least two cups a day having a slight edge. Research from the Netherlands provides remarkably similar data, with a 70% reduction in the risk of a fatal heart attack in those drinking at least one to two cups of tea daily.

Also from the Netherlands comes research that suggests that tea may reduce cholesterol deposits, or plaque, in the aorta. Although a single daily cup of tea was protective, the greatest benefit was found in people drinking more than four cups of tea each day.

Studies from the United Kingdom have not validated these findings, but it turns out that when it comes to the heart, certain British idiosyncrasies may be counterproductive. First, most Brits add milk to their tea, which appears to neutralize the heart-protective effects. In addition, the heavy tea drinkers in these studies were also more likely to be smokers and eat a high fat diet, thus skewing the findings.

Some scientists have speculated that the antioxidants in green tea may prevent damage to arterial walls and inhibit the formation of cancer cells, although the evidence is considerably stronger for a protective effect against cardiovascular disease than against cancer. One Japanese study reported that green tea lowers total cholesterol and triglycerides and raises HDL cholesterol (especially in those drinking at least ten cups a day). Another found only a reduction in total cholesterol.

A collaborative study between scientists from Vanderbilt University and China reported a hefty 16% drop in LDL cholesterol when healthy people were given a capsule of green tea extract enriched with theaflavins, which are the antioxidants found in black tea. There was no real improvement in HDL or triglycerides.

This sounds great, but before you rush off to brew a pot of tea, I should point out that the capsules, marketed as TeaFlavin, contain the antioxidant equivalent of about thirty-five cups of green tea without the caffeine.

THE TEA BAG

- Black, white, green, and oolong tea all supply antioxidants, although they are most abundant in green and white tea.
- Decaffeinated tea is a little weaker in antioxidants, but still a good source.
- Adding milk to tea may neutralize its antioxidants.
- Herbal "teas" do not count as tea; they are more correctly termed tisanes.
- Drinking at least one cup of tea every day appears to reduce the likelihood of cardiovascular disease by 40% or more. Tea may help boost bone strength, reduce cancer risk, and protect against kidney stones.
- Green tea may boost metabolism very slightly, by less than 5%.

ALCOHOL: HERE'S TO IT

As long as humans have celebrated the secrets of fermentation, so too have the joys and sorrows of alcohol been known. While the enjoyment of wine has long been a part of many cultures, its effects on the heart were not scientifically validated until the 1970s. To date, more than sixty studies have affirmed the heart-healthy benefits of moderate drinking, and the list continues to grow.

Enjoyed in moderation, any type of alcohol can help to protect against heart disease. A report published in 2003 followed more than 38,000 American men between the ages of 40 and 75 for twelve years. Compared with non-drinkers, men who drank alcoholic beverages three to seven times a week had a heart-attack risk that was 35% lower than their teetotaling counterparts, even when other risk factors for heart disease were taken into account. The type of alcohol was not important. A number of studies around the world have come to similar conclusions. Although the studies in women are smaller, the results are comparable.

While it's never too late to start, there's no point in trying to make up for lost time, since binge drinking does not offer any benefit. In fact, there is a higher risk of heart attacks and high blood pressure in binge drinkers.

Alcohol taken in moderation also appears to reduce the risk of congestive heart failure, even among the elderly. What's more, people who have already suffered a heart attack may reduce their risk of future mortality from heart disease by about 20% to 30%. Moderate drinkers (one to two drinks a day) fare a little better than light drinkers (less than one drink daily), regardless of the type of alcohol consumed.

The heart isn't the only organ that appreciates a little tipple. The brain, a highly vascular structure, usually benefits from anything that helps the heart. This appears to be true in the case of alcohol in general, but perhaps even more so with wine.

A study from Copenhagen found that drinking as infrequently as once a month was associated with a greater than 15% reduction in stroke risk. Weekly and daily drinkers' risks were about 40% and 30% lower, respectively. Other researchers have reported similar findings. Compared to those who abstain, people who drink one to six drinks per week are about half as likely to suffer from dementia later in life. There is evidence that women who drink moderately (no more than two drinks per day) may benefit even more than men.

But more is not always better. When it comes to alcohol, those who drink more than fourteen drinks a week have a 20% higher probability of dementia.

Alcohol seems to improve the body's sensitivity to insulin, resulting in a lower risk of diabetes. The metabolic syndrome (see chapter 13) is also reduced in mild to moderate drinkers. Even full-fledged diabetics may benefit substantially. Diabetic women who drink less than half a drink a day may be able to cut their chances of heart disease by nearly 30% compared to non-drinkers; those who drink one or two drinks daily appear to lower their risk by about 55%.

HEY, BARTENDER!

One drink is:
- 5 ounces of wine
- 12 ounces of beer
- 1 ounce of hard liquor

RED WINE: A HEART-WARMING STORY

We cardiologists hold a special place in our hearts for red wine. Red wine is rich in chemicals known as phenols, which give it its characteristic body and taste. These phenols are powerful antioxidants and include flavonoids such as catechins as well as non-flavonoids, one of which, resveratrol, is found only in grapes. These antioxidants are not found in beer or spirits and occur at much lower concentrations in white wine.

A Danish study of more than 27,000 people reported that light drinkers who did not drink wine had about a 24% reduction in heart disease risk compared to non-drinkers. Although this sounds impressive, when wine drinkers were singled out, the risk declined by a striking 42%. Other European studies have also found considerably more potent effects of red wine than other types of alcohol, although most studies done in the United States have not. One key difference may be in the way that wine is enjoyed. In European countries it is more common to drink wine with meals. This difference may be important, particularly with high fat meals, because it appears that wine, via its antioxidant properties, actually alters the LDL cholesterol that is released into the bloodstream after a meal, rendering it less harmful to the arteries.

Studies have shown some wines to be higher in natural antioxidants, with wines from a specific province in Sardinia, Italy, and those from southwestern France having the most potent effect on blood vessel function. Not surprisingly, people who live in these regions have greater than average longevity.

There are a number of other ways in which light to moderate alcohol use may improve heart health. It may raise HDL cholesterol by about 12%. Triglycerides may also decrease 8% to 10%. Moderate drinkers have lower levels of C-reactive protein and Lp(a), substances that in high levels are associated with the development of heart disease (see chapter 3). Alcohol reduces the blood's tendency to clot by reducing the stickiness of blood platelets, which are involved in the clotting process. Red wine probably has a more powerful blood thinning effect than other types of alcohol.

It seems that wine can even help keep your tummy trim. A study of more than 2,000 men and women found that light drinkers who drank wine regularly had smaller waist sizes than non-drinkers. The pattern of alcohol use is important, since binge drinkers tended to have the biggest beer bellies.

THE DARK SIDE

It would be foolish to discuss all the wonderful properties of alcohol without acknowledging its dark side. Heavy drinkers who regularly drink more than three drinks a day are at risk for severe weakening of the heart muscle, which can lead to congestive heart failure, disability, and death. In addition, high blood pressure and high triglycerides are common among those who drink more than two drinks daily. Heavy drinkers are also more likely to have strokes due to bleeding into the brain. Binge drinking can provoke an erratic and rapid heart rhythm called atrial fibrillation, a scenario we cardiologists term "holiday heart," and which may lead to strokes.

Many women are unaware that drinking alcohol may raise their risk of breast cancer substantially. Those of us who regularly drink more than one drink daily have a 28% higher risk of breast cancer than women who drink less or no alcohol. Women who drink this much and take hormone replacement therapy double their risk of breast cancer. For this reason, women should limit their alcohol to less than one drink per day, on average.

The often disastrous personal and social consequences of alcohol abuse are well known. The human tragedy and needless loss of life associated with drunk driving cannot be overstated.

A tendency towards alcoholism may be inherited, so if our parents or siblings are alcoholics we should be especially judicious when it comes to drinking. Fetal alcohol syndrome, which is a birth defect characterized by mental retardation and certain physical abnormalities, is a heartbreaking consequence of drinking during pregnancy. For these reasons and others, alcohol is not for everyone.

Smokers should be cautious since smoking combined with moderate to heavy alcohol use is associated with a higher risk of cancers involving the throat and gastrointestinal tract.

Given all the dangers involved, there is no doubt that if it were invented today, alcohol is a "drug" that would never make it through the FDA's stringent approval process.

Since alcohol can be associated with such dire consequences, researchers have begun to study grape juice to see if it might share some of the same properties as wine. Overall, the results are encouraging. Red wine that has been de-alcoholized increases blood levels of the antioxidant catechin at least as much as red wine itself. Purple grape juice also appears to help improve the ability of the arteries to dilate and has been found to have antioxidant effects on LDL cholesterol.

However, red wine contains far more flavonoids than juice does. This is because the wine-making process involves extracting these substances from the seeds and skin of the grape, where they are concentrated. Nevertheless, 4 to 8 ounces a day of purple grape juice is a practical alternative to wine or alcohol for those who prefer not to imbibe.

CLOSING TIME: WHAT YOU SHOULD KNOW ABOUT ALCOHOL

- Three to seven drinks a week may cut your heart attack and stroke risk by 25% to 40%, with red wine drinkers having the edge.
- Alcohol in moderation raises HDL and lowers triglycerides, C-reactive protein, and Lp(a).
- Mild to moderate alcohol consumption will reduce the likelihood of dementia. But drink fourteen or more drinks a week, and your risk will begin to rise.
- More than three drinks a day will increase your chances of heart failure, high blood pressure, high triglycerides, and abnormal heart rhythms.
- Red wines from the southwest region of France and from Sardinia, Italy, have the most potent antioxidants, but any kind of alcohol is protective.
- Women who drink more than one drink daily, on average, have a higher likelihood of developing breast cancer than women who don't drink.
- Smokers who drink are more prone to cancers of the mouth, throat, and digestive tract.
- Grape juice is a good alternative to alcohol, although it doesn't supply the full complement of antioxidants found in red wine.

TOBACCO: THE EVIL WEED

When I first met Krystal in the ER several years ago, the pack-a-day smoker was pale, clammy, and clutching her chest in pain. The EKG confirmed that this 58-year-old architect was suffering a heart attack. She was rushed to the cardiac catheterization laboratory and the artery was opened up beautifully.

Krystal thought she was home free until a routine chest X-ray disclosed a mass in the right lung. Fortunately, we had caught the cancer very early—she had experienced absolutely no symptoms, and the cancer had not spread. In short order, Krystal was seen by the cancer specialist, chest surgeon, and lung doctor and plans were made to treat the tumor aggressively. I thought for certain that two life-threatening illnesses diagnosed in the span of one week would convince her to lay off the smokes.

To my surprise, Krystal insisted she was not ready to stop yet. "I'm way too stressed out," she told me. "I'll stop when I feel better." Despite surgery to remove half a lung and intensive exercise therapy in cardiac rehabilitation, Krystal continued to smoke for more than a year. Whether it was my nagging that finally wore her down, or that she woke up one day and realized how fortunate she was to still be among the living, I'll never know, but she finally did quit.

The irrational struggles with tobacco addiction faced by this rational and educated woman opened my eyes to the immense hold that this killer can have on a person's life.

Another patient, Claire, is a pretty brunette who suffered a heart attack at the ripe old age of 39. She is a two-pack-a-day smoker with a stale haze of smoke that seems to hang over her like a bad aura. I see her every six months, treat her with medications, and do my best to convince her to stop smoking, but to no avail. I was dismayed, but not surprised, when she showed up in the emergency room with a second heart attack just days before her forty-second birthday.

So much misery in the world is caused by tobacco. In this country alone, more than 430,000 lives are lost each year as a direct result of smoking and other forms of tobacco use. That means that tobacco contributes to about one out of every five deaths. Worldwide, nearly 5 million deaths a year are due to tobacco.

Half of all smokers die prematurely, cutting their lives short by an average of fourteen years because of a senseless but powerful addiction to tobacco. A quarter of smokers die before the age of 70.

About 80% of people who currently smoke want to quit, but most are unable to break the addiction. A pack-a-day habit costs over $1200 per year and nearly $25,000 every twenty years, in today's dollars. Despite these grim statistics, it is estimated that over 1 million people, mostly teens, join the ranks of smokers each year, and 66 million Americans use tobacco regularly.

Tobacco kills in many ways. Cigarette tobacco contains more than 4000 naturally-occurring compounds and scores of additives, many of which cause cancer. Not surprisingly, smoking is responsible for most cases of lung cancer in this country. Chronic lung disease, such as emphysema, is endemic in smokers, often chaining its victims to lifelines of oxygen tubing. Fully one in four smokers will eventually develop chronic lung disease.

Don't Smoke Out Your Heart

While smoking's effects on the lungs are well-known, many people are unaware that smoking is a major contributor to heart disease. Smoking even one cigarette per day increases the risk of a heart attack at least 50%. Smoking more than forty-five cigarettes a day may raise the likelihood of heart disease to six times normal, and smokers who keep smoking after a heart attack are nearly twice as likely to die suddenly from a fatal heart rhythm disturbance. One hundred thousand deaths from heart disease each year can be blamed on tobacco alone.

There is no such thing as a low risk cigarette. Don't be fooled by "low tar" or "light" smokes. They do nothing to reduce the risk of smoking-related illnesses. Not surprisingly, trendy unfiltered cigarettes are even more dangerous than conventional filtered brands.

Smoking affects heart health on many fronts. It increases dangerous LDL cholesterol and triglycerides and lowers the heart-healthy HDL cholesterol. C-reactive protein levels and homocysteine are higher in smokers. Tobacco smoke contains dangerous oxidants that may generate free radicals in the bloodstream, leading to widespread damage to the lining of the blood vessels. It brings down blood levels of a number of vitamins, including B-vitamins, vitamin C, beta carotene, and vitamin E.

Smoking also enhances the blood's susceptibility to clots and, at the same time, reduces the effectiveness of aspirin as a clot preventer. It is probably this vulnerability to blood clots that causes women smokers who use the birth control pill to have an astounding heart attack risk of forty times normal—a risk that few realize they are taking. Smokers on the pill are also more likely to have a stroke, and the risk increases dramatically after the age of 35.

Smoking is responsible for many disabling and fatal strokes and is a major cause of peripheral vascular disease, or blockage of the arteries of the legs and arms. Diabetics are especially susceptible, and the condition may eventually lead to amputation due to poor healing of infections of the skin and bones. Indeed, smokers are more likely to become diabetic, since they are more prone to insulin resistance.

Smoking Hurts You and Those You Love

Smoking will bring on menopause about two years earlier, depriving women of valuable years of natural estrogen. Smokers are 50% more likely to develop osteoporosis, a disabling weakening of the bone structure that increases vulnerability to bone fractures. And while lung cancer kills three times as many women as breast cancer, smoking also increases the likelihood of breast cancer by up to five times the usual rate. Smokers' risk of ovarian cancer is more than doubled, and cervical cancer is more prevalent as well. Even second-hand smoke can harm the reproductive organs. A study from Johns Hopkins University found that non-smoking women who live with smokers are more than twice as likely to have precancerous cells in the cervix when compared with women who are not exposed to smoke at home.

Smoking has an enormous impact on the health of an unborn child. Smokers are more likely to give birth to underweight babies. Cleft palates, holes in the heart, and other birth defects are more common in the children of smokers. Those children whose moms smoke while pregnant are more likely to suffer from serious psychiatric illness later in life.

Infants in a smoking household are at greater risk for sudden infant death syndrome, or SIDS. Kids who grow up in a household where people smoke are much more likely to develop asthma and painful ear infections, and smokers' kids are more apt to develop cancer and heart disease as adults, even if they never smoke.

Smokers and people who use other forms of tobacco also dramatically increase their risk for a variety of nasty and disfiguring cancers of the head and neck. Cancers of the stomach, esophagus, pancreas, kidneys, and bladder are all legacies of tobacco use.

Periodontal disease (inflammation of the gum tissue) and bad breath are common side effects of smoking. And for men, smoking at least doubles the chances of developing erectile dysfunction.

Smoking affects everyone. One patient I will never forget was Patty, a 38-year-old stay-at-home mom with three beautiful children. Patty took low-dose birth control pills. She was not a smoker, but her husband was, and he chose to smoke in their home. Patty came into the ER early one morning in the throes of a heart attack, her frantic husband and children at her side. Fortunately, she survived with no long-term damage, and after exhaustive evaluation, the only risk factor we could find was her birth control pills. Combined with exposure to her husband's tobacco smoke, this was a nearly lethal mix.

PIPES AND CIGARS

Once the choice of stodgy old men, cigar smoking suddenly became fashionable in the mid 1990s, even among women, and is still considered cool in some circles. Since cigars are decidedly not cigarettes, many believe that the risks are negligible. Unfortunately, they are mistaken.

Regular cigar smokers and pipe smokers are 30% to 70% more likely than non-smokers to develop heart disease. Nevertheless, cigarette smokers who switch to cigars or pipes do reduce their risk of heart disease by about half, which is probably because they are less likely to fully inhale the tobacco smoke.

TOBACCO: KEEP IT TO YOURSELF

- Second hand smoke raises the heart attack risk by 25%.
- Babies of mothers who smoke during pregnancy are more prone to low birth weight, cleft palate, holes in the heart, and other congenital defects.
- Children of smokers are more likely to suffer from psychiatric disorders.
- Children of smokers are more likely to die of SIDS and to develop asthma and ear infections.

TOBACCO: HOW TO GIVE UP THE GHOST

On average, the person who quits using tobacco decreases her risk of dying prematurely by more than one third. Quitting before the age of 30 will eventually bring your risk down to that of a never-smoker, but even quitting by the time you hit 50 buys you several more precious years, not to mention an enhanced quality of life and the gratitude of your friends and loved ones.

Nearly half of all smokers will try to quit each year; most are not successful. I wish I knew a foolproof way to tell you how to stop smoking. Unfortunately, there isn't one. Tobacco is highly addictive in all of its forms. Nicotine, the addictive part of tobacco, affects a complicated array of brain chemicals in many ways. It acts as both a stimulant and a depressant. For some people, it improves the ability to concentrate. It may suppress the appetite, which is one reason that modest weight gain often follows smoking cessation.

Simply throwing the cigarettes away and resolving never to smoke again works for some people, but not for most. Nicotine replacement products are a reasonably safe option for the short term, even for people with heart problems. They are certainly safer than tobacco, which we know to be highly toxic. These products include nicotine gum, lozenges, and patches, which can be bought over-the-counter, and prescription nicotine inhalers and nasal spray. Usually, these should be used for several months. The important thing is to give it time, which many people fail to do. Even when used properly, their effectiveness is modest, with about only 20% to 25% of tobacco users quitting by about three months. No one product is substantially better than the others, so the choice is up to you.

Buproprion (marketed as Wellbutrin-SR and Zyban) has been approved by the FDA to assist in tobacco cessation. Usually this is taken for several months. When combined with a healthy dose of motivation and determination, the quit rates are on the order of 50%. Unfortunately, at least half of the quitters will backslide by a year, so a strong commitment to your health and well-being is essential.

Combining buproprion with a nicotine replacement product may boost your chances of quitting. Some people just feel horrible on this drug, in which case it should be discontinued. Since there is a very small (less than one-tenth of one percent) risk of seizures with buproprion, people with a seizure disorder or a history of anorexia nervosa or bulimia should avoid this drug, as they are more likely to suffer this side effect.

Varenicline (marketed as Chantix) was developed by Pfizer as a smoking cessation aid. A prescription drug, it helps to block the receptor in the brain that is associated with tobacco cravings and with symptoms of tobacco withdrawal. Because it can also cause slight nausea, it is not usually associated with weight gain. In a clinical trial, nearly half of those who used the drug quit in the first month (compared to 33% with buproprion and 17% with placebo in the same time frame). Treatment with the drug continued for three months.

At the one year mark, only 14% remained abstinent. This sounds dismal, but in this particular study it was far better than with buproprion (6%) or placebo (5%). Patients who have taken this medication successfully have told me that they simply "forgot to smoke." Chantix is a relatively safe drug, but should not be used during pregnancy or breast feeding. A few people may develop depression or other psychological problems, so it's important to follow-up with your doctor while on the drug.

Hypnosis may be a reasonable option for those willing to try it. Despite claims to the contrary, there is really not much in the way of good medical research to back up the use of hypnosis for smoking cessation. However, when administered by a credentialed practitioner, hypnosis may be effective for as many as 20% of smokers.

HAVE YOU SMOKED A CADILLAC?

Please don't tell me that it is too expensive to quit. Add up what you spend on your cigarettes, and you will see that the investment is well worth it. A day's worth of nicotine patches or Chantix costs about as much as a pack of smokes. As a lovely and genteel Southern lady once told me, "Honey, I have smoked an entire Cadillac." Another patient put it even more bluntly when she told me that quitting is cheaper than chemotherapy.

If your spouse or roommate smokes, you are much more likely to quit if you do it together. Being around other smokers is a powerful trigger and a quick way to sabotage your best intentions. When you do quit, be forewarned that you may gain weight. The average person who quits gains about 5 to 10 pounds, mostly because the oral fix that comes from smoking is transferred to food. The younger you are when you quit, the less likely it is that you'll gain weight. If you do put on a few pounds, know that you can lose it. Add more fruits and vegetables to boost your antioxidants, increase your exercise, and enjoy the fresh air that you are now free to breathe.

TOBACCO: THE NAILS IN THE COFFIN

- 430,000 Americans die each year from tobacco-related causes. One in four smokers dies before the age of 70.
- Smoking even one cigarette per day will raise your heart attack risk by 50%. Smoke more than forty-five cigarettes daily, and the chance of a heart attack is six times normal.
- If you smoke and take birth control pills, your heart attack risk is forty times normal.
- Smoking is linked to the development of a wide variety of cancers, emphysema, osteoporosis, strokes, blockage in the arteries of the legs, and premature aging.
- Smoking raises LDL cholesterol, triglycerides, CRP, and homocysteine and lowers HDL cholesterol.
- There is no safe tobacco.
- You can quit, but you will probably need help doing so. Ask your doctor about your medical options. Hypnosis is also worth a try. Cold turkey usually doesn't work.

ILLICIT DRUGS: YOUR HEART SAYS NO

It has been estimated that more than 80 million Americans have used marijuana at least once, over 25 million have tried cocaine, and at least 5 million have experimented with amphetamines. Exactly how many people continue to use illicit drugs is a matter of some debate. Understandably, many people will not 'fess up to their drug use, but regular marijuana users number around 5 million and cocaine-users about 1.5 million or more.

Many of these folks, especially pot-smokers, are everyday working people. They may be your neighbors, your grocers, or even your stockbrokers. Most have no clue about the harm these substances can cause. Perhaps as troubling, most people who use illicit drugs have absolutely no idea where their drugs originated, in what unsavory or downright disgusting fashion they were transported, what sorts of additives they might contain, and what level of potency they might provide. Of course, there is no way of knowing. The illegal drug trade is not a regulated industry.

There are many reasons to avoid illicit drugs. Everyone knows that heroin and other narcotics are harmful, but most people don't realize that marijuana, cocaine, and amphetamines can be damaging to the heart.

While there is no good evidence that smoking marijuana affects the heart arteries in the same way as tobacco, we do know that in the first hour after smoking pot, the risk of a heart attack increases to five times normal. That means that high risk people like cigarette smokers, diabetics, and people with high blood pressure are especially vulnerable.

Some people enjoy the sensation of being "mellowed out," but the heart is far from relaxed when exposed to marijuana. Heart rate and blood pressure rise, but standing up will often cause the blood pressure to fall precipitously, resulting in severe light-headedness and sometimes even fainting.

One patient of mine, a corporate recruiter and self-confessed former hippie who had smoked more than her share of pot in her younger days, visited Amsterdam on vacation to enjoy the legal marijuana available there. Minutes after smoking what she described as "a big fat doobie," she stood up and fainted dead away. She was rushed to a hospital where she endured a number of expensive medical tests before being pronounced safe to travel back home to the States. Her husband was not amused.

Cocaine poses special dangers to the heart. Over time, cocaine may cause cumulative damage to the heart arteries, resulting in widespread cholesterol plaques and aneurysms. In the first hour after using cocaine, the heart attack risk rises to a staggering rate of twenty-four times greater than normal. Twenty-five percent of heart attacks that happen before the age of 45 are due to cocaine use. Life-threatening heart rhythm disturbances and congestive heart failure are also well-known side effects of cocaine. Repeated use of the drug can lead to numerous injuries to the heart arteries, causing widespread cholesterol plaques and aneurysms.

Jack and John, two well-respected and highly sociable businessmen, regularly indulged in cocaine, sometimes using it to help them through grueling workdays and even longer evenings spent entertaining clients. They thought it made them feel hip and young. Both required bypass surgery before the age of 50 for multiple blockages in the coronary arteries. Neither man had any other risk factors to explain such extensive disease.

Amphetamines are similarly risky. They raise both blood pressure and heart rate, increasing the risk of heart attacks and heart failure. Amphetamine use has also been associated with an increased risk of bleeding into the brain, which can have the disastrous outcome of a disabling stroke or even death.

STEP FOUR

SMART WOMEN KNOW THEIR ALTERNATIVES

It's a fact of life that good health doesn't always come naturally. Smart women know that there is a world of options and alternatives available to help support, maintain, and protect our well-being. We also understand the value of a good doctor and how to make her an ally for optimal health. The challenge lies in learning how to make the right choices and knowing whom to trust.

While vitamins and minerals are essential for a healthy heart, recent medical research suggests that we need to be very careful when considering high-dose supplements. In most cases, when it comes to nutrition, Mother Nature really does know best. Nutritious, natural food is usually the best source of the vitamins and minerals our bodies crave.

Supplements and herbs are big business, and manufacturers aren't always the best sources of information. Learning to unravel the truth from the myths will help us make the smartest choices for ourselves and for those we love.

10

VITAMINS AND MINERALS FOR A HEALTHY HEART

Vitamins and minerals are essential to keeping these marvelous hearts, brains, and bodies of ours healthy, happy, and in prime working condition.

A vitamin is a chemical that typically cannot be made by the body, but that is required to keep the body in good working order. Since our bodies don't make vitamins (with the exception of vitamin D), ideally we should acquire them through the foods we eat, as Mother Nature intended. The next best option is a multivitamin pill.

There are thirteen major vitamins, four of them fat soluble (A, D, E, and K) and nine water soluble. While we store the fat soluble vitamins in the liver and fatty tissues, water soluble vitamins are usually washed out quite efficiently by our kidneys. Each vitamin has its own role, and we need all of them to function normally. Fortunately, severe cases of vitamin deficiency are very rare in the United States, although sadly common in the Third World. However, people with diabetes, alcoholics, and the elderly may be at higher risk for mild, but important, deficiencies of vitamins and minerals.

Provitamins are vitamin precursors that our bodies are able to convert into active vitamins. Two examples are beta-carotene (found in dark green, yellow, and orange vegetables), which is converted into vitamin A, and ergosterol (found in some yeasts and mushrooms), which becomes vitamin D.

Minerals are basically metallic elements, such as iron, calcium, and magnesium, and account for about 4% of our body weight. At least twenty-two different minerals are essential to our health. Minerals are involved in just about every function of our bodies, including muscle contraction, normal functioning of our nervous systems, proper regulation of hormones, and of course, development of our bones.

I'll walk you through the vitamins and minerals that are relevant to the maintenance of a healthy cardiovascular system.

WHY ARE ANTIOXIDANTS SO IMPORTANT?

Vitamins E and C, the provitamin beta-carotene, and the mineral selenium are antioxidants, which means that they help to neutralize free radicals, effectively disarming them. Free radicals are atoms and molecules with an unpaired electron. They will try to "steal" electrons from other molecules through a process called oxidation. It is the oxidized form of LDL cholesterol, for example, that is so damaging to the heart and blood vessels.

Free radicals come from many sources, including the food we eat. Nitrite preservatives, which are often found in pork products, are highly potent sources of free radicals. When we eat fat, the process of metabolizing, or breaking it down, churns out free radicals like a little factory. Cigarette smoke and air pollutants are also good sources of these wicked little assailants. Even exercise, particularly when we're out of shape and deconditioned, can produce free radicals due to muscle tissue breakdown.

Dietary antioxidants help to curb these constant assaults on the vital cells of our bodies. In the 1980s and 1990s, there was a lot of optimism that these nutrients, when taken in megadoses, might impact health and save lives. But recent well-done medical research has shown us that it is best to be circumspect. It seems that sometimes more is just too much.

VITAMIN E

Vitamin E, or alpha-tocopherol, is a fat-soluble vitamin that comes from plants. Vegetable oils, nuts, and whole grains are the best sources of vitamin E. Wheat germ oil is a vitamin E powerhouse. This vitamin has two major functions: the first is to defend our cells against oxidation, and the second is to help keep our red blood cells flexible. Vitamin E also helps counter the production of some of the factors involved in blood clotting and may lessen the amount of C-reactive protein that flows through the bloodstream after a high fat meal.

THE TRUTH ABOUT SUPPLEMENTAL VITAMIN E

Foods that are rich in vitamin E are also chock full of other important nutrients, and in all likelihood, these other nutrients work in concert with vitamin E to help protect and strengthen our cardiovascular and immune systems. Supplements are a different matter.

The minimum amount of vitamin E required to support normal physiologic function is 15 IU (international units) daily, but dietary supplements are available in doses ranging from 100-1200 IU and beyond. Both natural and synthetic vitamin E capsules are available. The synthetic form is less expensive, but it appears to be less accessible to the body than the natural form.

While foods high in vitamin E are clearly linked to improved cardiovascular health, scientific studies have failed to establish a concrete cause-and-effect relationship between supplemental vitamin E and heart disease, stroke, and cancer.

Although many people take the supplements in hopes of protecting their hearts, at least one study actually showed a slight increase in the risk of congestive heart failure in people taking high doses of vitamin E. In another, supplemental vitamin E was found to reduce the effectiveness of drugs designed to lower cholesterol, and under certain conditions, there was evidence that it might even promote a slight increase in cholesterol buildup.

Most studies of vitamin E have shown no effect on cancer prevention, although there is some evidence of a possible protective effect against prostate cancer. However, a Canadian study of people with cancer of the head and neck found that those who were treated with 400 IU of vitamin E daily had an increased risk not only of recurrence of the original cancer, but also of developing a second cancer.

The most disturbing news about vitamin E surfaced in late 2004, when an analysis of nineteen studies involving more than 130,000 people concluded that those who took 400 IU or more of supplemental vitamin E every day had a 10% greater risk of dying than people who took no supplement at all. Even doses of 150 IU were associated with a slight increase in mortality. Taking megadoses of 2000 IU or greater raised the risk to 20%.

Extremely high daily doses of vitamin E (more than 1000 IU) are known to increase the risk of potentially fatal bleeding, particularly in the brain. That is one reason why people who take certain prescription blood thinners, such as warfarin, should avoid high-dose supplements of this vitamin.

While it might appear that the supplement question is closed, there are still some legitimate questions being raised about the possibility that less common types of vitamin E supplementation might be useful in heart disease and cancer prevention. Although most supplements, natural and synthetic, contain alpha-tocopherol, this form is only one of eight different vitamin E compounds.

Gamma-tocopherol is actually the most common form of vitamin E in our diet. It is found in walnuts, peanuts, pecans, corn oil, sesame oil, and soy bean oil. Some scientists believe that the difference could be important, particularly in the prevention of cancer and Alzheimer's disease. Another form of vitamin E is found in palm oil and may have promise in the prevention and treatment of breast cancer. So far, these are just interesting questions and speculation.

VITAMIN C

Unlike vitamin E, vitamin C is water soluble. Consequently, unlike vitamin E, it is not incorporated into LDL cholesterol. It does, however, function as an electron donor to vitamin E. What this means is that when vitamin E acts as an antioxidant, it transfers one of its electrons to a harmful free-radical molecule, rendering it inactive. In turn, vitamin C (also known as ascorbic acid) kindly donates one of its electrons to vitamin E, essentially reactivating the vitamin E.

Every school kid knows that vitamin C is found in citrus fruits, but peaches, strawberries, broccoli, and tomatoes are also excellent sources. It is critical for the normal development and maintenance of the connective tissues in our bodies, as well as our nervous systems. While some people fall short of the recommended daily value for vitamin C, true vitamin C deficiency, also known as scurvy, is very rare in this country.

To prevent deficiency-related complications, most women should get, at the very least, 75 mg of vitamin C each day; men, being generally larger, require a minimum of 90 mg. Smokers have been estimated to require 100 mg daily, and those who exercise vigorously should probably take in 100 to 500 mg. And while it's important to know the minimum threshold for vitamin C, full saturation of the blood and tissue does not occur until you reach a daily intake of 200 to 400 mg. This amount of vitamin C is easily obtained from the foods we choose.

Whenever possible, enjoy your fruits and veggies at the peak of freshness since the vitamin content may decline as much as 50% after just a week of storage. Frozen fruit and vegetables are a surprisingly good choice since freezing preserves the vitamins. Boiling vegetables can literally wash away the vitamins, so if you have to cook them, try a quick steaming or a brief spin through the microwave.

To Supplement or Not to Supplement

If you eat your eight servings of fruits and veggies each day, you will never lack for vitamin C. In fact, you'll be way ahead of the curve. Just 4 ounces of red peppers will give you up to 215 mg of vitamin C, along with a tremendous infusion of important phytonutrients (another word for plant-based nutrients). Other foods, including cantaloupe, strawberries, and broccoli, supply on the order of 50 to 110 mg of vitamin C with each serving.

This sounds easy, but although we may be smart women in many ways, most of us get less than 200 mg of vitamin C from the foods we eat.

Obviously, it shouldn't take a vitamin pill to meet our body's needs, but when it comes to matters of the heart, a supplement is better than nothing.

High doses of vitamin C are another matter. There is no compelling evidence to justify the use of high-dose vitamin C, either alone or in combination with other supplements, as a means to prevent heart disease. In fact, a multinational study found that diabetic women who took high doses of vitamin C supplements were even more likely to develop heart disease, although vitamin C from foods posed no such risk.

Evidence in favor of vitamin C as a cancer preventative is poor. There is really no good data to support the use of vitamin C to prevent colds, although it is still possible that vitamin C might reduce the severity of cold symptoms.

Fortunately, vitamin C supplements rarely cause side effects, but kidney stones, anemia, and diarrhea may result from extremely high doses. Vitamin C doses in excess of 1500 mg daily are essentially wasted, since the body will excrete surplus vitamin C through the urine.

Without a doubt, your diet is the best and safest way to get the vitamin C you need. Nature creates our food in an exquisitely balanced package, combining vitamins with hundreds of other phytonutrients. Science is only beginning to understand how these substances work in harmony, and in most cases, our clumsy attempts to thwart Mother Nature with mega-supplements have backfired, causing more harm than good.

VITAMIN A AND BETA-CAROTENE

Vitamin A is a fat soluble vitamin. While it is not much of an antioxidant itself, one of its precursors, or pro-vitamins, beta-carotene, is renowned for its powerful antioxidant properties. Beta-carotene provides the rich orange pigment to carrots, sweet potatoes, and cantaloupe but is also found in spinach, broccoli, and other dark-green and yellow fruits and vegetables. Deficiencies of beta-carotene and vitamin A are rare in this country, but in third world countries, vitamin A deficiency is an all too common and easily preventable cause of blindness.

Beta-carotene is a potent antioxidant. Women whose diets are rich in beta-carotene have up to 26% less heart disease and a considerably lower risk of cancer when compared to those whose diets include little or none of the nutrient. Foods high in beta-carotene may even help to prevent diabetes.

If a little is good, shouldn't a lot be even better? You may have caught on by now that when it comes to supplements, the answer turns out to be a heartfelt "no." A study of nearly 40,000 women who were followed for two years and also given beta-carotene supplements found no effect on heart health or cancer risk.

That particular study was cut short when a large study of male smokers from Finland reported a chilling 28% increase in lung cancer in those who were given high-dose beta-carotene and vitamin A supplements. A similar increase in the risk of lung cancer was later reported in the Journal of the National Cancer Institute from a study of smokers in six different centers in the United States. (Despite these very compelling and sobering statistics, I was stunned to discover that a Web site selling beta-carotene supplements claimed that this very study actually reported a reduction in cancer deaths.)

How could it be possible that an antioxidant could increase the risk of cancer? Scientists are still studying the problem, but the theory is that once the beta-carotene becomes oxidized (that is, after it donates an electron to neutralize a free radical), it becomes lodged in the lungs and bloodstream and then acts as a pro-oxidant itself, causing harm to the surrounding tissue.

High levels of vitamin A, although not beta-carotene, have been associated with other complications, including an increased risk of bone fragility and bone fractures. Extremely high doses of vitamin A taken in the form of supplements may even, over time, cause permanent liver damage. Dietary beta-carotene has not been found to have this effect. You can literally eat enough carrots to turn your skin orange, but your levels of vitamin A will remain normal, thanks to the body's remarkable ability to self-regulate.

The recommended Vitamin A intake for women is 700 mcg, or 2300 IU; men require 900 mcg, or 3000 IU. You have to take more than 3000 mcg of vitamin A per day (or 10,000 IU) before it becomes harmful to the bones. Over time, daily doses of 7500 mcg (25,000 IU) or more are known to cause liver damage.

Vitamin A is found in liver and other organ meats, egg yolks, fortified dairy products such as milk and cheese, and vitamin supplements. Someone who eats liver regularly could easily exceed the recommended amount since 3 ounces of beef liver contains more than 30,000 IU of vitamin A. By comparison, one cup of fortified milk supplies 500 IU, and an ounce of cheese provides about 250 IU.

Beta-carotene is not the only precursor to vitamin A. There are more than 600 different dietary carotenoids, all of which have antioxidant properties and fifty of which have pro-vitamin A activity. Lycopene, found in tomatoes and other red fruits and vegetables, is another example of a carotenoid that may help protect against cancer and heart disease. It is thought that the carotenoids work in conjunction with one another—as a team, so to speak—and that this may explain why taking one in isolation may have unintended, unbalanced consequences.

While supplements may be dangerous, especially for smokers, there is no evidence that eating foods high in beta-carotene and other carotenoids is harmful; to the contrary, many studies have shown that these foods help to protect against heart disease and certain forms of cancer.

SELENIUM

Selenium is a trace element that is a vital component in many important antioxidant proteins in the body. Most of the selenium in our diet originates in the soil and comes to us not only through plants but also through the muscle tissue of grazing animals such as cattle and sheep. Seafood is also an excellent source of selenium, although mercury, a pollutant found commonly in the bodies of the fish we eat, can bind it up so that it is not available for our cells to use.

Brazil nuts and grains are potent plant-based sources of selenium, but it is possible to overdo it. Just 1 ounce of Brazil nuts supplies 840 mcg, or twelve times the required daily intake of 70 mcg. Just 3.5 ounces of tuna supplies more than 100% of the daily recommended intake, and two slices of whole wheat bread deliver about 30%. The Institute of Medicine recommends a maximal daily limit of 400 mcg, in order to avoid potential toxicity such as intestinal upset, thyroid abnormalities, hair loss, and damage to the nerves.

When selenium levels are adequate, there is no special benefit to heart health in taking supplements. Extremely low dietary levels of selenium have been a problem in some European countries and may lead to weakening of the heart muscle. High blood levels of selenium have been associated with a possible slight increase in cancer risk.

At one time, selenium was thought to be protective against diabetes, but a seven-year study in which people were given a daily supplement of 200 mcg of selenium found the incidence of diabetes was more than doubled. Since selenium deficiencies are extremely rare in the United States, it makes sense to get this mineral from the food you eat, unless you have a true medical need for a supplement.

WHAT YOU NEED TO KNOW ABOUT ANTIOXIDANTS

- Antioxidant vitamins and minerals include vitamins A, C, E, beta-carotene, and selenium. Antioxidants neutralize many harmful substances we bring into our bodies.
- Antioxidants in the diet are associated with a decreased risk of heart disease and stroke, but very high-dose vitamin E supplements may actually increase heart disease and cancer risk.
- High-dose beta-carotene supplements raise the risk of lung cancer in smokers.
- Selenium supplements may increase your risk for diabetes and cancer. Your best bet is to get your antioxidants from the foods you eat.

THE B VITAMINS

The B-vitamins are a family of water-soluble vitamins that help break down the food we eat into usable energy. Although all of them are essential for heart health, folic acid (B9), B6, B12, and niacin (B3) deserve special attention for their important preventive properties.

FOLIC ACID, B6, AND B12

Also known as folate or folacin, folic acid works in combination with vitamins B6 and B12. Folic acid is found in a wide variety of foods, including dark green leafy vegetables, whole grains, brewer's yeast, and liver, so a healthy diet will usually net you plenty of this nutrient. Alcoholics, who may get most of their calories from alcohol, are vulnerable to deficiencies, as are people with serious gastrointestinal illnesses. In addition, certain prescription drugs may counteract folic acid, necessitating the use of supplements to maintain normal levels. During pregnancy, folic acid is vital for the healthy development of the fetus' nervous system, so pregnant women are routinely supplemented with this vitamin.

In 1998, the Nurses' Health Study reported that women who had the highest intake of folic acid and B6 had about half the risk of heart disease of those women whose diets were deficient in these vitamins. Women whose diet included 500 mcg of folic acid and 3 mg of B6 daily appeared to benefit the most. In another report from the same study, greater daily intake of folic acid was linked to a lower likelihood of high blood pressure.

GET YOUR FOLIC ACID HERE

In 1998 the FDA mandated fortification of food grain with folic acid, in large part to help prevent birth defects caused by inadequate folic acid in the diets of pregnant women. As a result, average consumption was boosted to about 300 micrograms daily. Although this is still less than the daily 500 microgram dose that seemed to offer the most benefit in the Nurses' Health Study, a major study reported by the Centers for Disease Control and Prevention estimated that simply enriching flour and other grain products with folic acid prevents 48,000 strokes and deaths every year.

FOLIC ACID SUPPLEMENTS AND HEART HEALTH

There is some evidence that high dose B-vitamins might help prevent blockages from coming back in people who have undergone a coronary balloon angioplasty procedure. However, the balloon angioplasty procedure is now considered quaintly old fashioned, and implanted coronary stents have nearly supplanted this treatment for heart artery blockages. Stents are tiny metal mesh tubes that are used to open up blockages; since they are embedded in the wall of the artery, they are much more effective than simply blowing up a balloon. In this setting, high-dose folic acid supplements (on the order of 800 mcg of more) increase the likelihood that the stent will close up over time, and that a repeat procedure will be required.

Although homocysteine levels drop by an average of 28% with extreme vitamin therapy, there is actually a slight increase in the likelihood of a second heart attack or stroke in people with heart disease who take mega doses of B vitamins. In high doses, the supplements may even raise the risk for cancer, since folic acid appears to enhance the growth of all cells, both healthy and malignant.

Many cardiologists now consider homocysteine an "innocent bystander," or a marker for other risk factors, rather than a risk factor itself. Smoking, saturated fat, and coffee in excess of three cups a day are all known to raise homocysteine levels.

If your diet is heart healthy, you won't need to worry about getting enough of this nutrient. If you don't get enough folic acid from your diet, a vitamin supplement is reasonable. Doses of 400 micrograms a day, typically the amount found in a good multivitamin, appear to be safe and effective; pregnant women need at least 600 micrograms.

THE BUZZ ON B6 AND B12

In combination with dietary folic acid, Vitamin B6 is thought to help maintain healthy arteries and is important in the production of red blood cells and platelets. B6 also helps to normalize blood glucose levels, although there's no advantage to supplementation above the recommended daily requirement.

B6 is found in fish, brown rice, whole grains, soybeans, and organ meats, and true deficiencies are uncommon in otherwise healthy people, with the exception of alcoholics. Smoking, advanced age, and kidney failure are all associated with a reduction in levels of B6. Interestingly, low B6 levels are associated with high levels of CRP, a marker of inflammation that we discussed in chapter 3. The recommended daily intake is 1.3 to 1.7 mg, depending on age and gender (elderly men need the most), but research studies have used 5 to 50 mg daily with no adverse effects; 10 mg is the dose most frequently used.

The National Institute of Medicine recommends that doses of B6 should not exceed 100 mg daily, as higher doses may cause permanent nerve damage.

Vitamin B12 is critical to many of the body's functions, including heart health, normal function of the nervous system, and metabolism of carbohydrates, proteins, and fats. It is also important in the maintenance and production of DNA, the genetic blueprint of our cells. High-dose B12 along with folic acid may even help lessen the risk of hip fractures in vulnerable elderly people. The U.S. recommended daily intake of B12 is 2.4 micrograms, although most research studies have included 400 to 1000 micrograms of B12. There are no known adverse health effects of taking B12 at these levels.

In order for dietary B12 to be absorbed and utilized by the body, it must combine with a special protein in the stomach known as intrinsic factor. People who cannot absorb B12 can suffer serious consequences, including anemia, numbness of the extremities, and weakness. As people age, less intrinsic factor is produced, so deficiencies are much more common in the elderly.

The form of vitamin B12 that is found in vitamin pills is usually crystalline B12, which does not require gastric acid for absorption, so it is generally effective even for those who are deficient in intrinsic factor. Even so, people who are unable to absorb B12 from the stomach are often treated with injections, usually monthly. Symptoms of B12 deficiency in elderly people can be very vague, including just a general sense of malaise. Fortunately, a simple blood test can easily determine if a person is deficient in this vitamin.

Vegans must pay special attention to B12, since it is not found in plants, but is produced by bacteria in the intestines of grazing animals. It is found in all manner of animal products, including meats, egg yolk, poultry, and milk. It makes sense for vegans to add B12 supplements to their diets. Most vegans have not gotten the message, and up to 92% of them have been reported to be B12 deficient. Since it may take twenty to thirty years to deplete the body's stores, a B12 deficiency may not show up right away in a recent vegan convert.

Regardless of diet, it is critically important to add B12 when taking folic acid supplements, since higher doses of folic acid in someone who is B12 deficient may increase the likelihood of nerve damage.

NIACIN

Niacin, also known as vitamin B3, nicotinic acid, and nicotinamide, is important in regulating metabolism and maintaining healthy skin, nails, and gastrointestinal functions. Good sources include protein rich foods such as meat and fish, as well as peanuts and brewers' yeast.

At the usual dietary doses, niacin really doesn't play a major role in heart health. The recommended daily intake of niacin is 14 to 16 mg per day. However, at much higher doses (500 to 2000 mg), niacin morphs into a powerful cholesterol-altering drug which can lower LDL, raise HDL, and reduce triglycerides. Niacin in this prescription-strength range should never be taken without a doctor's supervision since it can cause undesirable side effects, including flushing, itching, headaches, nausea, and muscle cramps. Liver abnormalities are an uncommon but potentially serious side effect of high-dose niacin, so routine blood tests to evaluate liver enzymes are mandatory.

Prescription-strength niacin may also interact with other drugs. We'll discuss high-dose niacin more in chapter 13.

B-VITAMIN BINGO

- Pregnant women need about 600 micrograms of folic acid daily.
- High-dose folic acid supplements (more than 800 micrograms) may increase heart risk, especially if taken after a coronary stent has been placed.
- High-dose folic acid supplements may also increase the risk of cancer.
- More than 90% of vegans are deficient in B12, as are many elderly people; these people should take supplemental B12.

- Prescription strength niacin may help improve cholesterol levels but should be taken only under a doctor's supervision.

CALCIUM AND VITAMIN D

Most of us understand that we need calcium and vitamin D to keep our bones healthy and strong, but both nutrients are also essential for good cardiovascular health.

Vitamin D is unique in that it is manufactured in the skin, when we are exposed to ultraviolet (UV) rays. While sun worshippers may end up with sun-dried skin and troublesome skin cancers, they hardly ever have to worry about missing out on vitamin D. For those who shun the sun, or who cover up when out of doors, deficiencies are much more common and supplements are often required.

As we age, our vitamin D requirements increase. Until we reach our 50s, adults need about 200 IU daily, including pregnant and lactating moms. After menopause, our daily requirement surges to 800–1000 IU.

A sunny day is not the only way to boost your stores of vitamin D. There are dietary sources as well. Fatty fish, including salmon and tuna, are excellent sources of vitamin D, as well as healthy omega-3 fatty acids. Milk is usually fortified with vitamin D, as are most brands of soy milk and many breakfast cereals, so getting the vitamin is as easy as fixing yourself a bowl of whole-grain cereal and milk.

Low levels of vitamin D have been linked to a higher risk for cardiovascular disease, especially in people with hypertension. Too much vitamin D can be harmful as well, resulting in dangerously high levels of calcium. This in turn can cause mental confusion, abnormal heart rhythms, and deposits of calcium and phosphate in the soft tissues of the body.

The maximum safe daily dose of vitamin D is considered to be 2000 IU, although much higher doses are sometimes prescribed for people with serious deficiencies. A cup of milk supplies about 100 IU, and 4 ounces of salmon will buy you 400 IU. Fish oil capsules generally do not contain vitamin D. But for those who choose to take old-fashioned cod liver oil, one tablespoon of the slick stuff provides 1360 IU of vitamin D, leaving little wiggle room for more.

Calcium can also be overdone. Most people need about 1200 mg for optimal health. Take too much calcium (more than 2500 mg daily), and you run the risk of kidney stones. Calcium supplements can also cause stomach upset and constipation in some people, although many antacids contain calcium. If you are on antibiotics, avoid taking them at the same time as a calcium supplement, since calcium can prevent these drugs from being absorbed through the intestine.

It's best to get most of your calcium from the foods you eat, since dietary calcium maintains bone density better than calcium supplements. Dairy products are a great source of calcium, but molasses, tofu, and dark green leafy vegetables also supply reasonable amounts.

A diet high in calcium (1000 to 1500 mg/day) may help to lower blood pressure modestly (about 1 to 3 mm Hg), perhaps resulting in a 6% lowering of heart attack risk and a 13% reduction in stroke risk, since blood pressure is such an important factor in these conditions. A calcium-rich diet that includes low fat dairy foods may even help lower cholesterol and reduce the chance of developing diabetes. However, despite reports to the contrary, it probably won't help you lose weight unless you cut back on calories as well.

VITAMIN K

Vitamin K is found in virtually all green leafy vegetables and in soybeans. This vitamin is also made by bacteria living in our gastrointestinal tracts, so true deficiencies are rare. The major importance of vitamin K is its effect upon four critical clotting factors, all of which are manufactured in the liver.

Most people can eat food rich in vitamin K with impunity. However, for those people who take a blood thinner known generically as warfarin (the trade name is Coumadin), wide fluctuations in daily vitamin K intake can cause rather serious problems. This is because warfarin inactivates these vitamin K-dependent clotting factors, reducing the ability of the blood to clot. Warfarin is prescribed for people with a high risk of blood clots, such as people with an irregular heart rhythm known as atrial fibrillation, people with implanted mechanical heart valves, and people with a history of life-threatening blood clots.

For these people, consistency in vitamin K levels is extremely important. As long as vitamin K intake is kept steady, the dose of warfarin can usually be adjusted to accommodate it. That just means that some people may need to take higher than average doses of warfarin to overcome the effects of vitamin K. Given the tremendous health benefits of green leafy vegetables, the advice we used to give to warfarin patients years ago to limit their green leafy vegetables really does not make good medical sense. Of course, if you take a blood thinner and are planning to make changes to your diet, it's important to let your doctor know so your blood work can be monitored.

IRON

An essential mineral, iron is an integral component of hemoglobin, a protein found in all red blood cells. Through hemoglobin, iron helps oxygen to flow throughout the body, right down to the tiniest capillaries, keeping all our cells oxygenated and invigorated.

Our bodies are very good at squirreling away a little extra iron to use in case of a temporary shortage, so if we don't get enough iron every day, we can still get by, at least temporarily. The body is also incredibly efficient at self-regulation and can crank up absorption of dietary iron when our stores are running low and back off when supplies are plentiful.

However, excessive amounts of iron, often from high-dose supplements, can overload the system and may even be fatal to young children.

Beef, oysters, and chicken livers are good animal sources of iron, while soybeans, lentils, beans, and enriched grains provide reasonable amounts of plant-based iron. And just in case you don't eat enough of these naturally iron-rich foods, many cereals are fortified with iron.

While iron from animal sources is easy to absorb, plant-derived iron takes a little more work. Vitamin C assists with the process, so as long as vegetarians get enough vitamin C along with their iron, this does not pose much of a problem. Vitamin A is also important in maintaining a safe level of iron, since it helps to release stored iron during times when iron intake is low or when the body's demand for it is high.

Iron has been a controversial topic among cardiologists for many years. In the 1990s, researchers from Finland reported a link between high levels of dietary iron and coronary artery disease, but several large studies in the United States have found no significant correlation between iron and heart attack risk. In fact, we now know that people with pre-existing heart disease have a higher likelihood of heart complications, including heart attacks, angina, and heart failure, when the blood count drops too low.

Hemochromatosis is an inherited disorder associated with extremely high iron levels which can cause severe damage to the heart muscle and other organs. However, people with this disease do not have a higher rate of atherosclerosis. A simple blood test can detect this condition, which affects at least one in every three hundred people. Men are more likely to have the disorder than women, and Caucasians are most often affected. Treatment often involves what is known as a therapeutic phlebotomy; in essence, this is modern day blood-letting, with blood removed from the body in order to draw down iron levels.

POTASSIUM AND MAGNESIUM

Potassium and magnesium are critical to maintaining heart health. Normal heart and skeletal muscle function, normal electrical activity of the heart, and proper functioning of the nerves and nervous system depend in large part upon potassium and magnesium. In most people, the kidneys keep these elements in a delicate equilibrium, as too much or too little could have disastrous effects. However, diuretics ("water pills") and some other medications can upset this balance, as can kidney failure.

Diuretics are often used to treat high blood pressure and can be very effective, particularly in women, but monitoring is important, since diuretics can lower potassium, sodium, and magnesium. In those people who take diuretics and develop extremely low potassium levels, the risk of serious heart rhythm abnormalities may rise dramatically. Treatment with prescription potassium supplements usually corrects the problem. Mildly low blood levels of potassium may even contribute to high blood pressure. Potassium levels on the high end of the normal scale may decrease the risk of stroke and improve glucose tolerance, reducing the chance of diabetes.

Most American women take in less than half of the recommended 4.7 grams of potassium per day. Fortunately, it is very easy to remedy this. Fruits and vegetables are potassium dynamos. While your granny may have eaten a banana with her breakfast every morning, just about every fruit is chock-full of potassium. If you are not on diuretic medications, and you eat the recommended eight to ten servings of fruits and vegetables daily, it is unlikely that you'll ever lack for potassium.

While there are a few important medical causes of low potassium, if you are not on diuretic drugs, there is usually no reason to take a potassium supplement. Although potassium may be bought over the counter, it is really pretty dangerous to try to dose yourself. Some prescription medications, including blood pressure medications and certain birth control pills, may increase potassium levels, and the body may be unable to adequately rid itself of the excess. This becomes especially problematic in diabetics and those with kidney disease.

Magnesium works closely with potassium, and oftentimes low magnesium levels make it difficult to attain a normal blood level of potassium. Magnesium is involved in normal functioning of muscles and nerves, as well as energy metabolism and bone health. While magnesium has been shown to be involved in the health of the immune system, supplementation above and beyond normal levels does not improve it.

Green leafy vegetables, nuts, wheat germ, and avocados are good sources of magnesium; as luck would have it, so is chocolate. Refined foods tend to be relatively deficient in magnesium.

People with diabetes often have lower blood levels of magnesium and may require supplementation under a doctor's supervision. Excessive alcohol, diuretics, and chemotherapy may deplete magnesium stores, leading to heart arrhythmias, muscle dysfunction, and nerve impairment. Your doctor can run a simple blood test to check for a magnesium deficiency; if your magnesium is low, it's a good bet your potassium is as well. If supplements are needed, regular blood tests are important to be sure the dose is adequate but not excessive.

MINERAL MATTERS

- Iron helps to transport oxygen to our cells, so it's important to maintain normal levels. Vegetarians can usually get plenty of iron from green leafy vegetables as long as they also get enough vitamin C.
- Calcium is an important nutrient, but probably does not help weight loss. Many of us, especially kids and teens, don't get enough calcium from the foods we eat.
- Low levels of potassium can contribute to high blood pressure and can also trigger irregular heart rhythms. Fruits and vegetables are full of potassium, but most people don't eat enough of these foods.
- Magnesium works with potassium, and low levels can also contribute to irregular heart rhythms.
- Don't take supplemental magnesium or potassium without your doctor's approval. Blood tests can easily determine whether you are deficient in these minerals.

11

SUPPLEMENTS AND HERBS: SEPARATING FACT FROM FICTION

I can always count on Joanne, an energetic 54-year-old marketing executive with high blood pressure and elevated cholesterol, to arrive for her appointments balancing a stack of file folders brimming with the latest "breakthrough research" on supplements and herbs. Joanne always seems a little apologetic about her forays into self-care, but she is good-humored and respects my advice and medical opinion. I admire her initiative. Indeed, it was questions from inquisitive patients like Joanne that helped to motivate me to research and write this book.

Nutritional supplements can be found in the medicine cabinets of at least one in five Americans. They account for out-of-pocket expenses of more than $18 billion a year, with an annual growth rate estimated to be on the order of 20%. Another $5 billion or more is spent on herbal products. We're talking big business. More importantly, the wide-spread use of supplements and herbs highlights a desire that many of us have to take control of our own health, in terms that make sense to us and in a way that seems more in tune with nature.

I applaud the active participation in, and commitment to, preventive health care. All too often, supplements and herbs are taken on faith. Many times when I ask my patients why they are taking a particular supplement, the reply is simply: "It's supposed to help my heart." If I prescribed a medication for you and could give you no better explanation for it than this, you would probably be pretty skeptical. To help you to become your own health advocate and to choose supplements wisely, I want you to have some basic knowledge of dietary supplements as well as an understanding of the system that produces and markets them.

Most doctors don't know much about herbs and supplements. In defense of the medical profession, there are many good reasons for this. First, it is not usually a part of our training. More importantly, we are trained as scientists. This is a good thing. We demand proof of efficacy and assurance of safety before we prescribe a medication to our patients. That means that I am not going to recommend a supplement strictly based on hearsay, advertising, or tradition.

What many doctors don't know is that there is actually very legitimate, peer-reviewed research available on a good number of supplements, with many new studies currently in the works.

Supplements, Herbs, the FDA and You

We Americans depend on the Food and Drug Administration (FDA) to monitor and regulate the drugs that our physicians prescribe. While it is not perfect, the system now in place is designed to ensure both the effectiveness and the safety of the prescription and over-the-counter medications that we take. The FDA requires numerous well-controlled and scientifically sound research studies before it gives approval for a drug. These studies must include detailed assessment of risks and benefits, as well as potential drug interactions.

Despite the tremendous amount of time and resources a company may devote to bringing a drug onto the market, many are never approved. A perfect example is torcetrapib, a drug developed by the pharmaceutical giant Pfizer to raise HDL cholesterol. The company spent more than $800 million and many years developing and testing this very promising drug but, in the end, found an unacceptably high risk of side effects and withdrew the product from the FDA review process.

Once a drug actually makes it through, the FDA requires manufacturers to report all possible side effects that might be related to the use of the drug. Too many problems and a drug may be pulled from the market. By this process, the FDA does its best to ensure that the medications we take are as safe as possible and that they do what they are supposed to do.

Is the FDA infallible? Of course not. Occasionally a medication will be approved that is later found to have serious unanticipated interactions with other drugs or dangerous side effects that take many years to become evident. An example is the class of COX-2 inhibitors, including Vioxx, Bextra, and Celebrex. These drugs are associated with a higher risk of heart attacks, but that did not become apparent until several years and millions of prescriptions after their introduction.

To be sure, many drugs are known to have potentially serious side effects, yet approval is given because the benefits to a specific group of patients are important enough that they offset the possible risks.

Although it's far from foolproof, ours is arguably the best system in the world, and some drugs that are approved in other countries do not pass the FDA's muster. This lack of approval is not necessarily because the drugs do not do what they are claimed to do, but because the research to support the claims is not up to the FDA's high standards.

THERE IS A DIFFERENT STANDARD FOR SUPPLEMENTS

The FDA does not apply the same standards to dietary supplements as it does to prescription and over-the-counter drugs. Manufacturers of dietary supplements have a measure of latitude and autonomy not available to pharmaceutical companies. Supplements are broadly defined by the FDA as "any product that is intended for ingestion as a supplement to the diet," with a few exceptions. This definition encompasses vitamins, minerals, herbs and other plant-derived products, amino acids, and extracts from certain animal organs and glands. While these products may look like drugs, they are not considered by the FDA to be medications. As a result, they are not allowed to be marketed with the terms "diagnose," "treat," "prevent," "cure," or "mitigate."

TRUTH IN LABELING

It is fine for supplements to be sold with a type of health claim known as "structure-function" claims, as long as a clear relationship has been established between a given food product and health maintenance. For example, higher intake of fruits, vegetables, and fiber has been associated with a lower risk of heart disease, so this claim could apply to a supplement that contains these elements. Likewise, a product high in calcium could offer information regarding calcium's effects on bone protection. Manufacturers are required to include a standard disclaimer: "This statement has not been evaluated by the FDA. This product is not intended to diagnose, treat, cure, or prevent any disease." Nevertheless, these rules are frequently flouted, particularly on the Internet, where imposing regulation is very difficult.

By federal law, all products on the market must be considered safe, but specific information does not have to be provided to the FDA regarding any individual supplement product, and the FDA does not review or approve dietary supplements.

The only exception to this rule is something known as a "new dietary ingredient" that is not already commercially available in some form. In that case, the manufacturer must prove only that its product is safe if used as stated on the product's labeling.

It is very important to understand that the FDA does not ensure purity, composition, or quality of dietary supplements. This lack of regulation has created a wide-open market for these products and taken away a great deal of security for consumers.

Congress did pass a measure in 2006 requiring manufacturers of supplements and over-the-counter drugs to notify the FDA of any reported side effects. However, since there are so many manufacturers, there is no way to monitor the accuracy of reporting. By 2010, the FDA will require companies to confirm the safety of their products by testing for purity and authenticating the ingredients listed on the label. Given the wide variety of products and sheer number of companies in the supplement business, just how the agency will police the industry remains to be seen.

WHAT YOU SEE MAY NOT BE WHAT YOU GET

When it comes to supplements, investigations have exposed an abysmal amount of misinformation and mislabeling of these products. The amount of active ingredient stated on the label is frequently incorrect, sometimes drastically so. In fact, one Department of Health investigation found that 32% of Asian "herbal" medications actually contained measurable amounts of prescription drugs, including steroids, hormones, and anti-inflammatory medications. More than 10% contained dangerous heavy metals including lead, mercury, and arsenic. A 2004 study of Indian Ayurvedic herbal medicine products bought in the United States found that 20% of these products also contained heavy metals. Some so-called herbal medicines from Japan have been found to contain thyroid hormone, excessive amounts of which can cause tremors, life-threatening heart arrhythmias, and even heart failure. And more than a few supplements marketed for erectile dysfunction have been found to contain bootlegged versions of prescription drugs known to interact dangerously with other commonly prescribed medications.

Although it is the responsibility of the Federal Trade Commission to regulate advertising, there are simply too many products out there and not enough funding for enforcement, making supplements an industry that is nearly impossible to police. Perhaps even more important is the explosion of Internet Web sites offering dietary supplements for sale. Since many of these sites are not based in the United States, governmental oversight is nigh impossible. This is truly a case of "buyer beware."

A study from Johns Hopkins recently reviewed Web sites that offered herbal weight loss products for sale. Of thirty-two different sites offering thirty-two different products, 41% did not disclose potential adverse effects or contraindications to the use of the supplement, 53% did not include dose information, and 34% contained incorrect or misleading statements including claims of "100% safety" and "no harmful side effects," even when the supplements were known to be potentially harmful.

THE SPECIAL PROBLEMS WITH HERBS

Herbs are notoriously tricky since a single herb may contain hundreds of chemical compounds. Just which of these compounds is responsible for the purported benefit of the herb is often unknown. Furthermore, since there is no regulation of the industry and no requirement for product standardization, the active compounds in the herbs can vary by more than one-hundred-fold from one batch to another or from one brand to another. Different parts of the plant, different growing conditions, and different formulations can make an enormous difference.

It's important to be up-front with your doctor about supplements and herbs. Just because a product is natural does not mean it's safe—just think about those beautiful but deadly mushrooms you learned about in high school biology. Many supplements will interact with prescription medications, either by raising drug levels and increasing the risk of drug toxicity or by inhibiting the drug from working properly.

SUPPLEMENTS AND SCIENCE

In this chapter, we'll explore some of the more commonly used supplements marketed for heart health. Although the scientific data may be scant for some, for others, a substantial amount of legitimate medical research is available. As a physician, I found many of these reports to be eye-opening. Some theories that many of us accept as gospel have long been debunked, while others offer exciting new possibilities for prevention.

FUN FACTS TO KNOW ABOUT
THE FDA, SUPPLEMENTS, AND HERBS

- Prescription and over-the-counter drugs are strictly regulated, and not all new drugs are approved for sale.
- Government oversight of supplements is minimal due to the Dietary Supplement Health and Education Act of 1994 (DSHEA).
- Supplements cannot claim to treat or cure a problem but are allowed to include "structure-function" claims.
- Supplement labels are often inaccurate, especially when it comes to herbs.
- Make sure your doctor knows what supplements you're taking, since they can interact with prescription medications.

THE OMEGA-3S: FISH OIL AND FLAXSEED OIL

Cold-water fish are loaded with the heart-protective omega-3 fatty acids known as EPA and DHA (eicosapentaenoic acid and docosahexaenoic acid), a topic we dove into in chapter 5. There are probably many ways omega-3 fatty acids support heart health, including lowering triglyceride levels, reducing susceptibility to blood clots, and perhaps even improving blood pressure. The most important effect, however, appears to be protection against life-threatening heart rhythms that can sometimes lead to sudden death.

While fish oil is the best source of omega-3s, vegetarians and the fish-averse have options, too. Plant sources of omega-3 fatty acids include walnuts and flaxseed oil. In order to put them to use, our bodies must convert the plant-derived omega-3 fatty acid, alpha-linolenic acid (ALA), into DHA and

EPA; unfortunately, this biochemical process is quite inefficient and fairly unreliable. In fact, only about 6% of a given amount of ALA is converted to EPA and less than 4% becomes DHA. This cumbersome conversion process is further disadvantaged by the typical American diet, which is high in omega-6 fatty acids (from corn oil, safflower oil, and sunflower oil), since omega-3 and omega-6 fatty acids compete for some of the same enzymes. However, preliminary research suggests that such plant-based omega-3 oils may indeed help to prevent cardiovascular disease, particularly in people who do not get omega-3 fatty acids from fish sources.

Megadoses of flaxseed oil are to be avoided, since taking more than four tablespoons daily can interfere with normal function of the thyroid gland.

Unlike flaxseed oil, fish oil has been convincingly shown to be protective for the heart, especially in people who have recently suffered heart attacks. A large Italian study published in 2002 included more than 11,000 people who had suffered a heart attack within the preceding three months. The participants were randomly assigned to receive either one gram per day of highly purified prescription-grade fish oil (currently marketed under the brand name Lovaza) or placebo. After three months of treatment, there was a stunning 41% reduction in mortality in the fish oil group. The study was completed after forty-two months, with the fish oil group still way ahead of the curve.

Fish oil is often used to treat high triglycerides, and just one to two grams of purified fish oil daily will lower triglyceride levels by about 15%. In people who start out with high triglycerides (more than 150 mg/ dL), it is not unusual to see reductions of 30%. Read the label to find the EPA and DHA content of a supplement. The higher the sum of these numbers, the more potent the supplement will be. Prescription strength fish oil, containing over 900 mg of active ingredient per capsule, will lower triglycerides up to 45% when taken at the recommended dose of four capsules daily. (See chapter 13 for more about this FDA-approved medication.) While fish oil does not do very much for total HDL or LDL cholesterol, it does appear to reduce the harmful small, dense LDL particles and increase large HDL particles. Fish oil does not appear to affect CRP, even though it is known to have anti-inflammatory properties.

SO, WHO NEEDS 'EM?

Who, then, should take fish oil supplements, and how much is optimal? It is clear that people who have already had heart attacks are very likely to benefit from a dose of 1 gram daily. Substantial amounts of omega-3 fatty acids can easily be obtained from the diet. For instance, 3 ounces of wild salmon provides 1800 mg, and there is 1000 mg of omega-3s in 3 ounces of rainbow trout. Water-canned white tuna is also an excellent source, weighing in at 700 mg per 3 ounces, although the same amount of light tuna only provides 200 grams.

Someone who gets seven grams (or 7000 mg) of omega-3 fatty acids from fish each week probably will not benefit substantially from supplements. The exception is when triglycerides are too high, in which case higher doses may be helpful.

More than 3 grams of fish oil per day may be associated with a slightly higher risk of bleeding, so for most people the daily dose should not exceed 2 grams unless recommended by a physician. Fish oil may also cause fishy burps, although the more purified it is, the less noticeable the taste. Freezing the capsules might help to reduce the fishiness, although it's not known what effect this could have on the potency of the product.

While many omega-3-rich fish are contaminated with mercury, it is reassuring that *Consumer Reports* (July 2003) showed no significant mercury levels in the 16 top-selling brands of fish oil supplements. This is because mercury is water soluble and is removed during the purification process. This report also found that the labeling on these products was reasonably accurate, with most capsules containing the amount of omega-3 fatty acids claimed on the package. Due to the refining process, fish oil supplements tend to be low in other pollutants as well.

During pregnancy, omega-3 fatty acids are important to normal fetal neurological development. Expert panels from the World Health Organization and the National Institutes of Health recommend 300 mg of DHA daily for pregnant or lactating women. By comparison, the average daily intake of DHA and EPA in the United States is estimated to be 180 mg per day.

Since so much of our fish is contaminated with mercury and other pollutants, and since mercury is harmful to the developing brain, fish oil is probably a better choice for pregnant women. (See chapter 5 for more on fish, mercury, and pregnancy.) Of course, if you're pregnant or breastfeeding, it's important to check with your doctor before taking any supplement.

Is there anyone who shouldn't take fish oil? Of course, if you are allergic to fish, it makes sense to avoid fish oil. The use of fish oil is somewhat controversial in people with severe heart failure, but on balance it seems to be a safe option. As with any supplement, discuss your options with your physician before taking the plunge.

OMEGA-3 FATTY ACIDS: WHAT YOU NEED TO KNOW

- Supplements are made from flaxseed or fish oil.
- Fish-based supplements can be used readily by the body.
- Flaxseed oil requires a very inefficient conversion process, with less than 10% of plant-based omega-3s actually put to use by the body.
- A daily dose of 1000 mg of fish oil may reduce the risk of dying after a heart attack by 40%.
- Approximately 1000 to 2000 mg of fish oil will lower triglycerides by as much as 15% to 30%. Prescription fish oil, which is highly purified, can be used to lower severely elevated triglyceride levels.
- Fish oil will not lower cholesterol levels, although it may improve the composition of cholesterol particles.
- Omega-3s are good for the hair, the skin, and the brain, and may even support joint health and reduce inflammation.

- Mercury and other pollutants are generally removed during the fish oil purification process.
- Since mercury is toxic to the developing nervous system, supplements may be a better choice for pregnant and breast-feeding women.
- 3 ounces of wild salmon supplies 1800 mg omega-3, 3 ounces of rainbow trout provides 1000 mg, and 3 ounces of water canned white tuna will net you 700 mg.
- If you are getting less than 1000 mg of omega-3s daily, a fish oil supplement makes good sense. Look for one high in EPA and DHA.

SOY ISOFLAVONES

Soy is truly one of nature's "wonder foods," so it comes as no surprise that enterprising manufacturers have marketed soy isoflavones, or isolated soy extracts, as dietary supplements. But there is really very little data to back up the high-flying claims that often come with these products.

Most studies of soy isoflavone supplements show little or no meaningful effect on blood lipids. Since we know that adding soy-rich foods to your diet may help to improve your cholesterol profile, it seems that the improvement in lipids probably comes from the complete soy protein in combination with its associated isoflavones, packaged with love by Mother Nature.

An analysis of thirty-three commercial isoflavone products, published in the *Journal of Nutrition* in 2001, found that many did not contain the amount of isoflavone reported on the package label; furthermore, no two supplements were the same. Of even greater concern was the discovery that a number of the supplements contained unidentifiable chemical compounds, the safety of which were unknown. Another investigation of fifteen different products found that the isoflavone content of these supplements varied up to 2000-fold.

Nattokinase is another soy derivative often sold as a heart-health supplement. Manufacturers claim a number of heart-protective attributes, including inhibition of harmful LDL oxidation and reduction in incidence of blood clots. Nattokinase is based on a fermented Japanese food called natto, delicately described by its fans as cheesy, with a strong smell and slimy texture. Like most other soy-based foods, natto provides soy protein and soy isoflavones and is doubtless a fine addition to a heart-healthy diet for those strong enough to accept the challenge. However, there are no well-done human studies on nattokinase, despite the enthusiastic claims of its promoters.

SOY SUPPLEMENTS: SO-SO AT BEST

- While adding soy foods to your diet will improve your lipids, supplements have little to no effect.
- Labeling of soy supplements is notoriously inaccurate.
- Nattokinase is a fermented soy-based food. There is no convincing evidence that it is any better than any other type of soy food.

Supplements for Cholesterol Reduction

Psyllium

You may know psyllium as Metamucil, Konsyl, or Perdiem, but this soluble fiber, which comes from the husk of the blonde psyllium seed, is a true multitasker. Not only does it promote bowel regularity, but psyllium can also lower LDL cholesterol by about 10%. (There is no real effect on HDL or triglycerides.) Psyllium contains an aptly named substance called mucilage that allows it to increase in volume up to tenfold when exposed to liquids. This is one reason that it's such a great stool bulking agent. It also helps the body to get rid of cholesterol-containing bile acids through the stool and may directly interfere with the intestine's ability to absorb cholesterol and fat.

Studies of the effects of psyllium on cholesterol have focused mostly on a standard dose of about 10 grams daily. This is usually taken as two separate doses of 5 grams, but three 3-gram increments work just as well. Many forms of psyllium are available, all of which you can buy at the drugstore. Several high fiber breakfast cereals are made using psyllium, including Kellogg's Bran Buds.

There are several unpleasant and potentially embarrassing drawbacks to psyllium, including increased intestinal gas, soft stools, and abdominal discomfort. If fiber has not been a big part of your diet, it makes sense to go slow. You can usually take psyllium along with prescription medications, including cholesterol lowering drugs, but check with your doctor or pharmacist if you're not sure. In fact, by adding psyllium to a prescription cholesterol-lowering statin drug, the dose of medication required can often be reduced. If you have diabetes, psyllium may even help to lower your blood glucose. Psyllium does not appear to significantly affect absorption of vitamins or minerals.

Glucomannan

Glucomannan is a complex carbohydrate that comes from the Konjac root, an Asian tuber. Traditionally, it is used in jellies and noodles to give a rubbery texture, but it is indigestible, meaning it passes right through the intestinal tract. While it has been touted as a supplement for weight control, its real benefit appears to be in cholesterol reduction. Glucomannan is probably very similar to psyllium in the way that it absorbs bile acids in the intestine, thereby lowering cholesterol. It may lower LDL cholesterol by 7% to 22%, although reports of its effectiveness vary from study to study and, frankly, not a lot of research is available on this supplement. The greatest reduction in cholesterol was seen when people took it at doses of 0.5 to 1.2 grams three times daily with meals. Like psyllium, glucomannan also appears to help lower blood glucose levels modestly in diabetics.

Very little safety data is available on glucomannan. As with psyllium, the most common side effects are increased intestinal gas and bloating. However, a recent report of possible liver toxicity raises a red flag. Much more information and research are available on psyllium, so until we know more, psyllium is your better bet.

Plant Sterols and Stanols

Sterols and their derivatives, stanols, are naturally occurring plant-based products that bear a passing resemblance to cholesterol. As such, they compete with cholesterol in the intestinal tract, and by doing so, they limit the body's ability to absorb cholesterol from the foods we eat. Since stanols and sterols themselves are minimally absorbed, they basically just take up space on the special cholesterol receptors of the intestine, blocking the cholesterol molecules from getting in. As a result, total blood cholesterol levels are lowered by up to 10% and LDL cholesterol drops by as much as 15%.

Dietary sources include fruits, vegetables, nuts, legumes, and vegetable oils. Although stanols and sterols can be potent cholesterol blockers, they occur in such small amounts in nature that it is unusual to eat enough to make a dent in cholesterol by diet alone. On average, we consume 250 to 500 mg per day of sterols and 20 to 60 mg per day of stanols. At least 1 gram (1000 mg) per day is required to have much effect on lipids, and 2 grams per day seems to be optimal.

Sterols and stanols are often used in margarine, dairy products, salad dressing, orange juice, and other foods and are generally considered to be safe and well tolerated. There is no detectable smell or taste, and there are no gastrointestinal side effects. The small amounts of sterols that are absorbed through the gut are mainly excreted by the body through the bile, although there have been reports of plant sterols (but not stanols) being found in cholesterol plaques.

Despite this, there is no evidence to date that sterols increase the rate of cholesterol buildup in most people. Products containing sterols and stanols can be used by people on cholesterol-lowering drugs, and the effects on cholesterol are additive. That means that higher doses of prescription drugs might be avoidable if two grams per day of one of these products is added to the diet. (There is probably no benefit to taking more than 2 grams per day.) The effect appears to be greatest in people over the age of 50.

Several caveats do bear mentioning. First, sterols and stanols should be avoided by individuals with a very rare inherited disease known as "homozygous sitosterolemia." This disorder occurs in about 1 in 6 million people and is characterized by cardiovascular disease occurring at a very young age. People who suffer from this disorder generally have xanthomas, or large raised yellow lipid-filled bumps on the body, frequently around eyelids, joints, and tendons. They absorb sterols and stanols much more readily than most people, so theoretically their risk of heart disease could increase if they consume these products.

Stanols and sterols may decrease absorption of beta-carotene by up to 20%, with milder effects on vitamin E, lycopene and alpha-carotene of 7% to 9%. It makes sense, then, to eat more of the colorful fruits and vegetables if you are adding these products to your diet, and many experts also suggest adding a multivitamin to be on the safe side.

Finally, don't forget that the products containing sterols and stanols are not calorie-free. They should be used in place of other foods, not in addition. And since some margarine products with plant sterols and stanols also contain trans fats, label-reading is still important. There are lighter forms available that are trans fat free.

While no long-term studies have been done to specifically evaluate the effect of these supplements on the incidence of heart disease, it has been estimated that adding 2 grams per day of sterols and stanols to the diet might lower the risk of heart disease by as much as 25%, thanks to the cholesterol-lowering effect. Several studies have reported that after a few months of regular use, sterols lose their effectiveness, while stanols continue to keep cholesterol levels down.

Since we don't know for sure whether the very small amount of sterols our body absorbs may impact the risk for heart disease, and since we know that sterols can be found in cholesterol plaques, even when cholesterol levels are reduced, I suggest that you look for products specifically containing plant stanols. For instance, the Benecol brand of margarine and caramel chews are good sources of stanols, while several other national brands of margarine contain sterols.

Garlic

It stands to reason that something as pungent as garlic might affect the cardiovascular system as robustly as it does the nose. A "stinking rose," with the strength to deter vampires and the power to add character and passion to the cuisines of diverse cultures around the globe, surely ought to discourage atherosclerosis. For centuries, potent health benefits have been attributed to garlic, and for the past 30 or more years, its effects on cholesterol have been studied in earnest. The disappointing verdict: when it comes to cholesterol, garlic just doesn't pack much of a punch.

Although many animal studies have suggested that garlic lowers cholesterol levels, these findings have not been borne out in humans. Of the six studies considered to be the most scientifically valid, none showed a difference in lipids between garlic-takers and control subjects. Other studies have shown no beneficial effect of garlic oil, powdered garlic, or garlic extract.

Garlic does have antioxidant properties, and so theoretically it might reduce the ability of LDL cholesterol to do harm. In combination with other nutritious foods, garlic no doubt contributes to good health, but there is really no compelling reason to take a supplement.

Red Yeast Rice

Red yeast rice is a type of fermented rice on which Chinese red yeast (*Monascus purpureus*) has been grown. What makes red yeast rice so fascinating from the standpoint of heart health is its remarkable chemical composition. Not only does it include a substance known as a monocolin, which is identical to the drug lovastatin (the original prescription statin drug for cholesterol), it also boasts a variety of other statin-like substances, sterols, isoflavones, and monounsaturated fatty acids.

To date, several small-scale studies of the proprietary brand of red yeast rice known as Cholestin have shown a significant reduction in LDL cholesterol of about 20% when taken at doses of 2.4 grams daily. Some studies have also found an improvement in HDL cholesterol and triglycerides, and at least one Chinese study has reported a reduction in heart attacks and strokes in people taking this supplement.

The amount of lovastatin in the supplement is small: 5 mg as compared to 20 to 40 mg in the pharmaceutical strength. Since this small amount of lovastatin itself is unlikely to cause such a significant reduction in cholesterol, the sterols and isoflavones may also be important players. There are many different manufacturers of red yeast rice supplements, and since they are supplements, the FDA does not oversee or regulate the manufacturing process. An analysis by scientists at UCLA of nine different brands found dramatic variations in composition, with some containing virtually no monocolins at all. Therefore, the results seen with Cholestin may not apply to other brands.

Most studies of red yeast rice have reported no serious side effects of this supplement. However, the majority have included less than one-hundred people, whereas investigations of lovastatin and other statin drugs (which we will discuss in chapter 13) have enrolled thousands to tens of thousands of people.

In susceptible people, red yeast rice can cause liver abnormalities, since it contains a statin drug. In fact, I have seen this side effect in my practice, in a gentleman who had previously experienced serious liver problems with prescription statins and who had no idea that the supplement he was taking could do the same thing. Although liver sensitivity is uncommon, if you choose to take this supplement, you should be monitored with blood testing six to twelve weeks after beginning this supplement and every six months thereafter, just as we do for statin therapy.

Red yeast rice also has the potential to cause the rare but potentially life-threatening complication of muscle breakdown known as rhabdomyolysis, particularly in people who are on certain medications that are known to interact with statin drugs, including certain antibiotics and antifungal drugs.

All in all, red yeast rice appears to be a relatively safe supplement, but one that should not be started without a doctor's supervision. If you are already taking a statin drug, you should not take red yeast rice. It is important to recognize that red yeast rice will not produce the dramatic lowering of cholesterol levels seen with more potent statin drugs, but it may help bring mild to moderately elevated cholesterol down to a safe range. Long-term studies have not been done, and we don't know for sure whether the same reduction in heart disease seen with statin drugs can be expected from red yeast rice.

Policosanol

Policosanol is another supplement that has been championed as a cholesterol reducer. For years, studies funded by its Cuban manufacturer claimed substantial benefits to the lipid profile. But in 2006, a rigorous study of policosanol from a respected German research institute revealed that the supplement had no effect on LDL, HDL, triglycerides, or Lp(a). On the bright side, no major safety issues were identified.

Guggul

An extract from the resin of the mukul myrrh tree, guggul has been touted for its purported cholesterol-lowering effect and has been approved in India for that purpose. In the United States, guggul is marketed as a cholesterol-lowering dietary supplement, accounting for more than a million dollars in sales in 2002.

In 2003, a study by the University of Pennsylvania found that after eight weeks, there was no improvement in cholesterol readings in those who took guggul, regardless of whether they were on a high dose (2000 mg three times daily), or a standard dose (1000 mg three times daily). In fact, LDL cholesterol actually increased by 4% to 5%. Overall, there was no significant improvement in HDL, triglycerides, Lp(a), or hs-CRP. Although no abnormalities in liver or kidney tests were reported, 15% of the high-dose guggul group and 3% of the lower-dose group developed a rash.

Chitosan

Chitosan, an indigestible substance derived from the shells of crustaceans such as shrimp, lobsters, and crabs, is used in treatment of waste water, as a coating for glass fibers, as an additive for paper and photographic film, and as a component of wound dressings, among other things. Since the mid 1990s, it has also been promoted as a weight-loss and cholesterol-lowering supplement. A positively charged substance, it is thought to bind negatively charged molecules like fatty acids. Theoretically, taking chitosan with a fatty meal might prevent the fat from being absorbed through the gut. In reality, studies show the effects of chitosan on fat absorption and cholesterol in humans to be minimal to none.

Don't be fooled by advertisements with extravagant statements of chitosan's efficacy. Within the past several years, at least two manufacturers of chitosan have been sanctioned by the FDA for making false claims.

On balance, chitosan is unlikely to do much. It appears to be relatively safe, although nausea and constipation can be side effects, and there is also a risk of depletion of the fat soluble vitamins, A, D, E and K.

CHOLESTEROL AND SUPPLEMENTS:
TRUTH AND FICTION

- Psyllium (sold as Metamucil, Konsyl, and Perdiem, among others) can lower LDL by 10% with a daily dose of 10 grams. Psyllium may increase intestinal gas and bloating and cause soft stools.
- Glucomannan, at doses of 0.5 to 1.2 grams three times daily, acts similarly to psyllium, but there is little safety information available.
- Plant sterols and stanols block intestinal absorption of cholesterol and can lower LDL as much as 15% in doses of 2 grams daily. Stanols may be more effective, and possibly safer, than sterols.

- Garlic is a heart-healthy food, but it does little for cholesterol.
- Red yeast rice is the original statin drug, containing small amounts of naturally formed lovastatin (sold as the prescription drug Mevacor) as well as sterols, isoflavones, and monounsaturated fatty acids.
- Cholestin, a brand of red yeast rice, may lower LDL by about 20% at doses of 2.4 grams daily. Not all brands are the same, and composition may vary widely from brand to brand.
- If you take red yeast rice, you must have blood tests for liver function at least every six months and be aware of the risk of muscle aches and drug interactions.
- Policosanol does not do anything for cholesterol, despite manufacturers' claims to the contrary.
- Guggul does not lower LDL and may even raise it slightly.
- Chitosan neither lowers cholesterol nor blocks fat.

SUPPLEMENTS FOR HEART AND BRAIN PROTECTION

Coenzyme Q10

Coenzyme Q10, also known as ubiquinone, plays a critical role in energy production. It also has antioxidant properties. Coenzyme Q10 is produced by the liver with the help of B vitamins, along with vitamins E and C. Organ meats, salmon, mackerel, sardines, peanuts, and spinach are good dietary sources. (Maybe Popeye really was on to something.) Coenzyme Q10 has become one of the fastest-selling and most expensive dietary supplements in this country, fueled in part by claims from its manufacturers that it has the power to protect the heart against congestive heart failure.

In Japan and a number of other countries, coenzyme Q10 is mainstream therapy. A review of the supporting medical research is disappointing. Most of the studies on coenzyme Q10 supplementation are poorly done, include only 20 or so patients, and do not include a control group, making the results questionable.

The most well-done studies show minimal to no significant improvement in heart health in those people who already suffer from heart failure and are treated with appropriate twenty-first century medical therapy. Heart muscle function, exercise duration, and patients' perceived quality of life did not generally improve despite doses of coenzyme Q10 up to 200 mg daily. This lack of improvement may be explained by the fact that the prescription drugs we now have available do such a good job of treating heart failure that any additional impact of coenzyme Q10 is fairly minor.

Some advocates of coenzyme Q10 argue that statin drugs, used to lower cholesterol, also lower levels of coenzyme Q10, and that this may explain the muscle aches that some people experience with these drugs. This is logical, since part of the chemical pathway the body uses to make cholesterol is also involved in the production of coenzyme Q10. Although somewhat controversial, most studies of statins (including red yeast rice) have found lower coenzyme Q10 blood levels after a month of drug treatment. What we don't know is whether these reduced blood levels reflect what is going on in the muscle tissues.

It appears that some people are genetically susceptible to this side effect and therefore might benefit from supplemental coenzyme Q10 and possibly carnitine supplements as well (which I'll tell you about soon). One small study from Stony Brook University found a nearly 40% reduction in statin-related pain symptoms when 100 mg of coenzyme Q10 was taken daily.

Although coenzyme Q10 has been promoted as an energy booster for athletes, most studies, including an Australian study of endurance athletes, have shown no improvement in athletic performance.

Coenzyme Q10 is probably not harmful, and clearly some people may benefit from taking it. However, this is an expensive supplement, costing anywhere from $30 to $100 per month. Since the body manufactures its own coenzyme Q10, there may be limitations as to how much extra coenzyme Q10 it is able to put to use. As always, let your doctor know of any drug side effects that you experience, as well as any supplements that you choose to take.

Ginkgo

We all want to hang onto whatever brain power we can. It's no wonder that *Ginkgo biloba*, purported to improve memory, cognition, and blood flow, is the best-selling herb in the United States. In the laboratory, an extract of ginkgo leaves (which come from the maidenhair tree) has shown antioxidant, anti-inflammatory, and anti-clotting effects.

Unfortunately, most well-done studies of ginkgo in humans have failed to find any major effect on cognition or blood flow. In normal healthy people over 60 who took either 120 mg ginkgo or placebo for six weeks, no improvement was seen in learning ability, memory, attention, or concentration. For those suffering from Alzheimer's dementia, ginkgo may have some fairly subtle benefits, but these are far outpaced by the more potent prescription drugs available for patients with Alzheimer's. Likewise, people with blockages in the leg arteries may find a little relief with ginkgo, but the improvement seen is minimal.

Side effects of ginkgo include nausea, indigestion, headaches, and rashes. Bleeding inside the brain has also been reported with ginkgo. Ginkgo may interact with some prescription drugs, so check with your doctor or pharmacist before experimenting with this supplement.

Grape Seed and Pine Bark Extracts: The Proanthocyanidins

Proanthocyanidin is a million-dollar word that refers to the powerful antioxidants found in grape seed and French pine bark extracts. Similar antioxidants, including polyphenols, catechins, and flavonoids, are found in wine, tea, soy, chocolate, olive oil, and many fruits and vegetables. Since there is very good evidence that antioxidants are protective against heart disease and certain cancers, grape seed extract and pine bark extract (also known commercially as Pycnogenol) represent an attempt to concentrate high potency antioxidants into a pill-sized package. Indeed, in the test tube, the antioxidant effects of these extracts far surpass those of vitamins E and C.

Manufacturers of grape seed and pine bark extract supplements market their products aggressively. Grape seed extract, for example, accounted for

202

$40 to $50 million in sales in 2000, and the market continues to grow. But there are really very few studies in humans to support the use of either one of these supplements.

Rat studies suggest that grape seed extract may help prevent fatal heart rhythms in the setting of a heart attack, probably via the protective antioxidant effects. One study of Pycnogenol indicated that this supplement might protect smokers from harmful blood clots. Animal studies suggest that both extracts may also improve the flow of blood through the arteries of the heart and the body. A study of grape seed extract reported an improvement in the cholesterol profile in people whose fruit and vegetable consumption was relatively paltry, although there was no placebo group used for comparison. Some very preliminary research also points to a possible protective effect against cancers of the breast, lungs, and stomach, yet other researchers warn of a potential of these supplements to actually increase the risk of certain cancers.

As with most supplements, the potency and composition of the supplement may vary markedly from one manufacturer to another, and currently there is really no objective way to gauge the potency of any particular brand. Furthermore, we really don't know which, if any, component of these extracts may be the most useful. The National Institutes of Health has expressed an interest in studying grape seed and pine bark extracts. Until more data is available, my advice is to choose a diet rich in whole foods, including fruits and vegetables, and get your antioxidants naturally.

SUPPLEMENTS FOR HEART AND MIND

- Coenzyme Q10 probably does little for heart health in people already on medications.
- Coenzyme Q10 does not improve athletic performance.
- Coenzyme Q10, at doses of 100 mg daily, might help prevent muscle aches in people on statin drugs.

- *Ginkgo biloba* does not appear to help brain function and may have significant side effects.
- Grape seed and pine bark extracts are high in antioxidants, but there is very little valid research on these supplements.

Supplements for Energy and Weight Loss

Chromium Picolinate

For years, chromium picolinate has been breathlessly advertised as a weight loss aid that will also lower cholesterol and improve insulin sensitivity, cutting the risk of diabetes and other chronic diseases. What the vendors of this supplement fail to mention is that for the past ten years, numerous studies, including one done by the United States Navy, have shown absolutely no benefit of this supplement.

Our bodies do need chromium, but it is found in abundance in a heart-healthy diet. Natural sources include fruits, vegetables, whole grains, and seeds. Research has consistently found no improvement in metabolism, body fat, weight loss, strength, lipids, insulin, blood sugar, or any other parameter with the use of chromium supplements. And while no toxicity was reported in these studies, high doses (1200 to 2400 mcg per day) have been linked to kidney failure, blood abnormalities, and liver damage. Some preliminary research has suggested that even at typical doses, this supplement may actually cause the formation of harmful free radicals, so my advice is to sit this one out.

Ginseng

More than 5 million Americans have experimented with ginseng, the root of the Panax species, for its legendary enhancement of longevity, energy, and libido. Ginseng may be purchased as a whole root, an extract, a tea, a powder, or a tincture. There are several varieties of ginseng, including Asian, American, and Japanese varieties. (So-called "Siberian ginseng" is actually a different species altogether and shares little in common with the Panax species.)

Ginseng has more than twenty potentially active compounds, and exactly which of these components might be most responsible for the benefits attributed to it is not known. Many products that claim to be ginseng turn out to have absolutely none of these active ingredients.

Scientific studies on ginseng have yielded conflicting results. It does appear to have antioxidant properties and may even improve the lipid profile slightly. Most of the more positive studies come from China and Korea, where ginseng is sometimes used to treat heart failure. Studies done in the United States have found relatively minor effects on aerobic capacity and reaction times, but people over the age of 40 may be more apt to benefit from ginseng than younger people. Twelve weeks or more may be required to see any improvement. The standard ginseng dose is 200 to 400 mg daily of a 4% to 7% extract, or 1 to 2 grams of ginseng root daily.

Potential side effects of ginseng include high blood pressure, nervousness, and diarrhea. Ginseng may interact with blood-thinning drugs and cause an excessively high risk of bleeding. Siberian "ginseng" is known to cause high blood pressure and has few if any well-documented beneficial effects.

Ephedra

An adrenaline-like stimulant, ephedra comes from the Chinese herb ma huang. Ephedra is touted as a "thermogenic," meaning that it is supposed to create heat in the body by speeding up metabolism and burning fat. Does ephedra work as a weight loss aid? The answer is maybe.

An analysis of more than fifty studies published by the think tank RAND Corporation in 2003 revealed an average weight loss of about 2 pounds per month in people who took ephedra regularly for several months. However, this weight loss can come at a terrible price.

Ephedra has been associated with heart palpitations, high blood pressure, personality changes, anxiety, shakiness, and insomnia. Even worse, ephedra has been implicated in a number of cases of permanent disability and death due to heart attacks, life-threatening heart rhythm abnormalities, and strokes. These catastrophic events have often occurred during heavy physical exertion. When it's combined with caffeine, as it often is, the risk of serious side effects escalates. A randomized study of a supplement containing both ephedra and caffeine showed potentially dangerous changes in the heart's electrical patterns after a single dose was given to healthy young adults.

More than 160 deaths have been attributed to ephedra, and thousands more users have reported serious side effects. In 2004, after reviewing the numerous studies of the supplement and evaluating the reports of adverse events, the FDA prohibited the sale of ephedra in the United States.

Small amounts of ma huang may still be sold by Chinese herbal practitioners for treatment of respiratory disorders, but ephedra is prohibited by the International Olympic Committee, the National Collegiate Athletic Association, and the National Football League, among others. Despite the ban, a quick Internet search reveals business as usual, with multiple Web sites continuing to hawk ephedra as a weight loss and energy supplement.

Since ephedra and ma huang have earned such a bad name, and deservedly so, manufacturers of weight loss supplements are increasingly turning to other sources of the chemical. Watch out for ingredients like country mallow, joint fir, Mormon tea, and heartleaf, all of which may contain ephedra. Always read the labels of any supplement you take and be sure to share that information with your doctor.

Bitter Orange

Bitter orange, also known as *Citrus aurantium*, is an extract of the Seville orange, a beautiful and aromatic plant native to southeastern Asia, now found around the world. The extract of the bitter orange peel is the next generation thermogenic "ephedra-free" weight loss supplement. It is frequently combined with caffeine for a stronger kick. While manufacturers and purveyors of bitter orange claim that it has none of the dangerous side effects of ephedra, the facts suggest otherwise.

The active ingredient in bitter orange is synephrine, which is similar to epinephrine, also known as adrenaline. This chemical raises blood pressure, revs up the heart rate, and constricts blood vessels. Side effects are similar to ephedra and can include tremor, nervousness, anxiety, and headache. Bitter orange can also interact with prescription drugs, increasing the possibility of harmful drug reactions. Even worse, bitter orange in combination with high doses of caffeine will shoot a double-whammy to the nervous system.

Reports of life-threatening complications of bitter orange are becoming more frequent, including heart attacks, heart arrhythmias, and blackouts. Keep an eye out for ingredients such as zhi shi, kijitsu, citrus aurantium, sour orange, and neroli oil, all of which are alternate terms for bitter orange.

Hydroxycitric Acid

The key ingredient in a popular supplement, hydroxycitric acid is purported to burn fat and increase vitality. Hydroxycitric acid is derived from the rind of *Garcinia cambogia*, a yellow fruit native to India. It has been promoted as a weight loss aid, although traditional Indian healers use it for joint and intestinal problems.

Studies in humans have shown no effect on fat burning with exercise, even when doses of hydroxycitric acid used were more than ten times higher than the amount recommended by the manufacturer. What's worse, there have been reports of severe liver injury in people who took the popular supplement.

Hydroxycitric acid is also sold as brindleberry, gorikapuli, citrin, gambooge, and Malabar tamarind.

Hoodia

An Internet darling, Hoodia has been hyped and hawked by C-list celebrities and buttressed by reams of pseudoscience, but the truth is we really don't know much about this weight loss supplement. A succulent plant, *Hoodia gordonii* has been a part of the culture of the San tribe of South Africa since time immemorial. Before the encroachment of a Western life style, tribesmen chewed the plant to stave off hunger during long hunting treks and times of famine. The active ingredient, a molecule tagged "P57," apparently tricks the brain into thinking that the stomach is full. Presto! No more hunger.

The plant is extremely rare and very difficult to grow. There are other species of hoodia plants, but it is not known whether they have the same effect, or even if they are safe. It has been alleged that most, if not all, hoodia products on the market contain little, if any, of the active ingredient and that they often include other weight-loss supplements.

Even more problematic are the lack of safety data and the scarcity of published studies of the plant. At one time, pharmaceutical giant Pfizer acquired the rights to the active ingredient from the British company Phytopharm, which has a contract for developing the plant with the South African government. After investing more than $20 million, Pfizer dropped out of the project, citing difficulties extracting and synthesizing the active ingredients. Later, a Pfizer scientist also alluded to problems with potential liver toxicity. Hoodia rights were subsequently bought by Unilever, which manufactures Slim-Fast products, among others.

Because of concerns regarding toxicity, as well as the fact that buying hoodia truly is a crapshoot, my advice to you is to steer clear of this one.

WEIGHT LOSS AND SUPPLEMENTS: WHAT YOU SHOULD KNOW

- Studies of chromium picolinate have found no significant effect on weight loss, metabolism, muscle strength, cholesterol, or diabetes.
- Ginseng is an antioxidant. It might improve aerobic ability slightly but can raise blood pressure and cause nervousness and diarrhea.
- Ephedra might help you lose a little weight, but it has dangerous side effects, including heart attacks, heart rhythm abnormalities, and strokes. It is even more dangerous when combined with caffeine.

- Bitter orange (*Citrus aurantium*) is similar to ephedra. It can raise blood pressure and heart rate and cause anxiety, tremor, and headaches. Like ephedra, it has been linked to heart attacks and heart rhythm disturbances.
- Hydroxycitric acid does not help with weight loss and might hurt the liver.
- Hoodia may suppress hunger, but supplements on the market often contain little if any active ingredient. Hoodia may also cause liver toxicity.

AMINO ACIDS AND THEIR DERIVATIVES

L-Arginine

A semi-essential amino acid L-arginine has been touted as a treatment for disorders of the vascular system. It is considered semi-essential because our bodies are able to manufacture enough L-arginine for most of our needs. However, during children's growth phases, the body requires more than it can produce, making a healthy diet crucial to normal development.

L-arginine can be found in many different foods, including soy and other legumes, fish, meats, poultry, dairy products, and nuts. Spirulina, a type of algae, is a rich source of L-arginine, providing 4 grams per 3.5 ounce serving. By comparison, 3 ounces of turkey has 1.8 grams, 3 ounces of salmon supplies 1.4 grams, and half a cup of tofu has 1.3 grams. Most people get somewhere between four and ten grams of L-arginine daily. Since our adult bodies can manufacture L-arginine, there is no official minimal daily requirement.

Over the past five to ten years, several relatively small studies of L-arginine have been carried out in humans. Some have shown modest improvements in blood pressure with L-arginine, and rat studies even suggest that L-arginine may mitigate the high blood pressure seen in salt-sensitive individuals when exposed to a high salt diet. There is early evidence that this amino acid may also improve insulin sensitivity in adult-onset diabetes.

In the research lab, fairly high doses of L-arginine, generally on the order of 3 grams three times daily, appeared to improve blood flow in people whose arteries had already been affected by atherosclerosis. When researchers at Johns Hopkins University put this theory to the test in 2006, treating patients who had previously suffered heart attacks, they hoped to find improvement in heart function and reduced stiffness of the blood vessels. Instead, there was no improvement in heart or vascular function. In fact, the study was stopped early when more than 8% of those receiving the supplement died, compared to none of those taking the placebo pills. People taking L-arginine were also more likely to end up in the hospital with congestive heart failure.

Why did the facts of this trial not support the theory? The researchers noted that all the subjects involved already had normal levels of L-arginine, meaning that they were getting plenty from their diet and from their body's own production. Researchers also raised the possibility that high levels of L-arginine could actually cause the body to produce free-radicals, increasing the likelihood of harm to the artery walls.

Hopes have been raised that the supplement might be a natural treatment for male erectile dysfunction (ED). While there are many manufacturers who tout their L-arginine products as a remedy for ED, study results are mixed. Since a large percentage of men with ED have significant atherosclerosis, high-dose supplemental L-arginine carries the potential for significant risk.

There are some other important downsides to high-dose supplementation with this amino acid. A study of breast cancer patients given a whopping 30 grams of L-arginine daily or a placebo for several days prior to surgery found a disturbing increase in tumor growth and tumor activity in those women who took the supplements. Doses this high have also been associated with weight gain, stomach upset, and excessive sleepiness.

L-Carnitine

L-carnitine is technically not an amino acid, although it is frequently marketed as such. (D-carnitine, which is structurally similar and sometimes sold over the counter, cannot be used by the body.) L-carnitine is nonessential since our bodies are adept at manufacturing it, except in cases of very rare inherited deficiencies. People who are on hemodialysis for kidney failure may need to take L-carnitine supplements. For most of us, supplements are not necessary.

L-carnitine is abundant in meat, which supplies about 80 mg per 3-ounce serving, but is also found in poultry, fish, and dairy products. On average, most people get more than 100 mg of L-carnitine from their diet daily. Typical supplemental doses are 2000 to 3000 mg daily (2 to 3 grams.)

Since L-carnitine helps to transport fatty acids into the cells, and since it plays an important role in muscle function during exercise, it has attracted a lot of interest. Studies, however, have been disappointing, seeming to indicate that the supplement was not being taken up by the muscle tissue and showing no improvement in physical performance.

Studies are still underway to determine whether or not L-carnitine might help people who have had heart attacks. So far, there appears to be little or no benefit, although preliminary evidence suggests that it may help people with blocked leg arteries who have pain with activity. There may also be a role for L-carnitine in the treatment of statin-drug-related muscle aches, because about a third of people who experience this side effect may have genetic abnormalities of muscle L-carnitine.

Drawbacks to L-carnitine include a fishy body odor when taken in doses of more than 3 grams daily and an increased likelihood of seizures in people who have experienced seizures in the past.

Creatine

Creatine is a favorite of weight lifters and body builders for its reputed effects on muscle strength. It is found naturally in meat and fish, but our bodies are able to manufacture it quite readily from essential amino acids obtained from other dietary sources. Even vegetarians make enough creatine for their body's usual needs.

Most studies of creatine have found that it does indeed appear to improve muscle strength for tasks like weight-lifting, which require fairly short bursts of energy. Vegetarian weight-lifters may benefit more than meat eaters. Creatine does not, however, appear to affect aerobic or endurance training.

The supplement appears to be safe when taken in reasonable amounts. Creatine is usually taken in doses of 2 to 5 grams daily. One study of college football players who were dosed with an average of 5 grams of creatine per day for up to twenty-one months found no evidence of harmful effects on blood tests of kidney, liver, or blood cell function and no urinary abnormalities. However, higher doses have been linked to kidney disease. Like many supplements, not enough is known about creatine, but it appears to be safe when taken in moderation.

AMINO ACIDS AND THEIR DERIVATIVES: TRUTH AND CONSEQUENCES

- L-arginine is abundant in spirulina, turkey, salmon, and soy. It is important for normal function of our blood vessels.
- Adult bodies can manufacture L-arginine, but growing children need more, so they must get L-arginine from the foods they eat.
- High doses of supplemental L-arginine might increase the risk for heart attacks and heart failure in people who already have heart disease. High-dose L-arginine may also increase tumor growth in women with breast cancer.
- Our bodies usually make enough L-carnitine from scratch. We need l-carnitine to keep our muscles functioning normally.
- L-carnitine supplements might be helpful for people who get muscle pains with statin drugs. Side effects of L-carnitine include a fishy body odor and an increased risk for seizures in people with epilepsy.
- Creatine is involved in muscle energy production. It is found in meat and fish, but our bodies can make it from other foods we eat.

> • Creatine may improve muscle strength but doesn't affect aerobic fitness or endurance. Daily doses of 2 to 5 grams of creatine daily appear to be safe; higher doses have been linked to kidney disease.

FRUIT AND VEGETABLE CONCENTRATES

A perpetual darling of the multi-level marketing world, capsules containing dried fruit and vegetable juice concentrates have been hawked as the latest in anti-aging supplements since the 1990s. The proprietary product Juice Plus+ has been marketed aggressively by lay people as well as by some health professionals. Independent distributors of the product make money from their own sales as well as from the sales of the people they recruit. Since a year's supply of the product costs about $500, sales people are exceptionally motivated to acquire new customers. It is important to remember that although these salespeople may present themselves as medically savvy, most of them are not trained, educated medical professionals.

The idea behind juice and vegetable concentrates is not a bad one: package the antioxidants found in fruits and vegetables in a form that can be easily taken on a daily basis. Since we know that the majority of Americans do not choose to eat enough fruits and vegetables, this is one way to at least obtain some phytonutrients, including antioxidants, albeit without as much fiber. Basically what you are getting is dehydrated, de-sugared fruit and vegetable juice, along with a bit of fiber and other nutrients, packaged in capsule form.

To its credit, Juice Plus+ has sponsored medical research, some of which has been published in reputable journals. In 2003, the *Journal of the American College of Cardiology* published a study that demonstrated an improvement in blood flow after an extremely greasy fast food breakfast in people who took these supplements regularly. Arteries tend to constrict in response to high levels of fat in the bloodstream, which is one reason that a high fat diet can be so harmful, and it appeared that Juice Plus+ countered this effect. This research study has been cited by Juice Plus+ salespeople as proof that their product works.

While this certainly sounds like an important effect of the supplement, and it probably is, the same improvement in blood flow is seen in people who eat eight to ten servings of antioxidant-rich whole fruits and vegetables every day. Furthermore, eating fruits and vegetables in their whole forms supplies far more fiber and phytonutrients than does a capsule and also curbs the appetite, reducing cravings for less nourishing foods.

For someone whose diet is deficient in fruits and vegetables and who has no intention of changing, Juice Plus+ and similar products might be reasonable, though pricey, supplements to take. But if you truly want to support a healthy heart and body, it makes much more sense to eat the real thing.

FRUIT AND VEGETABLE CONCENTRATES:
THE STRAIGHT SCOOP

- Fruit and vegetable supplements are basically dehydrated, de-sugared fruit and vegetable juice, combined with fiber and sometimes other nutrients, and packaged into a capsule.
- These supplements may improve blood flow after a fatty meal and appear to be safe and well-tolerated.
- Fruits and vegetables clearly have the advantage, but if you don't eat enough of these foods, a supplement is reasonable.

12

Complementary and Alternative Medicine: Hope, Hype, or Healing?

Sometimes modern health care can seem so complicated, and the technology and science supporting it far out of our reach. We want answers about our health that make sense to us. Overwhelmed by the vast and sometimes impersonal medical infrastructure, many people have chosen to take their search outside the realm of conventional medicine. They seek treatments that will complement standard medical therapies, or perhaps even replace them with alternatives they hope will be safer and gentler. At least half of us have dipped our toes into the alternative healing pool at least once, and for many, it is truly a way of life.

A Word from Your Doctor

As a physician, I take my responsibilities to heart. Your health and well-being are my utmost concern, and I work hard to earn your trust. So if a therapy has the potential to harm, or if it will cost you some of your hard-earned money, I want to be absolutely sure that my recommendations to you are as well-researched and supported as possible. Yet I know that with or without the support of your physician, many of you will seek alternative care.

As trained scientists, we physicians are understandably skeptical of claims that lack sufficient scientific support. In general, complementary and alternative medicine (CAM) practices are not as thoroughly tested as most mainstream medical care. Over time, some have even been shown to be harmful. Now, spurred on by intense public interest, the scientific community is beginning to investigate some of these therapies with the same rigor it applies to traditional medicine.

The breadth of CAM is far too great for me to address fully in one chapter, but I will take you through some important CAM practices that relate specifically to the health of the heart.

Massage Therapy and Aromatherapy

I am a great fan of massage therapy, but its effects on the heart are fairly short-lived. Massage therapy is known to temporarily reduce tension and stress, and in conjunction with physical therapy, it may help injured muscles to heal. While blood pressure may drop during a session, the effect is not long-lasting.

You should avoid massage if you are prone to blood clots in your legs, if you have active inflammation or infection, or if you suffer from severe osteoporosis, or thin bones. If you are on blood thinners, especially warfarin, you should be sure to tell your masseuse, since some forms of massage can involve strong pressure that could lead to bruising in sensitive people. Choose a well-trained, certified therapist, and be honest with her about your medical history and about the benefits you hope to obtain from your session.

Aromatherapy, which uses volatile plant oils, is often used for stress reduction in conjunction with massage. Indeed, studies have shown that smell can affect mood and temporarily reduce anxiety levels. Aromatherapy may be beneficial for people with Alzheimer's dementia, and some people find that it can even cut cravings for food. While a recent American Heart Association survey found that 26% of women believed that aromatherapy could protect against heart disease, it simply does not hold that power. Most reputable practitioners of aromatherapy are careful to avoid making such claims.

CHELATION THERAPY

Chelation therapy is a specialized medical practice that involves infusing a chemical into the veins through a catheter to bind up and remove dangerous heavy metals from the blood. It is used to treat heavy-metal poisoning, including lead, mercury, and arsenic. In these fairly rare cases, only a qualified physician should administer the medication, and only after the diagnosis has been confirmed.

Chelation therapy is not approved for other conditions. There is no reliable evidence that it has any effect on atherosclerosis. Promoters like to claim that it will bind up free radicals in the bloodstream, preventing damage to the blood vessel walls, but that has not been proven and is probably not biologically plausible.

Scientists in the United States, Canada, and Europe have carefully evaluated chelation therapy in heart patients, evaluating both symptoms and vascular function. Multiple studies have shown that regular treatments for up to six months have zero cardiovascular effects.

Chelation therapy is not benign. It may deplete the body of zinc, which is important in immune function; it may seriously lower calcium levels; and it has the potential to cause life-threatening side effects.

Currently, a study of more than 2000 people is underway to objectively and scientifically determine once and for all whether there is any efficacy for chelation therapy in coronary artery disease. The study will also look at the effects of high-dose vitamin infusions. For now, considering the cost (about $4000 for 30 treatments) and the time commitment (three hours per treatment, generally twice a week), your time and money would be much better spent exercising, taking a stress-free vacation, and practicing healthy cooking with someone you love.

HYPNOSIS AND ACUPUNCTURE

While hypnosis has not been studied rigorously enough to draw firm conclusions, it appears to be as effective as nicotine patches for smoking cessation, with about 20% of people who undergo hypnotherapy quitting for good. Some studies have reported success rates of up to 60% in motivated individuals.

Hypnosis may also help you lose weight if it is included as part of an overall diet, exercise, and lifestyle modification program.

My advice to my patients is this: hypnotherapy is safe, it is more effective than doing nothing, and it may help you quit smoking or lose weight—but you must first be motivated to change your habits. Remember that nobody else can do that for you.

Acupuncture is widely used in treating addictions, chronic pain, and other health conditions. Medical interest has recently turned to the possible effects of acupuncture on the heart. Scientists at UCLA have reported potential benefit in people suffering from congestive heart failure, with decreased activity of the sympathetic nervous system in response to stress. Since activation of the sympathetic system leads to the "fight or flight" response, reduction of the activity of this system may help improve survival in people with weak hearts who respond poorly to stress.

Whether acupuncture can help lower blood pressure is debatable. A study of nearly two hundred people, funded by the National Institutes of Health, found no reduction in blood pressure with acupuncture when compared to a sham procedure. However, a German study of 160 patients with high blood pressure reported modest reductions, on the order of a three-to-five point drop in pressure. For now, there is simply not enough definitive information available, but acupuncture appears to be relatively safe and is unlikely to cause harm as long as the needles used are sterile.

If you do choose to pursue acupuncture for treatment of high blood pressure or heart failure, it is important that you not discontinue any ongoing medical therapy unless you do so under your physician's supervision. As with any type of CAM, count your doctor as your ally and keep her fully informed about all aspects of your health care. It will help her take better care of you.

COMPLEMENTARY AND ALTERNATIVE THERAPY:
A REALITY CHECK

- Massage is generally safe and effective for relieving muscle pain. Aromatherapy is relaxing, but it won't treat disease.
- Chelation therapy is not beneficial for the heart and may cause harm.
- Hypnosis may help up to 20% of smokers quit, and it may help with weight loss, especially when combined with lifestyle changes.
- Acupuncture may relieve pain; it has not been proven to lower blood pressure, but may have modest lowering effects.

13

THE POWER OF PREVENTIVE MEDICINE: MANAGING RISK, PREVENTING CONSEQUENCES

The lifestyle you choose can alter your destiny, protecting you from heart attacks, stroke, cancer, and dementia and granting you more time and energy to enjoy and contribute to all that life has to offer. Wouldn't it be nice if simply choosing a healthy way of life was all it took? Unfortunately, many of us carry within our genetic make-up a natural inclination for high blood pressure, high cholesterol, and diabetes—the most powerful risk factors for heart disease. Some people have none of these risk factors, yet come from a lineage fraught with heart disease and stroke. In every instance, how we take care of our bodies makes a tremendous difference. Still, sometimes healthy choices just aren't enough.

Thankfully, we live in an era of preventive medicine with unprecedented opportunities for treatment of these silent killers. As a physician, one of my most important responsibilities is the diagnosis and treatment of these common conditions. However, I cannot help you unless you take the first step. Get your blood pressure, cholesterol, and blood sugar tested. It is easy, and it just might save your life.

HYPERTENSION

People often confuse the word "hypertension" with the concept of being "hyper" or "tense." However, hypertension is simply high blood pressure. It is estimated that at least 65 million people in the United States have high blood pressure. That's one third of the population, or 35 million women and 30 million men. Hypertension is on the rise in this country, largely due to mounting obesity levels. The older you get, the more likely you are to have high blood pressure. After the age of 60, half of all men and women suffer from hypertension. In fact, older women are somewhat more likely than older men to have high blood pressure. If you live long enough, you will have a 90% lifetime risk of developing hypertension.

Why should you care that hypertension is such a big problem? Although the condition itself is usually painless, hypertension is a major contributor to more than 1 million heart attacks every year and is the most preventable cause of strokes. It increases the stress on the heart, causing the heart muscle to become thicker and less efficient. It also injures the blood vessels of the heart, brain, kidneys, and other vital organs, making them more rigid and vulnerable to cholesterol plaques. Women with hypertension have a dramatically higher risk for preeclampsia, a dangerous complication of pregnancy that can threaten the lives of both the mother and the unborn child.

People living with uncontrolled hypertension have a sevenfold increase in the risk of a stroke and are three times more likely to suffer a heart attack than people with normal blood pressure. Other devastating consequences include kidney failure, congestive heart failure, disease of the retina, and even dementia.

Many times, high blood pressure exists without symptoms, allowing years of silent damage, continuing unabated, to the heart, brain, and kidneys. Some people do experience headaches when their blood pressure is excessively high, especially if they have what is known as "labile hypertension," or widely fluctuating blood pressure.

Despite the widespread prevalence of hypertension, fewer than half of all people have sufficiently low blood pressure even when they do take medication for it. This is usually not because the blood pressure-lowering drugs don't work, but rather because the patient or her physician chooses not to treat the condition aggressively.

It is easy to get frustrated with the process of controlling high blood pressure. Sometimes it's a matter of trying several different drugs before we hit on the right choice or combination. We are all unique individuals, and there is no "one size fits all" treatment.

The only sure way to know whether your blood pressure is high is to test for it. Typically, your doctor's office performs this test using a blood pressure cuff, or sphygmomanometer. You can also easily do it yourself, but there are some important nuances worth understanding—so indulge me with this blood pressure primer.

HOW BLOOD PRESSURE IS MEASURED

Blood pressure is always given as two numbers, one above the other. The systolic, which is the first or top number, measures the pressure when the heart is contracting. The bottom reading, the diastolic pressure, represents the pressure in the arteries as the heart relaxes after the contraction. Both numbers are important.

Blood pressure readings should be taken after sitting quietly for about five minutes while you are in a seated position, feet on the floor, and your arm at heart level. The cuff is inflated briefly, preventing blood flow in the main artery that travels through the arm. As pressure in the cuff is slowly released, blood starts to flow in the artery, creating a pounding sound. The systolic blood pressure is the pressure at which this sound is first heard. The air is slowly emptied, and when the pulse is no longer audible, we have reached the diastolic blood pressure.

Generally, you should have at least three separate blood pressure readings on three different days before a doctor can make a diagnosis of high blood pressure—although this rule does not usually apply to people with extremely high pressures.

The ideal blood pressure is less than 120/80 mm Hg. (The abbreviation "mm Hg" refers to millimeters of mercury, which is the scale that is used to measure blood pressure.) A blood pressure between 120/80 and 139/89 is considered "prehypertension." A blood pressure in the prehypertensive range is associated with a twofold to threefold higher risk for heart disease. If you fall in this range, consider it a wake-up call to implement major lifestyle changes, including curbing salt intake, choosing a heart-healthy diet, and exercising. A blood pressure of at least 140/90 is considered hypertensive.

Systolic pressures as low as 90 may be perfectly normal, especially in smaller women. However, excessively low blood pressure may cause dizziness and lightheadedness and is often due to dehydration, blood loss, or over medication.

Both the systolic and diastolic blood pressures are important, but their relative importance changes with age. Below the age of 50, a higher diastolic pressure is associated with a higher risk of heart disease and stroke. Over the age of 50, the systolic pressure becomes more of an issue. In general, each increase of 20 mm Hg systolic or 10 mm Hg diastolic above 115/75 doubles the risk of cardiovascular disease.

Many people suffer from "white coat hypertension," or the phenomenon of higher blood pressure readings in the doctor's office. This problem is typically brought on by stress or anxiety. Often, the blood pressure can be rechecked a few minutes later, and it will be back in normal range.

Measure Your Own Blood Pressure

If you want to monitor your readings, it will help tremendously to obtain your own blood pressure cuff, since multiple measurements throughout the course of the day are much more helpful than a single pressure reading in the office. A home blood pressure machine is a great investment in your health, and most devices are easy to use. You can choose either an electronic or a manual cuff, but make sure you get it checked by your doctor to confirm that the readings are accurate. I recommend an upper arm cuff because pressures measured in the wrist or finger are much less reliable. The cuff should fit properly since an excessively large or small cuff may result in false readings. Most obese people will need a large cuff.

Blood pressure is not a static number; it is normal for it to vary by about 20% throughout the day. Measure your blood pressure in the middle of the day, as well as morning and evening, so you can get familiar with the range of your numbers during your most stressful and most relaxing times of the day. Once you have a good representative sampling (usually one to two weeks) you will not need to measure it as often, unless your doctor advises you to do so.

If your blood pressure is borderline or high, what should you do? Diet, exercise, and weight loss can help tremendously, especially in people below the age of 50 whose blood pressure is only mildly elevated. Up to one third of people with early-stage or prehypertension can bring their blood pressures down to the normal range with these simple lifestyle changes. If you are overweight, losing as little as 15 pounds can make all the difference. A diet high in fruits, vegetables, and low fat dairy products is particularly effective, especially when combined with a low sodium diet (see chapter 6 for more about salt and sodium).

Stress and chronic pain can influence blood pressure, but are usually less important than other lifestyle factors. Drinking more than two alcoholic drinks a day or more than three cups of coffee may also raise blood pressure.

Seemingly innocent prescription drugs and over-the-counter medications may affect blood pressure. Some women will find that birth control pills bump up the pressure, although this happens fairly infrequently. A wide range of prescription and over-the-counter anti-inflammatory medications, including ibuprofen and naproxen, may increase blood pressure and cause fluid retention. Over-the-counter decongestants and stimulants such as ma huang, ephedra, and bitter orange are also culprits (see chapter 11). It is a little known fact that an obsession with black licorice can raise the blood pressure.

Your doctor may also want to exclude some more obscure medical causes of hypertension. A good screening evaluation includes a complete physical exam and a blood chemistry profile, which may uncover other associated problems, such as kidney disease or thyroid abnormalities.

Despite the long list of blood pressure offenders, the great majority of people with high blood pressure that is not easily controlled with diet and exercise have what we call "essential" hypertension. Essential hypertension refers to high blood pressure with no identifiable cause.

Unlike infections and broken bones, essential hypertension is a condition that requires ongoing medical treatment and is usually a lifelong condition. Most of my patients are surprised when I tell them that the average person with high blood pressure requires two or three medications, and often more than that. Even if you have essential hypertension, you can minimize the number of medications you need with a healthy diet, appropriate body weight, and regular exercise. Considering the high cost of most medications, this investment in your health will quickly pay dividends.

HYPERTENSION BY THE NUMBERS

- High blood pressure affects one in three American adults, and the risk increases with age.
- Hypertension dramatically raises the risk for stroke, heart disease, kidney failure, retinal damage, and dementia.

- Hypertension is usually "silent," causing no symptoms.
- The ideal blood pressure is 115/75 for most people.
- Diet, exercise, and weight loss can often bring mildly elevated blood pressure back to normal without resorting to medications.
- The average person with high blood pressure requires three medications.

TREATING HYPERTENSION

While it is beyond the scope of this book to review specific medications, it is helpful to go over the general classes of drugs that your doctor may choose to prescribe. There are scores of antihypertensive drugs, but most will fit into one of the following categories.

Diuretics

Also known as "water pills," diuretic medications are often a great first choice to treat high blood pressure. Some women tend to retain fluid due to salt-sensitivity, and diuretics can help. Most diuretics cause potassium loss, so a doctor may also prescribe a potassium supplement. If you take a diuretic, it is important to have regular blood work at least once or twice a year to monitor your electrolytes.

Beta-blockers

The name refers to the receptors in the heart and blood vessels that these medications block, resulting in lower blood pressure as well as reduced heart rate. This class of drugs is especially important for people with heart disease. They reduce the risk of a heart attack and are highly effective for the treatment of heart failure. Beta-blockers are also extremely helpful in people with palpitations due to fast or irregular heartbeats.

Most people have no problems with beta-blockers, but these medications do have the potential to cause excessive slowing of the heart rate, depression, fatigue, and poor libido in a small percentage of people. As a result, metabolism may slow a bit, and motivation to exercise may diminish. These side effects are why beta-blockers are occasionally associated with weight gain in sensitive individuals, although we're talking an average gain of less than 3 pounds over about six months. Some beta-blockers can raise levels of triglycerides, although usually only to a mild degree. People who exercise vigorously may notice that their peak heart rate is somewhat constrained when taking beta-blockers.

If you experience these problems, it's important to discuss them with your doctor. In many cases, your doctor can substitute another drug for the beta-blocker.

Calcium Channel Blockers

Calcium channel blockers are medications that slow the flow of calcium into the cells of the heart and arteries, allowing them to widen and relax and thus reducing blood pressure. Like beta-blockers, some calcium channel blockers also slow the heart rate, so they are sometimes used for this purpose as well. Don't let the name of this class of drugs fool you. A calcium channel blocker will not lower the calcium level in your bones or bloodstream.

Most people feel just fine on calcium channel blockers, but somewhere between 5% to 10% of people will experience side effects such as fluid retention and constipation. The drugs diltiazem and verapamil can also cause an excessive slowing of the heart rate in people who are sensitive to this effect, most notably older folks.

Angiotensin-Converting Enzyme-Inhibitors

ACE-inhibitors, or inhibitors of angiotensin-converting enzyme, block the production of a chemical that, among other things, causes arteries to constrict. ACE-inhibitors are used to control blood pressure, treat heart failure, and prevent kidney damage in people with hypertension or diabetes. These medications help to relax your blood vessels, which improves the efficiency of the heart and lowers blood pressure. ACE-inhibitors also increase blood flow, which decreases the amount of work required by your heart.

This class of drugs is a mainstay of heart disease treatment and has been proven to lower the risk of heart attacks and congestive heart failure. They are also used to prevent kidney failure in diabetics. The most common side effect is a dry, itchy cough, which occurs about 5% of the time. Some people with advanced kidney disease may be unable to take ACE-inhibitors, as they may worsen kidney function in these folks. It's easy to test for this complication with a blood test. ACE-inhibitors should never be taken while pregnant since they can cause birth defects.

Angiotensin-2 Receptor Blockers

Angiotensin-2 receptor blockers (ARBs) work much like ACE-inhibitors but are associated with fewer side effects. For instance, these drugs do not cause a cough. Like the ACE-inhibitors, this type of medication is also a great choice for diabetics, since the ARBs help protect against kidney failure. As with the ACE-inhibitors, it is important to use blood tests to monitor kidney function in people with vulnerable kidneys. And like the ACE-inhibitors, these drugs can also cause birth defects, so should be avoided during pregnancy.

Alpha-blockers

These drugs help to relax the blood vessels, thereby lowering blood pressure. Alpha-blockers are not especially beneficial to the heart, so they are not usually our first line of therapy.

Direct Renin Inhibitors

This fairly new class of drugs targets an enzyme called renin, which is produced by the kidneys. High levels of renin contribute to high blood pressure by causing constriction of blood vessels. Kidney function should be evaluated with a blood test when one of these drugs is started.

Whatever blood pressure medication your doctor recommends, it is important that you take it as prescribed since most of these medications wear off in twenty-four hours or less. If you are pregnant or considering pregnancy, it's critical that you discuss this with your doctor before starting any blood pressure medication. If you experience side effects, let your doctor know. If your blood pressure is difficult to control, you may need a referral to a cardiologist or other blood pressure specialist.

Don't give up and just accept mediocre blood pressure control. There are many different medication choices available, and we can usually find one, or a combination, that will work well for you. Remember that the goal is to achieve not just a "number," but a blood pressure that will help to keep your heart, brain, kidneys, and the rest of your body safe, strong, and healthy.

LIPIDS: CHOLESTEROL AND TRIGLYCERIDES

LDL cholesterol (the "lousy" one) is influenced by genetics, but diet and smoking have a substantial effect. Trans fats and saturated fats are notorious for raising LDL cholesterol, whereas monounsaturated fats from foods like olive oil, nuts, and soy, and soluble fiber from foods like oatmeal and apples, can lower LDL. Unlike fat, dietary cholesterol itself plays a relatively minor, but still important, role in raising LDL. And adipose tissue (that is, body fat itself) increases LDL cholesterol levels.

In general, LDL should be less than 130 mg/dL; ideally, it should be below 100. If you have coronary artery disease or diabetes or are at very high risk for cardiovascular disease, your LDL should be under 70.

More than 40% of women and men over the age of 20 have LDL cholesterol levels over 130, and nearly 20% have dangerously high LDL levels over 160. While younger women tend to have lower cholesterol levels, the LDL starts to rise after menopause, contributing to a higher likelihood of heart disease and stroke. In fact, after the age of 45, women are more likely than men to have high LDL cholesterol.

Fortunately, we have HDL cholesterol, the good fairy. Exercise, moderate alcohol use (one or two drinks a few days a week), and a healthy diet will point HDL in the right direction. For women, soy foods may raise HDL slightly, and olive oil may have a favorable effect. Smoking, saturated and trans fats, and stress can lower HDL, as can a diet high in simple carbohydrates with a high glycemic load (refer to chapter 4 for more on this topic). When it comes to HDL, women tend to have an advantage over men, although menopause tends to level the playing field. Our HDL levels should be at least 50 mg/dL, but the higher, the better.

Triglycerides are also part of the lipid profile, and levels greater than 150 mg/dL are associated with a higher likelihood of heart disease, especially in women. Sweet, starchy, and fatty foods and heavy alcohol use (three or more drinks daily) will raise triglycerides, as will estrogen replacement pills (but not patches) and smoking. A diet higher in protein and lower in carbohydrates will help bring down the triglyceride level (see chapter 7). Soy, omega-3 fatty acids such as fish oil, moderate amounts of alcohol, and exercise are good ways to lower triglycerides.

For many people, careful attention to diet, exercise, and lifestyle will make a vital difference. It is possible to lower your LDL as much as 30% by following the simple recommendations I've outlined for you.

CHOLESTEROL CALLING

- LDL is "bad" cholesterol; you want to lower this one. HDL is "good"; you want to keep it high.
- Most people should have an LDL less than 130 mg/dL; ideally, it should be below 100. If you have coronary artery disease, diabetes, or are at very high risk for cardiovascular disease, your optimal LDL is less than 70.
- Trans fats, saturated fats, dietary cholesterol, smoking, obesity, and genetics raise LDL. LDL also rises after menopause.
- Weight loss, soluble fiber, and monounsaturated fats lower LDL.
- HDL should be above 50 mg/dL; the higher, the better.
- Exercise, moderate amounts of alcohol, soy foods, and monounsaturated fats raise HDL. Smoking, saturated fats, stress, and high glycemic carbohydrates lower HDL.

- Triglycerides should be less than 150 mg/dL.
- Sweets, starchy foods, fats, heavy alcohol use, and smoking raise triglycerides. Estrogen replacement pills (but not patches) raise triglycerides. A high protein, low carbohydrate diet lowers triglycerides.

TREATING LIPIDS

The sooner high cholesterol is treated, the greater the opportunity for prevention and a life of good health. In 2003, a group of British researchers published an analysis of more than 200 studies and reported that by reducing cholesterol just 10% at age 40, the risk of heart disease could be lowered 50%. If we start at age 70, the same cholesterol reduction translates into a 20% lower risk.

If your heart disease risk is high, or your cholesterol or triglycerides are substantially elevated, prescription drugs are often needed to improve the lipid profile enough to bring it into a safe range. It's important to remember that even if you do require medications to reach your lipid goals, diet and exercise are crucial in maintaining and supporting the health of your body. Taking a pill does not absolve you of your responsibility for your own health.

One word of warning: if you are pregnant, breast-feeding, or considering pregnancy in the near future, be aware that you should not take cholesterol-lowering drugs, since these drugs may be harmful to the fetus or baby.

Statin Drugs

Statins are truly modern miracles. They reduce the risk of heart attack, stroke, and other life-threatening cardiovascular events by an average of 25% to 30%; with long-term use, the benefits may be even greater. This means not only a reduction in risk of death but an equally important reduction in the likelihood of disability due to stroke, congestive heart failure, and life-threatening heart rhythm abnormalities.

Statins are the most commonly used and most effective cholesterol-lowering drugs available. These drugs, which include such well-known names as Lipitor, Zocor, Pravachol, Lescol, Mevacor, and Crestor, work primarily via the liver. The drugs work to prevent the manufacture of cholesterol while improving the liver's ability to clear LDL cholesterol out of the bloodstream. The amount of LDL lowering depends on the specific drug, the dose used, and the individual response, but reductions of 50% or more are typically achievable.

Statin drugs help to stabilize pre-existing cholesterol plaques, making them less prone to rupture and cause a heart attack or stroke. They also prevent formation of new plaques. At high enough doses, statins may even help to shrink cholesterol buildup. Statins also lower hs-CRP, probably through antioxidant and anti-inflammatory mechanisms, although this has not been studied to the same extent as cholesterol. HDL is generally minimally affected by statins, although some statins can raise HDL by 5% to 10%.

The benefits of statin drugs may extend beyond heart health. Newer evidence on statin drugs points to a lower risk of senile dementia in statin-users. This stands to reason since the brain is a vascular organ, and many cases of senile dementia are due to a series of tiny, almost imperceptible strokes.

A seven-year study from the Harvard School of Public Health also found lower rates of anxiety, depression, and hostility in long-term statin users, although the study could not definitively establish cause-and-effect. Preliminary research suggests that statins might even reduce the likelihood of multiple sclerosis and certain cancers and help prevent bone fractures.

Who should take statins? Anyone who has suffered a heart attack or stroke or who has cardiovascular disease is a prime candidate. People with diabetes are at the same high risk for heart disease and should usually take a statin drug. Two-thirds of people with high blood pressure also have high cholesterol; if the cholesterol cannot be sufficiently lowered with diet and exercise, a statin drug is an important preventive medication since the combination of high blood pressure and high cholesterol can be deadly.

Talk with your doctor, and be sure that she or he has a firm understanding of the importance of prevention. Experts estimate that nine out of ten adults with high cholesterol are not adequately treated, and less than a third of women who are at high risk for cardiovascular disease are not on any treatment at all. Although it is never too late to start a statin drug (seniors age 80 and up can use these drugs safely), the longer someone takes the drug, the bigger the benefit.

Are Statins for Everyone?

If statins are all that, why don't we all take them? Indeed, that is a question asked by many a cardiologist. These drugs have been studied extensively for many years. When used appropriately, they save lives and are associated with a low risk of side effects. However, many people are afraid to take a statin drug for fear of liver damage.

Statins may raise liver enzyme blood tests in certain susceptible individuals. We can think of this simplistically as irritation of the liver. Liver test abnormalities will usually happen in the first three months of treatment, so it is important that your doctor check blood work during this time. It is routine to check cholesterol and liver tests every six months thereafter.

Liver test abnormalities are more common in women, people more than 60 years of age, people with liver disease, and people who use alcohol regularly. Frequent use of acetaminophen, the active ingredient in Tylenol, will also raise liver enzymes. The higher the statin dose, the more likely you will have elevated liver enzymes. Less than 3% of people will need to discontinue treatment because of liver abnormalities, and the lab tests virtually always normalize by one to three months.

Newer statins, such as Lipitor and Crestor, appear to be associated with less liver enzyme abnormalities than older statins. Since statins are all a little different, an alternative statin can be tried once the blood levels are back to normal, as long as blood work is followed closely.

Liver failure is a completely different matter from liver enzyme elevations. Concern about liver failure is a fear that I address with my patients nearly every day. Although the media has done a good job of frightening people away from statins, the truth is that the odds of true liver failure in patients on statin drugs is 1 in 1.14 million people per year. That is the same likelihood we all have of randomly developing liver failure and in all probability has no relation to statin use at all.

An extremely small percentage of people may experience problems with memory loss on statins, although in general statin drugs appear to reduce the risk of dementia.

A more realistic concern with statins is the issue of muscle pains. Up to 5% of people who take a statin will experience aching muscles or joints; however, nearly an equal number of people who take placebo pills in research studies of statins report the same thing. If you develop muscle pains on statin drugs, your doctor may order a blood test to determine if there is muscle injury.

A blood test may not always detect the source of the problem. We can develop aches and pains for many reasons, but if the discomfort begins after the introduction of the drug and stops when the drug is withdrawn, the statin is the likely culprit, regardless of the blood test results. For relatively mild pain associated with statin drug therapy, it is worth considering coenzyme Q10 supplementation. Refer to chapter 11 for more information on this supplement.

Rhabdomyolysis is a very uncommon but dangerous side effect of statin therapy. This life-threatening complication is due to acute breakdown of muscle tissue. The breakdown products can overwhelm the kidneys and cause kidney failure. Symptoms include profound weakness and severe muscle pain. The urine may appear brown due to toxins from the damaged muscle tissue. Fortunately, this is a rare complication (less than 5 in 100,000), and the risk of death is even rarer (less than 1 in a million).

Symptoms of this problem can generally be caught early enough to avoid serious injury, and a blood test for muscle enzymes, known as CPK, will confirm the diagnosis. Higher doses of statins are more likely to cause this problem, and some people are more sensitive to certain statins than others.

Statin-related musculoskeletal problems, both mild and severe, are more common in women over 60, people with kidney or liver disease, and those in whom statins are combined with other drugs that compete for the same enzymes in the body.

Grapefruit juice may interact with some statins but appears to be safe to take with Crestor (rosuvastatin) and Pravachol (pravastatin). If you have questions about potential drug interactions, be sure to discuss them with your doctor or your pharmacist. And always be sure that your doctor knows what other medications and supplements you are taking.

Fibrates

Fibrates, also known as fibric acid derivatives, are a class of lipid-lowering drugs that includes gemfibrozil (Lopid) and fenofibrate (Tricor, Lofibra, and Antara). These medications are used to lower triglycerides, with reductions of approximately 20% to 50%. Even greater declines may occur if the baseline triglyceride level is higher than 500 mg/dL. People with triglyceride levels of greater than 1000 mg/dL are at high risk for pancreatitis, a dangerous inflammatory condition of the pancreas gland, which sits near the liver and stomach. In these cases, treatment of triglycerides is critical in order to lessen the risk of this dangerous condition.

A fibrate is generally chosen when a high triglyceride level is the principal lipid abnormality. Lowering triglycerides is of special concern for women, since a high triglyceride level appears to be up to twice as dangerous in women as it is in men. Fibrates also have modest LDL-lowering effects and may raise HDL cholesterol by 10% to 35%.

In certain high risk people with elevated triglycerides and high LDL cholesterol, a physician may recommend combining a fibrate with a statin. This pairing can be highly effective, but depending on the specific statin and fibrate used, the combination may increase the risk for serious side effects, including muscle aches, liver enzyme abnormalities, and rhabdomyolysis, so careful monitoring is a must.

Niacin

Niacin, also known as nicotinic acid, is an important nutrient in our everyday diet. However, at high doses, prescription-strength niacin is also a drug that has powerful effects on HDL cholesterol and triglycerides and moderate effects on LDL cholesterol. It is also the only drug available to date that will lower Lp(a).

When used appropriately, prescription niacin may reduce the risk of a heart attack by an average of 25%. Dosing generally starts at 500 mg and increases to a maximum of 2000 mg. The drug comes with a few caveats, the most important of which is the need for close monitoring of liver tests, just as with statin drugs.

People with uncontrolled diabetes may find their blood sugars more difficult to control if they take some forms of niacin, although prescription niacin generally does not cause much trouble. Just about everyone who takes high-dose niacin will experience facial flushing at some time, particularly if the drug is combined with alcohol, hot foods, or spicy foods. Red food coloring may also trigger this side effect. This side effect is why it is usually best to take niacin just before bedtime, preferably with a low fat snack.

While it is easy to find inexpensive nonprescription high-dose niacin supplements, these products are problematic. Since they are sold as supplements, they are not approved for lipid lowering by the FDA (see chapter 11 for more information about the FDA's approach to supplements) and are not regulated like FDA-approved pharmaceuticals.

Although "no-flush" niacin products may sound appealing, researchers from the University of Washington reported in 2003 that this form of niacin contains none of the active form of free nicotinic acid needed to treat lipids, even though it is the most expensive variety of nonprescription niacin.

Short-acting niacin is the least expensive niacin supplement available. Although it is less likely to cause liver problems than the long-acting niacin supplements, short-acting niacin tends to cause much more severe flushing and is usually not as effective as the prescription drug for improving the cholesterol profile. The longer-acting sustained-release supplements are associated with a significantly higher likelihood of liver toxicity than are the prescription forms, since they are primarily metabolized through the liver.

The prescription niacin known as Niaspan is in an intermediate-release form and is safer and more effective than any of the niacin supplements. Niacor is a prescription form of immediate-release niacin. Whether you take prescription niacin or over-the-counter high-dose supplements, regular (every three to six months) tests of liver enzymes are important. Although niacin can be extremely effective when combined with a statin, the combination may increase the risk of side effects. As always, it is vital for your doctor to know what supplements you are taking so she can give you the best care possible.

Bile Acid Sequestrants

The bile acid sequestrants (BAS) include cholestytamine, colestipol, and colesevelam (Welchol). They may come in a powder form that mixes with liquids or in a capsule.

BAS drugs bind to cholesterol-containing bile acids in the intestine, so they cannot be reabsorbed by the body and put back into circulation. They are weaker than statin drugs, lowering cholesterol levels about 15% to 30%. In some people, BAS drugs will raise triglycerides, so they are not a good choice when high triglycerides are a problem.

BAS drugs often work well in conjunction with statins, but they have the unfortunate side effects of constipation, bloating, and flatulence. The powder forms should not be taken at the same time as other drugs, as they may interfere with absorption. It is best to take most other medications either one hour before the BAS or four hours afterwards. Since these drugs do not get into the bloodstream, musculoskeletal side effects are not an issue with them.

Ezetimibe

Ezetimibe, also known as Zetia, works to lower LDL by inhibiting its uptake through the intestine. Unlike the bile acid sequestrants, it does not "bind up" cholesterol, but rather it works at the cellular level. By itself, ezetimibe can lower LDL by about 20%.

Since ezetimibe does not work through the liver, it won't generally cause the muscle pains that can occur with statin drugs. The lack of this side effect allows us to use a lower statin dose to achieve the same lipid-lowering results, potentially avoiding significant side effects. Studies of cardiovascular outcomes with ezetimibe are scarce, but it does not appear to be as effective as the statins at preventing heart disease; for that reason, it is not considered first-line therapy. The side effect profile of ezetimibe is quite low, although it may cause abdominal pains and allergic reactions in a few people.

Prescription Fish Oil

Prescription fish oil, specifically the drug Lovaza, is used chiefly to lower triglycerides. It is refined and purified to an extent that is above and beyond the level of supplemental fish oil. Since it is considered a drug, the manufacturing process is regulated by the FDA, so the amount of active ingredient is standardized from one batch to another. The purification process renders Lovaza much more active than most supplements and also reduces the likelihood of side effects like the "fishy burp" that is so common with many nonprescription fish oils.

At the usual dose of 4 grams daily, triglyceride levels are typically lowered 20% to 45%. HDL may increase with Lovaza, but usually less than 15%. Since Lovaza does not interact with other drugs, it can be safely combined with other lipid medications. If triglycerides are severely elevated, Lovaza may raise LDL cholesterol as the lipids rebalance.

DIABETES AND INSULIN RESISTANCE

The American Diabetes Association estimates that every sixty seconds someone is diagnosed with diabetes. The disease affects upwards of 24 million Americans, including nearly 6 million who don't know they have it. By far, the most serious problem caused by diabetes is heart disease.

A man with diabetes doubles his risk of heart disease, but if you are a diabetic woman, you are up to five times as likely to suffer from cardiovascular disease or a stroke as a woman who is not diabetic. Even as deaths from heart disease are declining in diabetic men, there has been no such improvement in women.

Every year more than 230,000 lives are lost in this country to the complications of diabetes. Fully two thirds of diabetics will ultimately die of cardiovascular disease. In fact, a diabetic person with no history of heart problems has exactly the same risk for a heart attack as a non-diabetic person who has already had a heart attack. Despite these grim statistics, most diabetics do not realize that they are at risk.

While cardiovascular disease is the major cause of death, the ravages of diabetes are not limited to the heart. Every year, 100,000 diabetic people go on dialysis for kidney failure. People with diabetes are at high risk for peripheral vascular disease, or disease of the blood vessels of the limbs, a condition that may ultimately lead to amputation. Blindness is yet another devastating complication of diabetes.

The Centers for Disease Control and Prevention (CDC) estimates that the costs for treatment and management of diabetes and its complications, including lost productivity, surpass $132 billion each year. The average annual health care expense for an American with diabetes in 2002 exceeded $13,000, compared with the health bill of $2,500 for those without the disease. Given the soaring costs of health care, these figures will continue to rise.

Who is at risk for diabetes? The figure is staggering. About 60 million Americans are highly vulnerable to developing diabetes, mainly due to lifestyle factors including diet, obesity, and lack of exercise. Diabetes is an equal opportunity disease, with at least as many women as men afflicted. Currently more than 8% of adults can count themselves among the ranks of diabetics, including nearly 25% of folks over age 60. Black and Hispanic men and women are even more likely to be diabetic than are Caucasians.

The vast majority (95%) of diabetics are Type 2, or adult onset. The prevalence has more than doubled during the past forty years, thanks to our sedentary lifestyles and burgeoning obesity. Just between 1997 and 2004, the number of newly diagnosed cases of diabetes increased by more than 50%. Approximately 1.4 million new cases were diagnosed in 2004 alone. It has been estimated that at the rate we are going, of those born in 2000, a mind-boggling one in three will eventually develop diabetes.

Defining Diabetes

Insulin is a hormone that allows the body to utilize the glucose that comes from the food we eat and from the stockpiles our bodies keep in the liver and muscle tissues. Insulin holds our blood sugar levels steady and enables our cells to do their work safely and efficiently. In diabetes, the body either doesn't make enough insulin or isn't able to effectively use the insulin it manufactures; oftentimes it is a combination of both problems.

The hallmark of diabetes is a blood sugar, or glucose, level that is consistently high. Elevated levels of sugar in the blood can lead to serious problems with the cardiovascular system, eyes, kidneys, nerves, gums, and teeth, particularly when the problem continues unchecked over a long period of time.

There are two types of diabetes: Type 1, which typically develops in childhood, and Type 2, also known as adult onset diabetes.

Type 1 Diabetes

Our cells must have insulin in order to use glucose properly. Insulin also helps the cells use amino acids, the building blocks of proteins, which are vital to life. The pancreas is the source of insulin and releases it in response to high blood levels of glucose, typically after a meal or snack.

When the insulin-producing cells in the pancreas are destroyed, the result is Type 1, or juvenile diabetes.

Type 1 diabetes usually begins in childhood and is thought to be the result of an immune response to a viral infection gone amuck, causing the body to attack its own cells. Type 1 diabetics must take insulin shots since there is no way for their bodies to produce their own insulin. Without insulin, a Type I diabetic will die.

Type 2 Diabetes

In adult onset diabetes, the cells of the body are unable to process the glucose that is circulating though the bloodstream, despite the fact that there is insulin available. We call this insulin resistance. Over time, the pancreas may begin to fail, compounding the problem by producing less and less insulin. Genetics can play a role, but obesity and a high caloric diet are the major contributors.

People who store their body fat in the abdominal area are especially prone to Type 2 diabetes. Eighty percent of adults with Type 2 diabetes are overweight or obese. Fat is actually a functioning organ of the body that manufactures a variety of harmful substances, some of which increase inflammation in the body and contribute to insulin resistance. Because of this, even a modest weight loss of 5% to 10% of total body weight may substantially improve blood sugar control.

In fact, if you are at risk for diabetes, you can reduce your likelihood of getting the disease by more than 50% simply through weight loss and thirty minutes of aerobic exercise daily.

Lest you think that you can wait until you are older to worry about diabetes, consider this: for women, weight gain in early adulthood (between the ages of 25 and 40) confers a greater risk for diabetes than weight gain later in life. Particularly troubling is the recent rise in Type 2 diabetes in children, thanks to a toxic culture of fast food, television, and sedentary lifestyles.

As with many other insidious processes, millions of Type 2 diabetics are undiagnosed and have no idea that they suffer from this slowly devastating disease. The hallmark symptoms of excessive thirst and hunger, frequent but normal-volume urination, and unexpected weight loss often go unrecognized, and the typical delay from diabetes onset to diagnosis is somewhere between four and seven years.

My father, who was a specialist in endocrinology (a branch of medicine that includes diagnosis and treatment of diabetes), did not, or would not, recognize that he was diabetic until his disease was far advanced. Many of the devastating health problems that plagued him in the last years of his life could have been avoided had his diabetes been treated early on. Like my dad, many people with Type 2 diabetes are genetically susceptible, and sometimes despite a lifetime of good habits, diabetes just happens. The best way to know whether you might be diabetic is to be screened with a simple blood test.

DIAGNOSING DIABETES

Adults should be screened for diabetes with blood tests at least once every three years, but more often if they are obese or have a history of borderline elevated blood sugar. A fasting blood sugar of more than 125 buys you a ticket into the diabetic club. Your doctor may order a hemoglobin-A1-C to monitor your progress or to help to make this diagnosis. This blood test is like a crystal ball in reverse. It allows your doctor to assess your average blood glucose during the past ninety days.

Less commonly, your doctor might order a glucose tolerance test in order to evaluate your body's response to a sugary drink. If you do not clear the sugar from your bloodstream quickly enough, this would indicate either impaired glucose tolerance or diabetes. This test is used more typically to test for gestational diabetes, or diabetes of pregnancy.

Twenty percent of middle-aged adults and 35% of adults over 65 have glucose intolerance, also referred to as insulin resistance or pre-diabetes, with fasting blood sugars more than 100 but less than 126. When tested with a glucose tolerance test, the blood sugar response is not normal, but it is not as impaired as that seen in full-blown diabetes. Most people with glucose intolerance are at least 20% overweight, and within five years, somewhere between 10% and 25% of them will become true diabetics.

DIABETES IN PREGNANCY

Gestational diabetes is a condition unique to women and, by definition, occurs during pregnancy. It is more common in obese women over the age of 25, and even more so if there is a family history. Fortunately, gestational diabetes can often be controlled with a healthy diet, but it requires close monitoring throughout the pregnancy. Women who have gestational diabetes are more likely to become true diabetics later in life. Babies of women with gestational diabetes are often born unusually large, increasing the likelihood of birth-related complications, and they are more likely to become obese kids.

COMPLICATIONS OF DIABETES

How can a little extra sugar be bad for you? Sadly, "the sugar" is not so sweet. Elevated levels of blood glucose contribute to stiffness and damage of the artery walls and make blood vessels more susceptible to harmful free radicals. This damage then makes the arteries more vulnerable to cholesterol buildup, increasing the propensity for heart attacks, strokes, and kidney failure. When the blood sugar is high, the risk of blood clots goes up, as does the risk of high blood pressure and lipid abnormalities. The heart muscle itself may become stiff and non-pliable, leading to congestive heart failure. The typical diabetic has high triglycerides and low HDL cholesterol, further stacking the odds against her.

Insulin itself may be harmful in large amounts, although this is still open to debate. Many Type 2 diabetics make excessive amounts of insulin in an attempt to overcome the insulin resistance. Some scientists believe that excessively high levels of insulin may predispose the coronary arteries to spasm. Insulin may also stimulate the growth of the smooth muscle tissue that lines the walls of the arteries, making them more vulnerable to injury and development of cholesterol plaques. However, if you need insulin shots to control your blood sugar, it's important that you take them, since it is well established that elevated blood glucose levels are dangerous.

Diabetes commonly affects the small blood vessels, including those of the feet and hands, impairing the body's ability to heal itself. This condition may in turn lead to skin ulcers, which may become deep and badly infected. Since many diabetics suffer neuropathy, or nerve damage, it's not unusual for a very nasty infection to go unnoticed when the pain receptors fail to function normally. In the worse case scenario, this can lead to gangrene, bone infections, and eventual amputation of a limb.

Ignorance is not bliss. Because of poor nerve function, a diabetic may not feel chest pain when she has a heart attack and may not recognize other symptoms of a troubled heart such as fatigue and shortness of breath. Once a heart attack happens, a diabetic person is twice as likely to die within a year as someone without diabetes.

Diabetes, insulin resistance, and obesity can also contribute to a liver abnormality known as "fatty liver." This typically occurs when the fat content of the liver surpasses 5%. Most of this fat is in the form of triglycerides, and while it may not be harmful in and of itself, extensive testing is often required to rule out other types of liver problems. A small percentage of people with this condition will go on to develop cirrhosis of the liver and liver failure.

HOW CAN I REDUCE MY RISK?

First, maintain your weight in the optimal range by keeping your BMI less than 25 (see the appendix). To do this effectively, it's going to take both diet and exercise. You've got to do both. Exercise will improve your body's sensitivity to insulin, reducing the amount of insulin you require to process the food you eat. Both aerobic and anaerobic (weight training) exercise can help, since greater muscle mass and muscle strength are associated with a lower likelihood of diabetes. A Mediterranean-style diet rich in whole grains, fruits and vegetables, nuts, and unsaturated fats will help keep blood sugar levels steady.

Commit to staying away from fast foods and so-called "convenience" foods, since these foods are chock full of the bad stuff. Fast-foodies who eat typical burger-palace or fried-chicken meals more than twice a week are twice as likely to develop insulin resistance as those who rarely visit fast food joints.

A habitual diet of red meat and processed meats, including bacon and hot dogs, will also boost your risk for diabetes. If you choose to enjoy alcohol, drink moderately. People who drink too much alcohol (more than two drinks a day), as well as complete abstainers, are more likely to become diabetic than moderate drinkers. Stay away from the smokes. For reasons that are not clear, smoking doubles the risk of becoming diabetic.

DIABETES: WHAT YOU NEED TO KNOW

- Diabetes increases the risk of heart disease up to fivefold in women and doubles the risk in men.
- The majority of diabetics are Type 2, or adult onset.
- Type 2 diabetes is usually brought on by obesity, an unhealthy diet, and a sedentary lifestyle, although some people are genetically predisposed.
- Nearly 10% of adults are diabetic, including nearly 25% of those over age 60. Twenty percent of middle-aged adults are pre-diabetic, as are 35% of those over 65.
- To avoid diabetes, keep your BMI less than 25, exercise regularly, and choose a Mediterranean-style diet. Stay away from fast food, processed meats, and tobacco.

TREATING DIABETES

If you are diabetic, your doctor will probably recommend medical treatment. There are eight major types of medication prescribed to people with diabetes; most Type 2 diabetics will ultimately require two or more medications. Several new classes of drugs are currently in the pharmaceutical pipeline, some of which may also prove to impact lipids and weight management. Blood sugar control is critical and has been proven to reduce the likelihood of such dreaded diabetic complications as heart disease, blindness, kidney failure, and amputation.

Insulin

The body needs insulin in order to put glucose to work. Since Type 1 diabetics are unable to produce this hormone, insulin shots are mandatory for this condition. However, many Type 2 diabetics require insulin injections as well, which happens because either the pancreas produces an insufficient amount of insulin or, more commonly, the body is so resistant to insulin that higher levels of it are needed in order to push glucose into the cells where it belongs.

Most insulin used in this country is human-type insulin, although older, less commonly used forms come from extracts of pig or cow pancreas and are referred to as "natural" insulin. Human insulin is generally made from a process using yeast (Novolin) or bacteria (Humulin). There are at least six varieties of insulin, classified according to onset of action, peak of activity, and duration. Usually two or more types of insulin are combined to create a custom fit for an individual.

Type 1 diabetics may use an insulin pump that injects insulin through a catheter and allows fine tuning. Although most insulin must be injected under the skin in order to be effective, slow release skin-patch forms of insulin are currently being studied. Frequent finger-stick blood tests are required in order to dose insulin appropriately.

One major drawback of insulin therapy is the possibility of overshooting by administering too much insulin, leading to hypoglycemia, or low blood sugar; this may cause lightheadedness, confusion, or even loss of consciousness. Changes in diet, exercise, and general health can affect insulin requirements, so daily glucose monitoring is essential.

Sulfonylureas

Sulfonylureas work by stimulating the pancreas to produce more insulin and by improving the body's ability to use insulin. Examples include glyburide

(DiaBeta, Glynase, and Micronase), glypizide (Glucotrol), and glymepiride (Amaryl). Side effects may include an allergic rash, weight gain, and low blood sugar. There is also some evidence that glyburide and perhaps glypizide might increase the likelihood of abnormal heart rhythms in susceptible people. Other studies have suggested that these two sulfonylureas may actually worsen outcomes after heart attacks. Glymepiride appears to be safer for the heart, although this is still a controversial issue.

Meglitinides

Repaglinide (Prandin) also works by stimulating insulin secretion. It is faster acting than the sulfonylureas, so is usually taken before a meal. This type of medication allows more flexibility with mealtimes than longer-acting drugs. Potential side effects include low blood sugar and weight gain.

Alpha-glucosidase Inhibitors

Alpha-glucosidase inhibitors include miglitol (Glycet) and acarbose (Precose). They work by delaying the absorption of carbohydrates in the intestine, resulting in a slower rise of blood sugar after a meal. These drugs should be taken with meals. Side effects include diarrhea and flatulence, but not low blood sugar.

Thiazolidinediones

This class of medication includes rosiglitazone (Avandia) and pioglitazone (Actos). Thiazolidinediones (TZDs) work by improving the cells' sensitivity to insulin. They generally do not cause low blood sugar. Studies have found improvements in CRP, HDL cholesterol, and triglycerides, in addition to lower blood glucose. However, TZDs can cause fluid retention, which may lead to congestive heart failure. There are also concerns that at least one TZD, rosiglitazone, may increase the risk for heart attacks, although not all studies of the drug have found this to be the case.

If you take a TZD, it is important to have regular monitoring of liver function blood tests, since TZDs can cause liver abnormalities in a small percentage of people. Anemia and weight gain may sometimes occur on these drugs, and they may increase the risk for bone fractures in women.

Biguanides

Metformin (Glucophage) is the only biguanide currently available. This drug reduces the amount of glucose produced by the liver and increases sensitivity to insulin. (The body stores excess glucose in the liver and muscle tissue. In diabetes, there is a malfunction in the regulation of glucose release from the liver.) Unlike many other diabetes medications, metformin may actually cause a modest amount of weight loss.

However, it has a slew of potential side effects, the most common of which are gastrointestinal, including nausea and vomiting. Metformin may also cause a deficiency in vitamin B12. More serious side effects include lactic acidosis, in which dangerously high levels of acid in the blood may result in kidney damage. Although this usually occurs in people with pre-existing kidney damage or heart failure, use metformin with caution if you drink more than moderately, since excessive alcohol may increase the risk of side effects.

Dehydration and acute medical illness will also increase the likelihood of problems. Iodine contrast dye and metformin do not play well together. It is critical that if you have a radiology test using intravenous iodine contrast dye, such as a CT scan or cardiac catheterization, you should avoid taking metformin for at least forty-eight hours following the procedure to avoid potential kidney damage. The dye and the drug are both processed by the kidneys and in combination may cause harmful levels of metformin to build up. The elderly are more vulnerable to these side effects.

While the potential for harm with metformin clearly exists, the prevalence of life-threatening side effects is low in those without contraindications, ranging somewhere between one and five cases per 100,000 people taking the drug. Your doctor should check your kidney function and blood sugar control regularly with a blood test to be sure that this drug is safe and effective for you.

D-phenylalanine Derivatives

Nateglinide (Starlix) stimulates the pancreas to produce more insulin and works quickly and for a short duration. It should be taken before a meal.

Other than the potential side effect of low blood sugar, this drug appears to be very safe and well tolerated.

Dipeptidyl Peptidase-4 Inhibitors

Dipeptidyl peptidase-4 (DPP-4) inhibitors increase the production of a group of hormones called incretins, which are produced in the gut. Incretins signal the pancreas to make insulin and tell the liver to stop producing glucose. In diabetics, levels of incretins tend to be low. DPP-4 inhibitors such as Januvia are often used in conjunction with other drugs for diabetes. Side effects are not common, but can include headache and gastrointestinal problems. Typically, we don't see weight gain or low blood sugar with this class of drugs.

Incretin Mimetics

Exenatide (Byetta) is designed to mimic the effects of incretins, enhancing the body's own release of insulin in response to a meal and preventing the liver from overproducing glucose. What's more, it can slow down the emptying of the stomach contents into the small intestine to reduce the rate that glucose is released into the bloodstream. Byetta is an injectable drug that is usually used twice daily, almost always in conjunction with other diabetic medications. It is not a substitute for insulin. Side effects may include nausea and weight loss. In fact, it is the weight loss associated with this drug that makes it so attractive to many doctors and diabetic patients.

THE METABOLIC SYNDROME

The metabolic syndrome is a collection of health risks related in large part to lifestyle choices, which increases the likelihood of developing cardiovascular disease. While several definitions have been put forth, the strictest and most relevant criteria were developed in 2005 by the International Diabetes Federation. To meet the definition, you must have a waistline measurement of 37 inches or more if you are a man (35.5 inches for Asian men) and 31.5 inches if you are a woman. In addition, two of the following criteria are required:

- A blood pressure of 130/85 mm Hg or higher
- A triglyceride level above 150 mg/dl
- A fasting blood glucose (sugar) level greater than 100 mg/dl
- A high density lipoprotein (HDL) level less than 40 mg/dl (men) or under 50 mg/dl (women)

Having the metabolic syndrome will increase the probability of developing heart disease by nearly 40% in nondiabetics and more than 50% in those with diabetes when compared to people without these risk factors.

While cardiovascular disease risk increases over time, a study of people with metabolic syndrome aged 55 and younger found that the vast majority, nearly 90%, already had evidence of early cholesterol buildup in the carotid arteries, which supply blood to the brain. Since carotid artery disease is also a marker for vascular disease elsewhere in the body, it is likely that many of these folks also had significant cholesterol buildup in the heart arteries.

Metabolic syndrome is increasingly common in the United States. An estimated 27% of adults, including 29% of women, are affected by this largely preventable disorder. Most Type 2 diabetics have the metabolic syndrome. Up to half of Americans over the age of 60 qualify for this diagnosis. Sadly, women are acquiring the metabolic syndrome at rates far greater than men. Even more worrisome is a recent report that metabolic syndrome may be found in 14% of young teens.

Metabolic syndrome is widespread amongst obese people, nearly two thirds of whom meet the criteria. This compares to less than 6% of individuals with normal body weight.

Notice that the definition of metabolic syndrome does not include body mass index, but rather waist circumference. The point is that not everyone with metabolic syndrome is obese by BMI standards. The most dangerous fat in your body is the visceral fat, or deep abdominal fat. Some normal weight people have a thick waistline, and some obese people have a normal amount of this type of fat. Think of the round-bellied "apple" shape, as opposed to the "pears," who carry more fat in the hips and buttocks and are less likely to have the metabolic syndrome.

This visceral type of fat is so important because, unlike subcutaneous fat (fat under the skin), it is actually a functioning organ of the body. It produces a host of hazardous chemicals such as CRP, that promote inflammation, as well as other products that can trigger dangerous blood clots. Fat also produces chemicals that block the action of insulin and interfere with proper function of the insulin receptors in the body's cells, preventing insulin from being used properly. The result is insulin resistance. Fat tissue raises LDL levels, lowers HDL, and raises triglycerides. Binge eating, a common problem in people who suffer from obesity, is also associated with high insulin levels and insulin resistance. For all these reasons, tackling the obesity problem is a major focus of efforts to prevent and treat the metabolic syndrome.

There is probably a genetic predisposition towards the metabolic syndrome. There appears to be an inherited tendency towards storing fat in the abdominal area. For example, Hispanic women have much higher levels of the metabolic syndrome, hovering around 35%, which is not entirely explained by diet or activity levels.

PREVENTING THE METABOLIC SYNDROME

Unlike many chronic diseases, the metabolic syndrome is highly preventable. Exercise can reduce a thick middle, if you stick with it. Just thirty minutes, five days a week, when combined with a healthy diet, can work wonders. And when it comes to diet, studies have found that the Mediterranean diet may be the best way to lower your risk of the metabolic syndrome. Flip to chapter 7 to learn more about this delicious and healthy way of eating.

Exercise and diet take time, and if you're in need of help, your doctor may choose to prescribe metformin. This drug helps to sensitize the cells to insulin so that they are better able to use it.

But don't give up on lifestyle modification. A 2002 study of more than 3000 people from the Diabetes Prevention Program Research Group showed a decided advantage of diet and exercise over drug therapy in treating the metabolic syndrome. In this study, people were followed for an average of three years; they were assigned to receive a phony placebo pill, metformin, or to follow a diet and exercise program.

The program included a weight loss goal of 7% or greater of body weight and thirty minutes of exercise five days a week. At the end of the study, 29% of the people who received placebo tablets had become diabetic, while 22% who were given metformin developed diabetes. A pretty good response, but not earthshaking. The most exciting finding was the fact that only 14% in the diet and exercise group were diabetic by the study's end.

Put another way, a healthy lifestyle resulted in a greater than 50% reduction in the incidence of diabetes without the use of potentially harmful and costly drugs. This was despite the fact that only half of the people studied actually achieved their weight loss goal and less than three quarters were fully on board with the exercise recommendations. The benefits were there regardless of gender, age, or race.

THE METABOLIC SYNDROME: FACTS AND FIGURES

- Metabolic syndrome is a pre-diabetic state associated with abdominal fat, high blood pressure, lipid abnormalities, and elevated blood sugar.
- If you are an "apple" shape, carrying your fat in your middle area, you are more likely to develop the metabolic syndrome than a "pear," who is bottom-heavy.
- Nearly 30% of Americans have the metabolic syndrome, including up to half of those over the age of 60 and nearly 15% of kids.
- The metabolic syndrome is associated with cholesterol buildup in the arteries at a much younger age than would normally be expected.
- Exercise and diet are the most effective treatment for the metabolic syndrome.

THE POLYCYSTIC OVARY SYNDROME

Metabolic syndrome is common in women who suffer from polycystic ovary syndrome (PCOS). PCOS strikes about 5% to 10% of women of reproductive age and includes irregular menstrual cycles, acne, facial hair growth, infertility, ovarian cysts and, frequently, obesity. It turns out that fat tissue can manufacture estrogen, and this may interfere with normal functioning of the ovaries, where estrogen is usually produced. PCOS is not the same thing as run-of-the-mill ovarian cysts, which occur without the syndrome in 20% of women.

More than half of all women who suffer from PCOS are obese, and upwards of 75% of obese women with PCOS have insulin resistance. About a third of normal-weight women with PCOS will also have insulin resistance. By the time of menopause, many women with PCOS will be diabetic, so if you suffer from this disorder, regular screening for diabetes is important.

PCOS is associated with other features that double or even triple the heart disease risk, including elevated levels of CRP and lipid abnormalities, which occur in most women with the syndrome. Thickening of the carotid arteries is also more common in women with PCOS and portends a higher likelihood of strokes and heart disease later in life. Obese women with PCOS also tend to have high levels of the male hormone testosterone, which is responsible for the acne and facial hair that plague women with this disorder.

Infertility, facial hair, and heart disease. You wouldn't wish it on your worst enemy, but the good news is that PCOS is treatable, and often preventable. The first and most important step is lifestyle modification. You guessed it: diet and exercise.

Losing even 10% to 20% of body weight may substantially improve all aspects of the syndrome. If that is not sufficient, the drug metformin may be helpful. By lowering insulin levels, reducing testosterone, and improving rates of ovulation, metformin may be a real lifesaver. However, fertility rates may improve just as much, if not more, in women who choose to take control of their PCOS with diet, exercise, and weight loss.

ASPIRIN: THE TRUE WONDER DRUG?

Aspirin has been in use, in one form or another, for more than 2000 years. In 1897, aspirin as we know it was created in the laboratory of the Bayer Company. By 1900, the drug had hit the market and the rest is history.

As a blood thinner, aspirin works by inactivating platelets in the blood. These small, oblong-shaped cells are a vital part of the clotting process. Remember that a heart attack is usually caused by the rupture or fissure of an unstable cholesterol plaque in a heart artery. The body interprets this disruption as a wound, and platelets rush to the site to help close off the injured area by forming a clot. This clot, formed by the well-meaning platelets, is what ultimately closes off the artery.

The loss of blood flow to the portion of the heart muscle that depends on that artery for its oxygen supply is what causes the heart attack, or what we doctors call a myocardial infarction. If blood flow is not restored quickly, then permanent damage follows. When we disable the platelets, this series of catastrophic events is less likely to take place. Since aspirin permanently inhibits platelets, its blood-thinning power lasts a good eight to ten days, which is the life span of a platelet.

If you think you might be having a heart attack, it makes sense to pop a full-strength chewable aspirin (for immediate release) in your mouth while waiting for help to arrive, since aspirin reduces the risk of a full-blown heart attack or death by nearly half in this time-critical situation.

In 1988, a study of more than 22,000 healthy male physicians aged 40 though 84 reported a remarkable finding: one 325 mg aspirin taken every other day lowered the risk of a heart attack by 44% at five years. The benefits were seen chiefly in men over the age of 50. It is fair to say that this study profoundly changed the way we look at heart disease prevention, offering a simple, relatively safe, widely available, and cheap drug that could measurably save lives.

While this study focused on men, other studies of aspirin that included relatively small numbers of women suggested a protective effect for women over 50 who carried at least one risk factor. But in 2005 the Women's Health Study researchers found that, once again, women are not just "little men," but biologically and physiologically different creatures.

Healthy women older than 64 with no personal history of heart disease who took 100 mg of aspirin every other day achieved a 34% reduction in heart attacks and 30% reduction in strokes. Conversely, in women aged 45 through 64 who had never been diagnosed with heart disease, aspirin had no significant effect on the risk of heart attack or stroke.

Aspirin-takers have other reasons to celebrate. The drug may provide additional heart-healthy benefits, including antioxidant effects and the ability to protect the vulnerable lining of the blood vessels. Studies show that men with a high CRP reduce their heart attack risk by 55% when given aspirin, suggesting an important anti-inflammatory role.

Is There a Downside?

In the Women's Health Study, aspirin increased the risk of severe intestinal bleeding, although this side effect was very uncommon, occurring in 6 out of every 1000 women treated with aspirin for ten years, compared to 5 in 1000 of the women who received placebo pills. Nosebleeds, bruising, and other bleeding problems were also more common in the aspirin group.

Aspirin probably does not reduce the risk of colon cancer or breast cancer, despite speculation to the contrary. It may help lower the risk of prostate cancer in men, and there is a chance that it could reduce the risk of lung cancer, although no one knows for sure.

When to Avoid Aspirin

How do you make the decision whether to take aspirin? First, check with your doctor to be sure that there are no medical reasons you should avoid aspirin. If you have been diagnosed with any sort of bleeding disorder, you should, as a rule, stay away from aspirin, unless directed to take it by your doctor.

If you have problems with stomach ulcers, don't take aspirin unless the ulcers are healed and your doctor clears you to do so. People on other blood thinners and anti-inflammatory medicines are more prone to bleeding, but depending on the situation, your doctor may decide that the benefit outweighs the potential risk. Some asthmatics and people with nasal polyps are sensitive to aspirin and may even suffer severe allergic reactions to the drug. If you are pregnant, only take aspirin under the supervision of a doctor.

Who Should Be Taking Aspirin?

While aspirin may not help low risk, healthy, younger women without a history of heart disease, there is a proven benefit for women under 65 with a heart disease history. Regardless of age, most high risk women, including diabetics, should consider taking aspirin at a dose of 81 to 325 mg daily. If you have already been diagnosed with heart disease, a daily dose of aspirin will lower your risk of dying from cardiovascular disease by a full 25%. If you have two or more risk factors for heart disease, or you are age 65 or older, you may also benefit from aspirin. As always, it is important to discuss your treatment options with your doctor.

Coated vs Non-coated

Should your aspirin be enteric-coated or non-coated? Somewhere between 5% and 30% of people are resistant to the effects of aspirin. This aspirin resistance may be genetic in the way the body handles aspirin, but it also appears that 20% of normal-weight adults simply do not absorb enough aspirin when it is given in enteric-coated form. The problem worsens in obese people, who require more aspirin to achieve an adequate concentration of the drug, and in smokers.

If you are able to take aspirin without it causing stomach upset, it makes sense to take a low-dose of non-coated aspirin with food in the morning. Avoid taking it before bedtime, since there is a greater likelihood of the aspirin tablet spending the night camped out in your stomach, which could cause ulcers. And remember that acetaminophen (Tylenol), ibuprofen (Advil, Motrin), and other pain relievers are no substitute for aspirin when it comes to matters of the heart.

ASPIRIN: NOT JUST FOR ACHES AND PAINS

- High risk women, including diabetics and women with heart disease, should usually take aspirin daily to lower heart attack risk.
- Most women 65 and over will also benefit from low dose aspirin (81 mg), with a 30% to 35% reduction in heart attack and stroke.
- Low dose aspirin is less likely to be of benefit to smokers and to people who are obese. These people may need to take a full strength, non-coated pill (325 mg).
- Check with your doctor before starting a daily dose of aspirin to be sure it's right for you.
- Take an enteric-coated aspirin if you have a sensitive stomach. If you notice any signs of bleeding, stop the aspirin immediately and contact your doctor.
- Taking an aspirin at the first sign of a heart attack may save your life.

Do Antibiotics Prevent Heart Disease?

It might sound far-fetched, but heart disease has been linked to *Chlamydia pneumoniae*, a bacterium that frequently infects the respiratory system. This bacterium has been found in cholesterol plaques, and animal studies suggest that it has the ability to worsen atherosclerosis. Based on preliminary studies, some doctors have even chosen to treat their heart attack patients with antibiotics.

In 2005, two large randomized trials of heart patients reported absolutely no benefit of treatment with antibiotics, even when therapy continued for two years. Scientists have not ruled out the possibility that infection with *Chlamydia pneumoniae* or other organisms may stimulate the onset of atherosclerosis, perhaps by causing inflammation in the arteries, and research in this area is ongoing. Meanwhile, there is no compelling reason to take antibiotics for the prevention of coronary artery disease.

PREVENTIVE MEDICINE: IT'S UP TO YOU

As vital as medications are to those who need them, up to 20% of people who are hospitalized for a heart attack stop their medications within six months, often with dangerous consequences. I recall Marguerite, a 68-year-old retired secretary who came to our hospital with a heart attack in progress and was treated with a cardiac stent to open a critically blocked artery. She was prescribed a regimen of drugs, including aspirin and another blood thinner, Plavix, which were essential to keep the artery open.

I sat down with Marguerite and her family before she left the hospital and reviewed with them the importance of taking her medications exactly as prescribed. Everyone seemed comfortable with the plan, and Marguerite assured me she would follow doctor's orders. But after a few weeks, Marguerite decided she was tired of taking her pills. They were too expensive, and, anyway, she felt just fine, so why bother? She also decided that she really didn't have the time to go to my office for her check up and wasn't interested in cardiac rehabilitation, even though the cost was covered by her Medicare health plan. Unfortunately, three weeks after she stopped her medications, the paramedics rushed her back to the emergency room in severe distress with a second major heart attack. Marguerite now suffers from congestive heart failure and from the knowledge that she could have prevented her condition had she just taken a little more responsibility for herself.

Whether you take pharmaceuticals for cholesterol, high blood pressure, or diabetes, it is vital to your health and well-being that you take your medications as prescribed. If your doctor recommends aspirin, treat it with the same importance as you would any of your prescription drugs.

Side effects can happen with just about any medication, so be sure to let your doctor know if you have concerns. We can usually find alternatives. Be honest with your doctor if you are concerned about the price of your medications. As your doctor, I want to help keep your costs down, but sometimes I choose a specific drug for you based on its unique virtues that simply don't apply to the whole class of drugs. While a generic may not always be the best choice, many times a similar drug can be substituted that will allow you a lower insurance co-pay. With hundreds of different health plans out there, your doctor often won't have that type of information at her fingertips. Make the effort to research the options yourself. If you are truly needy, many drug companies have programs to provide drugs at low or no cost, so be sure to ask if you need assistance.

No matter how many medications you take, it is critical that you do all you can to reduce your risk of heart disease through diet, lifestyle, and exercise. Not only will you feel better, you will drastically reduce your personal cost of health care. Obesity and a sedentary lifestyle powerfully increase the risk of high blood pressure, high cholesterol, diabetes, arthritis, lung disease, and cancer. All of these diseases will cost you money, not to mention years of life and health. Take responsibility now, and it will pay off for the rest of your life.

STEP FIVE

SMART WOMEN GET
A MOVE ON

Exercise makes us look good and feel great. It keeps our hearts pumping and our minds clear. Smart women know that time is precious and not to be wasted in front of the TV or computer. When we get up and move, we are tapping into a force for health that is more powerful than almost any drug the pharmaceutical industry could dream up. It can be virtually free of charge, making for a brilliant return on a very small investment.

Heart-savvy women lift dumbbells, walk like they mean it, practice yoga, take the stairs over the elevator, and dance to their own music.

14

Exercise and the Active Lifestyle

No matter what your passion—horseback riding, tennis, golf, yoga, walking, or any other activity that gets you up and moving—let it inspire you to make fitness a way of life.

Ever Wonder How Long You'll Live?

To achieve a healthy heart, mind, and body, exercise is not an option. It's a necessity. Your exercise capacity, or the amount of exercise that you can do before reaching the point of exhaustion, is a more powerful predictor of your life span than high blood pressure, diabetes, smoking, or even pre-existing heart disease. If you exercise, chances are you will live longer.

THE GOOD NEWS ABOUT EXERCISE

If you commit to exercise, you are half as likely to become obese as your couch-bound neighbors. People who exercise regularly have lower levels of triglycerides and higher levels of beneficial HDL cholesterol. Although total LDL cholesterol levels don't usually change with exercise alone, LDL subclasses do improve, so that the LDL that you have is less likely to harm your arteries. And if you lose weight, your LDL will probably fall as well. CRP levels may be reduced by up to 40% with exercise, indicating a reduction in inflammation.

Aerobic fitness improves the body's sensitivity to insulin so that diabetes is much less likely to develop. This is due in part to the fact that aerobic exercise is one of the best ways to get rid of harmful deep abdominal fat or "belly blubber." Men who exercise regularly are up to 30% less likely to develop erectile dysfunction than those who are inactive—good motivation to get your man to the gym. Researchers at the University of Washington found that exercise might even help prevent the common cold.

Regular workouts will make you smarter and happier, and over time you'll be less likely to suffer from depression, dementia, and insomnia. People who exercise handle stress better, both physically and mentally. For menopausal women, exercise may be one of the best ways to deal with the capricious effects of fluctuating hormones.

What's more, exercise is nearly free of charge. Most people can put on a pair of walking shoes and head outside or to a nearby mall for a brisk walk. The Centers for Disease Control and Prevention has estimated that if the 88 million or so sedentary Americans would get up off their cabooses and exercise, health care costs could be slashed by more than $75 billion. That would go a long way towards reducing our national health care costs and, at the same time, would improve our quality of life.

For older people, maintaining physical fitness helps preserve a higher level of functioning and greater independence. Exercise may help slow the progression of dementia in people at risk for the condition. Even folks well into their 80s, including those with physical disabilities, will reap benefits from regular physical training. However, the earlier you start exercising, the greater the rewards will be.

Many people believe exercise will increase their appetite and consequently sabotage their attempts to lose weight. This isn't necessarily true. Scientists have found that exercise actually has a fairly weak effect on appetite as long as you are getting sufficient calories for your body's needs. One important exception is people who engage in vigorous exercise. Research shows that after moderate-intensity exercise, like brisk walking, people generally eat about 35% of calories burned, whereas high intensity exercisers, such as fast joggers, often eat 90% of the calories they worked so hard to sweat off. This just means that if you're trying to lose weight, you need to be more vigilant about your calories after a hard workout.

GETTING A MOVE ON

To optimize your health and well-being, commit to two and a half hours of exercise each week. Ideally, this will be at least thirty minutes of exercise five days a week, since sustained exercise is best for heart health. Incorporating brief bursts of physical activity into your daily life will burn some extra calories and modestly improve fitness, but for true cardiovascular impact, the heart must work for a minimum of twenty minutes straight.

If you haven't been very active for a while, consider using a pedometer to track your steps, and aim for at least 10,000 steps per day. Climb the stairs at work instead of taking the elevator, take a long walk across the parking lot instead of circling to find the closest spot, and choose a walk break instead of a smoke or coffee break. Although they don't take the place of regular exercise, these mini-workouts are well worth the effort. For example, climbing stairs just five minutes a day could net you a three-pound weight loss over the course of a year, as long as you don't reward yourself with a cookie.

If you are working on weight loss, you will probably need to exercise more—perhaps up to one hour a day to achieve and maintain a healthy weight. If you need a motivator, plan in advance—new clothes, a CD for every 10 pounds you lose, a trip to the movies, or whatever else gets you moving. Just keep it calorie-free. In time, your reward will be improved health, increased energy, and a fit and toned body.

While you should aim for two and a half hours every week, any regular exercise will put you ahead of the curve. The more you exercise, the better off you will be. In people ages 40 to 68, those who exercise more than two hours every week have a 60% lower likelihood of developing heart disease than those who do not exercise at all. Just one to two hours a week reduces the risk a respectable 40%, but even a little exercise still promotes a 15% reduction in heart disease risk compared to no exercise at all.

AEROBIC EXERCISE

Aerobic exercise gets you breathing more deeply and makes your heart pump faster and stronger. If you are exercising aerobically, you are working the large muscle groups of your body, typically your arms and legs, and you're probably breaking a sweat.

Brisk walking, jogging, biking, skating, and swimming all get you moving and pull more oxygen into your body. Aerobic exercise classes also fit the bill, as do dancing, mowing the lawn, and playing tennis. Whatever you choose, the ideal aerobic activity is one that you can keep up for at least thirty minutes without stopping.

To be aerobic, exercise needs to let you reach a target heart rate of 60% to 85% of your age-adjusted maximal heart rate. How do you know what your target heart rate is? It's simple.

First, subtract your age from 220; this will give you your age-adjusted maximal heart rate. To figure 60% to 85% of that, multiply it by 0.6 and then by 0.85. This will give you your range. For example:

If your age is 40, then 220 - 40 = 180

180 x 0.6 = 108 (60% of your maximum predicted heart rate)

180 x 0.85 = 153 (85% of your maximum predicted heart rate)

Your target heart rate range is 108 to 153 beats per minute.

To learn what your heart rate actually is at any time, you can check your pulse either at your wrist (the radial artery) or at your neck (the carotid artery). Count how many beats occur in fifteen seconds, then multiply by four.

For example, at rest, you may count twenty beats in fifteen seconds. Multiply 20 x 4 = 80, or eighty beats per minute. You can also buy a monitor to wear on your chest or wrist to check your heart rate, but be aware that these can sometimes misread the heart rate due to interference from muscle movements and contractions.

WHAT'S MY HEART RATE RIGHT NOW?

Check your pulse at the wrist or neck. Count how many beats you feel in fifteen seconds, and then multiply by four.

WHAT'S MY TARGET HEART RATE FOR
AEROBIC EXERCISE?

The number 220 minus my age equals my maximum heart rate, based on my age. My target heart rate is 60% to 85% of that number.

As long as you have normal blood pressure, it is not usually necessary to monitor your blood pressure with exercise on a regular basis. However, if you have high blood pressure, check with your doctor before you launch into an exercise program. It makes sense for everyone to warm up and cool down for five to ten minutes when doing vigorous exercise to avoid abrupt changes in heart rate and blood pressure. Stopping suddenly can sometimes cause the blood pressure to fall too quickly.

In general, more energetic exercise is better, as long as you can keep it up without stopping. If you're a walker, pump up your pace to 3 miles per hour or more for an optimal cardiovascular workout. If that's too fast, don't despair. Even slow walkers are far better off than those who stay on the couch.

If you are just starting to work out, begin slowly and work your way up. Don't expect to be able to run an eight-minute mile or to bike for two hours straight if you hung up your "tennies" right after high school graduation. Overdoing is often counterproductive since you are apt to get sore and discouraged and just give up. And don't wait for a sunny day to strut your stuff. Blaming the weather is a tired old excuse for not exercising that will get you nowhere.

Find something that you can do despite the weather or the time of year. An exercise bike or treadmill is a great investment in your future, especially if you are not able to get to a gym regularly. If you have physical limitations, learn to work around them, perhaps with the help of a good physical therapist. Arthritis sufferers or those with back trouble can search out a local pool to swim laps or do water aerobics. Some of the fittest patients in my practice are paraplegics and amputees who don't let their disabilities get in the way of good health.

It's fine to start out at just fifteen minutes a day, if you need to, and work your way up week by week. And despite what the hard-core gym rats might say, it's also okay to read a book or watch TV while you're exercising on a stationary bike or treadmill, as long as that doesn't slow you down.

If you are over 40 and have not exercised for years, see your doctor and get a thorough checkup before jumping into an aerobic exercise program. Not everyone will need a stress test, but for high risk people such as those with high blood pressure, diabetes, or pre-existing heart disease, it will be an important step towards good health. Knowing your aerobic capacity and the response of your blood pressure and heart rate to exercise will give you a good idea of your baseline level of fitness. This information will also help your doctor uncover and treat important risk factors or signs of significant heart disease and ensure your safety as you embark on your new lifestyle.

ANAEROBIC EXERCISE

Aerobic exercise is, by definition, exercise that uses oxygen. Anaerobic exercise, such as weight lifting, uses glycogen, a type of sugar stored in the muscle tissues. A by-product of glycogen breakdown is lactic acid. Contrary to popular belief, lactic acid is not responsible for the "burn" we feel after heavy exercise. We now know that it is lactic acid that helps to keep the muscle working past the point of fatigue. Weight lifting, sometimes referred to as resistance training, is a great complement to aerobic exercise, since it works the body and the muscles in a completely different way.

If you're planning to embark on a weight-lifting program, check in with your doctor first. People with hypertension are at greater risk for a stroke if the blood pressure is not controlled because the strain of weight lifting will briefly raise the blood pressure. With regular workouts, the rise in blood pressure will usually become less substantial, as long as your resting blood pressure is normal. Of course, people with untreated heart problems, such as unstable blockages and congestive heart failure, should not exercise until their problems are under good control. A few heart conditions, such as serious heart valve disease and severely thickened heart muscle walls, make weight lifting unacceptably risky.

Weight training benefits are seen in men and women of all ages, ranging from teens to the elderly. It's never too late to start. One study showed striking improvements in muscle strength and ability to perform activities of daily living in a group of one hundred frail nursing-home patients whose average age was 87, most of whom required a cane, walker, or wheelchair to get around.

Besides strengthening the muscles, regular weight training actually increases your basal metabolic rate and will burn more calories even when you are doing nothing at all, because muscle tissue requires more energy to maintain itself than does fat tissue. Diabetics who combine weight training with aerobic exercise will often see incremental declines in blood sugar levels.

Some women fear that weight training will bulk them up, and so they avoid this type of exercise. That's not a worry as long as you follow my recommendation of twenty to thirty minutes of weight training twice a week. Believe me, I've been working out with weights for more than twenty years and have yet to find a muscle that I don't want to keep. On the other hand, weight lifting shouldn't be counted on as a stand-alone exercise.

Weight lifting uses less than half the number of calories as aerobic exercise in a given amount of time. However, adding weight lifting to aerobic exercise may protect your heart even more than aerobic exercise alone. What's more, you will feel great and look even better.

DON'T HURT YOURSELF

Most gyms will offer basic training on equipment use to new members. If they do not, investing in a few sessions with a well-qualified trainer is usually money well-spent. Proper technique is vital if you want to achieve optimal results and will also help you avoid injuries and muscle strain.

A good trainer recognizes that there is no such thing as a typical woman, and she will work with you to develop a plan that takes into consideration your personal goals, as well as your baseline strength and fitness.

YOGA

Yoga and Pilates are physical exercises that incorporate an awareness of the body and mind through the use of the breath. They are often referred to as "mind-body" disciplines. Through both forms, the body is stretched and suppled, lengthening the muscles and allowing greater flexibility. Tendons and joints become more flexible, the mind becomes calmer, and stamina increases. It is no wonder that professional athletes and dancers have flocked to yoga for years.

Yoga is accessible at all levels of physical fitness and can range from very basic meditative poses to extremely challenging postures that take years to perfect.

Yoga newbies need knowledgeable instruction. Some of the postures can cause back pain or injury to the ligaments if done improperly or if attempted before the body is sufficiently flexible. If you already suffer from back or joint problems, consult your doctor first. Researchers at the University of Washington have found that when done properly, with good instruction, yoga can be very effective for reducing chronic low back pain.

Studies of yoga have reported lower blood pressures, lower rates of anxiety and depression, and decreased levels of the stress hormone cortisol in yoga practitioners. Remember Dr. Ornish and his vegetarian high carb, low fat diet in chapter 7? The participants in his program also followed a strict regimen of yoga, aerobic exercise, and meditation. By five years, they had half as many heart attacks and other heart events as those who chose not to follow the program, as well as much less cholesterol buildup in their arteries.

There are numerous forms of yoga, some more spiritual, others purely physical. One school of yoga, known as Bikram Yoga, involves practicing in a room heated to more than 100 degrees Fahrenheit with 70% humidity. This type of yoga should not be attempted by someone who is not physically fit. People on blood pressure medications may also react badly to the hot and humid environment and develop dangerously high or low blood pressures.

PILATES

Like yoga, the Pilates techniques, developed by Joseph Pilates in the early 1900s, are also eagerly embraced by dancers and other athletes. Pilates, who believed that physical fitness was essential for true happiness, derived many of his exercises from yoga. Symmetrically strengthening the core muscles of the abdomen, along with the muscles of the lower back and buttocks, the Pilates method enhances balance, flexibility, and posture.

Many Pilates exercises can be performed quite effectively with minimal to no props. But in traditional Pilates, a contraption known as the "Universal Reformer" helps to isolate various muscle groups so that the muscles can be used most effectively. Although this and other time-honored Pilates devices, with their pulleys, straps, and head rests, may look like medieval instruments of torture, they really do work. By using this equipment, you can develop a sense of proper body alignment and learn to use each specific muscle group to its best advantage.

The best way to learn Pilates is through an accredited teacher who can help you learn proper body positioning. There are also some excellent DVDs available to supplement your practice.

Choosing an Exercise Plan

Since there are so many choices when it comes to exercise, it helps to define your goals. If the purpose of exercise is solely to prevent heart disease, then a brisk aerobic activity for thirty minutes five days a week is perfect. For body sculpting and fat burning, add a twenty-minute workout with weights two or three days a week. To help develop serenity, balance, and flexibility of mind and body, a thirty- to sixty-minute session of yoga or Pilates at least once a week will work wonders.

EXERCISE AND YOU

- Exercise reduces your risk of heart disease, diabetes, high blood pressure, osteoporosis, colon cancer, breast cancer, gallstones, depression, and insomnia.
- Exercise helps burn up belly fat, raise good cholesterol, and lower triglycerides and CRP.
- Aerobic exercise includes walking, running, swimming, and biking. Try to do at least two and a half hours of aerobic exercise weekly.
- Weight training is anaerobic exercise. Shoot for twenty to thirty minutes two or three days a week.
- Yoga and Pilates help to stretch and add suppleness to the body, calm the mind, and improve balance and coordination. A session once or twice a week can have lasting effects.

STEP SIX

SMART WOMEN LISTEN
TO THEIR MOTHERS

Whether it's getting a good night's sleep, keeping those pearly whites gleaming, or making time for our friends, smart women practice the daily wisdom our mothers always preached. And just like our mothers promised, a positive approach to life keeps us on the road to good health.

It's comforting to know that old-fashioned or not, motherly advice never goes out of style. What we do with our mothers' words of wisdom will be the legacy we share with the next generation of smart women.

15

MOTHER KNOWS BEST—ARE YOU LISTENING?

Whether you'd like to admit it or not, your mother probably did know best. Why is she always right? Although maternal wisdom may be mysterious in its origin, it is practical in its application. Here is a heaping helping of motherly advice that we should all take to heart.

DRINK UP

Your body is an expert at monitoring and maintaining fluid balance. The problem is that we often don't listen to what our bodies are telling us. Frequently, we misinterpret our thirst as hunger, and snack when we should be sipping.

While the 64 ounces of water per day paradigm has been challenged, if you are active, this amount is usually sufficient to maintain good hydration and heart health. People who drink at least five glasses of water a day are less prone to heart troubles than those who drink very little, probably because the fluid keeps the blood flowing smoothly.

Juice or other drinks, including sports drinks, run a distant second to water, and not only because of their higher calorie content. Some scientists suspect that they can be counterproductive to good hydration, by pulling fluid into the digestive tract and out of the bloodstream. The exception is marathon runners and other extreme sports enthusiasts, who can severely deplete their body's electrolytes, especially on a hot day. For these athletes, juice or sports drinks are a must.

It is possible, although rare, to genuinely go overboard, drinking water to excess, and diluting the natural balance of electrolytes. This problem is more common in the elderly, people with psychiatric illness, and those with kidney failure.

DON'T FORGET BREAKFAST

Breakfast is not optional. Your brain and body need healthy fuel for peak performance. Both adults and kiddos who eat breakfast tend to have a more positive mood, and they do better on tests of memory and attention span. Compared with people who eat a nutritious breakfast, breakfast skippers fare worse on tests of physical endurance, even though they often feel that they are working harder. Adults and kids who eat breakfast are also less likely to become overweight.

BRUSH THOSE PEARLY WHITES

You know your mother was right about this one, although she may not have known that poor dental health is associated with a measurably higher risk of cardiovascular disease and stroke. Periodontal disease, or disease of the gum tissue, is often caused by poor hygiene. People with this condition are up to 70% more likely to develop heart disease. The risks of carotid artery disease (which may lead to strokes) and disease of the leg arteries are also higher with poor dental habits.

Periodontal disease is associated with higher levels of C-reactive protein, indicating chronic inflammation. The theory is that this inflammatory condition may also cause inflammation in the heart arteries, making cholesterol plaques less stable and more prone to rupture. Adults who are obese and people with diabetes are more likely to have gum disease than people of normal weight.

Keeping your gums and teeth clean and shiny is not rocket science. See your dentist at least every six months, and brush at least twice a day for two minutes, preferably with an ultrasonic-type electrical brush. Don't cheat. Two minutes can seem like a long time when you've got a toothbrush in your mouth, but a healthy smile is worth the effort.

PLAY NICELY WITH OTHERS

Above my desk hangs a small framed cross-stitch I received from a dear friend and medical school classmate. My little keepsake declares: "A true friend is the rarest of all blessings." I know this to be true. Together, my friend and I survived gross anatomy lab and the rigors of our first nerve-jangling nights on call. I feel fortunate that we have been able to maintain this friendship, forged in fire, across the years and miles. A friend is a lifeline, both figuratively and literally.

When we are under stress, having a friend by our side will help keep the blood pressure and heart rate in line and lower the body's production of stress hormones. Perhaps not surprisingly, this effect is most powerful when the friend is a woman, regardless of whether the beneficiary of the friend's support is male or female.

As women, many of us are gifted with a natural ability to nurture our families and those we love, and to support each other through good times and bad with friendship and sympathy. For many men this role does not come easily, yet we all need love and acceptance.

Male or female, people with poor social support are more than twice as likely to die in the first year after a heart attack as people with a caring community of friends and family. People with larger social networks tend to be healthier and to live longer than those who are more solitary. For example, people who describe themselves as lonely are much more likely to suffer from high blood pressure and the associated health problems that come with this condition.

Elderly people who are lonely are more prone to develop Alzheimer's-like dementia, although their brain tissue may appear normal. This finding suggests that loneliness might actually alter our brain chemistry.

Marriage itself is an intriguing situation. Married or not, women stay healthier longer when they have supportive female friends. But for men, marriage can make all the difference. Single men are twice as likely to die after a heart attack as married men and are two to three times more likely to die prematurely from any cause. This does not necessarily hold true for women, whose health does not appear to benefit substantially from tying the knot, with one notable exception. Married women or women in a long-term relationship with a man who shows his affection with hugs and (yes!) massages tend to have lower blood pressures and a less intense physical reaction to stress.

Compared to women in bad marriages, women who are happily married are less likely to develop the metabolic syndrome, a spectrum of risk factors that includes obesity, high blood sugar, high blood pressure, and high cholesterol (see chapter 13). And while healthy disagreement and even heated discussions with a spouse can be constructive, married women who respond to arguments with downright hostility are more likely to build up cholesterol plaques; this is particularly true for women with confrontational personalities whose husbands are also hot-tempered.

GIVE A HOOT, DON'T POLLUTE

It is easy to see how air pollution might increase the risk of asthma, lung cancer, and chronic lung disease, but what many people don't know is that air pollution will also increase the risk of heart attacks, heart failure, strokes, and dangerous blood clots in the legs. It probably does so by triggering inflammation within the blood vessels as well as by stepping up production of fibrinogen, a blood product involved in clotting.

Pollution is powerfully tied to the foods we eat. Emissions from coal-burning power plants dump tons of mercury into our air and oceans each year, contaminating much of the fish that end up on our dinner plates. Our country's voracious appetite for meat also has environmental implications. According to a 2006 United Nations report, the livestock industry is responsible for nearly 20% of greenhouse gas emissions worldwide.

Pollution should concern us all. It has been estimated that people living in highly polluted cities lose an average of one to three years of life due to the effects of pollution. Children who live close to a freeway have substantial reductions in normal lung development. Limiting emissions and supporting research into alternative energy sources will not only help the environment, but is likely to have a direct effect on our cardiovascular and neurological health as well. It makes sense to do what you can to contribute to a solution.

Roll Up Your Sleeve and Say Ouch

Everyone knows that a case of the flu is a recipe for pure misery, but most people are unaware of the true devastation the virus can cause. The influenza virus, which strikes 25 to 30 million people in the United States each year, attacks the respiratory system, causing fevers, chills, body aches, cough, and a sore throat. Although most people recover from the illness, in this country more than 200,000 people are hospitalized and about 36,000 people die from the flu and its complications each year.

The flu can leave the lungs more susceptible to pneumonia. It is known to increase inflammation, raise the risk of blood clots, and to increase the heart rate, all of which can threaten heart health. In higher-risk individuals, the flu can actually trigger a heart attack. In fact, up to 30% of heart attacks are preceded by the flu or upper respiratory infections.

Not everyone who catches the flu is at the same high risk for a heart attack or pneumonia. Those who are more vulnerable to complications of the flu include people over 50 years of age, women who expect to be pregnant during the flu season, and folks with chronic medical illnesses, including heart disease and lung disease. For these people, studies show that getting a flu shot may cut the risk of a heart attack by 25% to 50%. The risk of stroke also decreases considerably, and the overall risk of death declines 50%. Tens of thousands of lives could be saved every year, and even more disability prevented, simply by vaccination.

Potential Problems with the Flu Vaccine

Many people refuse to be vaccinated. Some have an irrational fear of needles, while others are worried the shot will cause the flu.

Because the flu shot now in use is a killed virus, there is no way that it can cause the flu, so you should put this fear to rest. (However, the intranasal form does contain live virus and is not recommended for heart patients and others with chronic conditions.) If you have a severe allergy to eggs, you should check with your physician before getting the vaccine, as there may be risk of a reaction.

You might catch the virus if you are not vaccinated soon enough, but don't blame it on the flu shot. It takes about two weeks for the flu vaccine to work within your system to produce immunity.

Other people who avoid vaccination cite years in which they were vaccinated in plenty of time, but still caught the flu. This is often not a failure of the vaccine itself, but rather a failure of the vaccine's developer to anticipate the specific strain of flu virus for that year. Since the virus mutates easily, there are a number of different permutations of influenza, some of which dominate more than others in any given year.

Whether you catch the flu or just a nasty cold virus, stay home until the worst of it passes. People who work while they are sick are twice as likely to suffer a heart attack as those who stay home, and they are more susceptible to other infections. Keep your sniffles to yourself, cover your mouth when you cough or sneeze, wash your hands frequently, and everyone will be the better for it.

DON'T BURN YOUR FOOD

While it is important to cook certain foods, particularly meat products, at temperatures high enough to destroy harmful bacteria, we know that cooking fruits and vegetables at high temperatures can rob them of their vitamins. It now seems that cooking food at temperatures of more than 212 degrees Fahrenheit may produce high levels of a carcinogenic (cancer-causing) substance known as acrylamide. Starchy foods like French fries contain acrylamide in abundance. It has been estimated that acrylamide may be responsible for up to 1000 cancers each year in the United States alone, although the issue is far from clear.

Cooking food at high temperatures may form other chemicals known as advanced glycation end-products, which promote inflammation in the body and may raise C-reactive protein. These substances are found in meats, breads, and other foods that are browned in the oven. They react within the body to increase damage to arteries, nerves, and kidneys. Diabetics are particularly susceptible. Exactly what this means for those of us who enjoy cooking outside on the grill on an occasional sunny weekend is not clear, but this is an area of research that promises to heat up.

A DOG IS A GIRL'S BEST FRIEND

The first thing I see when I walk in the door after a long day at work is the joyful, goofy grin of my sweet greyhound. No matter what the day brought me, Rosie makes me smile, and I can feel the stress begin to slip away. While you and I may know firsthand the healing powers of pets, scientists have just begun to discover the ways that our furry friends can enhance our lives and improve our health.

Studies have found that older pet owners are more active and report a greater sense of well-being than those without animals. Adults of any age who have pets tend to experience less of an escalation in blood pressure and heart rate when exposed to mental and physical stress, especially when their pet is nearby. In fact, State University of New York researchers found that stress produced a milder physical reaction when a pet was near than when a spouse was standing by.

Even people who are already on high blood pressure medication experience lower readings when there is a pet around the house. Dog owners who suffer a heart attack are less likely to die in the first year afterwards than are those without dogs. There is no doubt that dogs are great exercise companions. Once you begin a daily walking routine, your dog surely won't let you forget it.

Of course, having a pet is an important responsibility, but for many people, this responsibility adds more meaning and purpose to life. I remember speaking to a stressed-out and lonely young law student who confided in me that if it wasn't for his cat, he probably would have committed suicide. Although his family on the other side of the country never knew it, he survived law school thanks, in large part, to his feline friend.

THANK GOD FOR GOOD HEALTH

Central to many religious traditions is the tenet that it is the spirit—or the soul—that joins the mind and the body together. The word "spirituality" is commonly used in a religious context, but it may also refer to a sense of connectedness with life or an experience of transcendence. People with strong ties to a wide variety of faiths and diverse beliefs need no convincing that their health is profoundly affected by their experience of the divine.

Older people who attend religious services regularly live longer than non-churchgoers. Simply listening to religious radio or watching a service on television doesn't appear to offer the same health rewards as actually being there. People who attend church tend to have lower blood pressure, while those who watch it on television are more likely to have high blood pressure. It may be the service itself, or it could be the community provided within the church, but there is no question that a rich spiritual life contributes to the well-being of the body.

Get a Good Night's Sleep

Sherone is a vibrant hard-working woman in her late 30s who sees me for high blood pressure. She is the mother of a 2-year-old son and works in a high intensity corporate environment. Sherone was not happy about having to take medication, but her blood pressure was too high to go untreated. She was about 50 pounds overweight, so I encouraged her to work on weight loss and exercise, with the hope that tuning up her lifestyle might bring down her blood pressure enough to allow her to come off the medicine.

This usually immaculate woman showed up one morning looking almost disheveled, her hair carelessly pulled back in an elastic band, her skin tone flat, and dark circles under her eyes. She had taken my advice to heart. She was starting her day an hour and a half earlier so she could fit in time to exercise while her family slept, but she still went to bed at her usual late hour. She hadn't lost weight, her blood pressure was higher than ever, and her work and home life were suffering. Sherone was miserable.

We all need to balance our busy lives with sufficient sleep. We cannot adapt to less sleep, no matter how hard we try. Not only does lack of sleep make us sleepy, it can stifle creativity and memory and limit our ability to work at optimum levels. People who do not get adequate sleep are also more likely to suffer from depression.

Women and men in their 30s through 50s who sleep less than an average of six hours per night have a twofold risk of hypertension. Their blood vessels may fail to respond normally to stress, and blood tests may show higher levels of harmful inflammatory C-reactive protein.

With a few exceptions, most of us do best with seven to eight hours each night. Sleep only six hours and you increase your odds of obesity by 23%. Those who sleep just four hours bump that obesity risk up by 73%.

Even short-term sleep deprivation may increase hunger pangs and result in cravings for starchy carbohydrates and sweets. Poor sleep habits may be an important contributing factor for diabetes.

Is there such a thing as too much sleep? Possibly. Some studies have found a correlation between increased risk of heart disease and regularly sleeping nine or more hours nightly. However, people who nap regularly, for at least thirty minutes three times a week, may actually decrease their risk for cardiac death by more than a third. Even occasional catnaps may lower the risk slightly.

Sleep Apnea, Obesity, and Snoring

Obese people, particularly those with thick necks, are at high risk for a condition known as obstructive sleep apnea (OSA), in which the airway becomes partially blocked during sleep. People with sleep apnea tend to snore heavily, followed by periods of not breathing at all, known as apnea, and experience frequent awakenings during the night. The quality of sleep suffers tremendously. It is estimated that at least 2% of women and 4% of men over 50 suffer from OSA, but many experts suspect that number is even higher.

People with OSA tend to suffer from overwhelming fatigue during the day and, consequently, fall into a dangerous and self-perpetuating rut of overeating and inactivity. OSA is associated with high blood pressure, elevated pressures in the lungs, weakening of the heart muscle, abnormal heart rhythms, and a higher risk for heart attacks and strokes.

Fortunately, OSA is easy to diagnose with an overnight sleep study and can usually be effectively treated with a special mask that is worn at night. In severe cases, surgery may be required. Often, once the OSA is controlled, weight loss and exercise become much easier.

Off to Dreamland

So how do you ensure a peaceful night's sleep? Avoid caffeine within six hours of bedtime. Exercise regularly, but not too late in the evening, or you may find yourself too wired to sleep. Stay away from late-night snacks, especially if you suffer from gastric reflux. Avoid drinking too much water before bedtime, and try to go to bed at around the same time every night.

Don't watch television or do office work in bed. Treat yourself to a relaxing bedtime ritual, such as soaking in a warm tub, reading a "mindless" magazine, or writing in a journal, and make your bedroom a place of tranquility and peace.

One glass of wine may be a pleasant way to end the evening, but for some people, alcohol can cause disordered sleep. So can many over-the-counter sleep aids, particularly diphenhydramine (also known as Benadryl). The supplement melatonin works well for some people, but we don't yet know much about its long-term safety. If you are a true insomniac, see your doctor. If everything checks out normally, a temporary prescription for a short-acting sleep medicine can sometimes help to reset your internal clock.

LISTEN TO YOUR MOTHER

- Drink 64 ounces of water every day; more if you're exercising.
- Don't skip breakfast.
- Brush your teeth for two minutes, at least twice a day—preferably with an ultrasonic toothbrush.
- Play nicely with others. Make good friends and keep them; cultivate a loving relationship with your spouse or partner.
- Try not to contribute to pollution. Avoid exercising in polluted air when possible.
- Stay away from burned or scorched food, particularly if you are a diabetic.
- Get a flu shot each year, and avoid spreading cold and flu germs.
- A dog is your best friend. Or maybe a cat.
- A healthy dose of spirituality can do wonders for your physical well-being.
- Sleep seven to eight hours every night, and squeeze in a nap when you can.

16

Attitude and Stress: Don't Let It Break Your Heart

On a busy Monday morning, I opened the exam room door to meet Tiffany, a slim and girlish 35-year-old, with a swinging red ponytail, sent to my office by her family doctor for symptoms of chest pain.

Tiffany looked so healthy and young that I doubted I would find anything wrong. Her blood pressure was perfect and, assuming she indeed was a low risk patient, her cholesterol was just right. But as her story unwound, it was clear that my first impression was way off the mark.

A mother of two, Tiffany had been devastated when she caught her husband in an affair a year earlier. She was now in the middle of a contentious divorce. Her financial affairs were a mess, forcing her to work a low-paying cashier's job to support her kids. At night, she attended a local community college to earn a degree in hopes of providing a better future for her family.

Overwhelmed with stress, Tiffany had recently taken up smoking, a habit she had quit ten years earlier. Despite all of this, she still found time to work out on her elliptical trainer at home after the kids were tucked in for the night. Recently, she had noticed a deep, nagging ache in her chest when she exercised. It was annoying, but she would try to power through this feeling, determined to finish her workout.

I scheduled a stress echocardiogram for Tiffany, an exercise test that includes imaging the heart with ultrasound. The study results were extremely abnormal—so much so, that I sent her straight to the hospital.

There was an 85% blockage in one of Tiffany's major coronary arteries. Two stents (small, flexible metal tubes) were required to open the vessel in order to restore normal blood flow. Thankfully, no permanent damage was done to her heart muscle, and a combination of medical therapy, smoking cessation, and stress reduction helped to get Tiffany back on track.

Tiffany illustrates the harm that stress can inflict. She was loaded down with a burden of anxiety and tension, which was nearing the breaking point. She had a couple of strikes against her already—smoking and a family history of heart disease. Unlike many younger women who develop heart disease, she was not on birth control pills, which can dramatically raise the heart attack risk in smokers, but her decision to smoke, even a couple of cigarettes a day, doubled her risk.

Stress made Tiffany feel like life was spinning out of her control. As much as I would have liked, I could give her no magic bullet to vaporize her stress. But, with some insight and understanding of the impact of the competing pressures in her life, she reached out to others—a key to reducing anxiety.

Tiffany learned to ask for help from her family, to choose foods for health rather than convenience, and to add yoga to her exercise routine. A financial planner at her community college helped Tiffany create a manageable economic roadmap, which gave her valuable peace of mind. With these important changes, along with a life-long commitment to medical treatment, Tiffany will probably do well for years to come.

Just as stress can trigger a heart attack, increased life stressors following a heart attack are associated with a greater threat of subsequent death and serious illness. Depression and stress may both play a role in destabilizing cholesterol plaques, increasing the heart's vulnerability. Tiffany is a case in point.

Most studies have shown that stress alone is not enough to cause a heart attack. Take my patient Joe, who first met me in the emergency room when he rolled in with a full-blown heart attack that struck right after he was handed his divorce papers.

Joe insisted I call his soon-to-be-ex immediately to tell her the heart attack was all her fault. I respectfully declined and explained to my unhappy patient that this heart attack was the outcome of a long series of events brought about not only by stress, but also by smoking, high blood pressure, and a lifetime of fast food.

THE BROKEN HEART SYNDROME

Although stress alone is not usually enough to cause a heart attack, there is a relatively rare condition known as Broken Heart Syndrome or Takotsubo cardiomyopathy that typically occurs as a result of severe and intense emotional stress. The condition is much more common in women over 50 than in any other group. In this disorder, the heart acts just as if it is in the throes of a heart attack. Severe chest pain, marked abnormalities of the electrocardiogram (a recording of the heart's electrical pattern), and characteristic blood test findings all point to a heart attack. The heart appears enlarged and weakened. Usually women (or men) with this syndrome will be taken urgently for a cardiac catheterization, or angiogram, to look at the heart arteries in anticipation of finding a blockage. In most cases of broken heart syndrome, there are no blockages at all. Exactly why and how this happens is not well understood, but it is probably related to a massive, toxic outpouring of stress-related hormones and chemicals. Fortunately, the condition usually resolves with medication, and in most cases, the heart muscle eventually returns to normal function.

THE SCIENCE OF STRESS

Job issues, family problems, financial worries, you name it—most of us, on any given day, are just trying to cope with what life throws our way. In a survey from the U.S. Department of Labor, more than 60% of working women, regardless of job or income, described stress as their number one problem.

As tension builds, stress may lead to a wide range of physical ailments, triggering the body's natural fight or flight mechanisms, which are designed to protect us in times of extreme danger. These stress-triggered systems work well in the event of an emergency, but it is easy to see how chronic and recurring stress may be harmful to your heart.

Your endocrine system doesn't know the difference between your angry boss and a marauding saber-toothed tiger. All the body knows is that you are in trouble, and so it does its best to prepare you to fight back or run away.

Adrenaline is one of the stress hormones our bodies release in response to acute anxiety. It causes a sudden surge in heart rate and blood pressure, which helps us to make our swift getaway, but adrenaline can also irritate the heart muscle, causing irregular heartbeats that may feel like an uncomfortable pounding or fluttering sensation in the chest.

Cortisol is another hormone our bodies churn out in response to physical or emotional stress. People who suffer from depression and anxiety tend to over-produce this hormone. Excessive cortisol production may also be triggered when we drink more than three cups of coffee in a day.

Cortisol, made by the adrenal glands, raises blood sugar, preparing the body for increased energy needs. As a result, blood sugar may rise precipitously in diabetics and in those pre-diabetics with glucose intolerance. At the same time, blood pressure and heart rate may soar to dangerous levels. People over 60 are especially vulnerable to such surges in blood pressure. Cortisol can even help to make you fat, since it boosts your cravings for high fat foods.

Cortisol, along with other hormones, has a diurnal variation, meaning that levels rise and fall throughout the day in a fairly predictable pattern.

Levels tend to be highest around 6 a.m. and lowest at midnight. It is thought that the early morning rise in cortisol may account for the fact that heart attacks frequently occur first thing in the morning.

IS STRESS ALWAYS BAD?

Anxiety, apprehension, and worry, particularly in women, often lead to overeating both during and after the stressful parts of the day. Highly stressed people are more resistant to the effects of medications used to treat blood pressure and heart conditions. Beneficial HDL cholesterol tends to be lower in highly stressed individuals. Stressed-out people tend to have a poor quality of sleep, which can lead to a plethora of mental and physical ailments.

Since stress is part of life, it is vital to understand that it comes in many forms, and it's not always harmful. What it all boils down to, it seems, is often control.

Women who work in positions of responsibility in which they experience stress, but can maintain control of their work and reach their goals successfully, are much better off, heart-wise, than many women in clerical jobs. Women in clerical jobs often have minimal control and may be at the mercy of an unsupportive boss, increasing their risk of stress-related problems. Homemakers with husbands who don't support them emotionally or are unreasonably demanding also tend to be less healthy than working women in positions of responsibility.

Chronic stress at work, with high demands, low control, and minimal social support, more than doubles the risk of developing the metabolic syndrome, a cluster of risk factors that includes high blood pressure, unhealthy levels of cholesterol and triglycerides, insulin resistance, and obesity (see chapter 13).

Feeling good about your work, whatever the work may be, and being supported and empowered to do your best will tend to balance out the type of stress that comes with the demands of the job.

GRANNIES AND STAY-AT-HOME MOMS

Not surprisingly, studies have found higher cortisol levels in mothers in the workforce, indicative of greater emotional stress. Yet stay-at-home moms who spend more than twenty hours a week caring for their kids have a higher risk of heart disease than women without children or those who are empty nesters. Grandmothers who spend at least nine hours a week with their grandkids also carry a higher risk of heart trouble.

STAMPING OUT STRESS

How do you cope with stress? First, recognize the problem and the factors that contribute to it. If you work, you may not be in a position to change jobs, but you can strive to improve your environment, or at least your mindset.

If you're a mom, accept that raising children is stressful, no matter how much joy the sweet things bring. Children are your most vital responsibility—nurture them and guide them, but don't neglect yourself. It's important to allow yourself time out to be your own person.

If your marriage is the problem, don't just accept the status quo. A credentialed counselor or trusted clergy person can provide vital insight and guidance.

Recognize stress triggers. Learn to tune in, to discover the sources of anxiety and stress in your life. Take ownership of the problem. If you are a procrastinator, know that it is your responsibility to take control of your schedule and to manage your life so that you have the time and space you need to get the job done on time, whether it is at home or in the workplace.

Get help from an expert if you need to get organized, either from within your company or from an organizational specialist. Develop supportive social networks at work and at home. Eat well. A diet high in sugar, simple starches, and saturated and trans fats will ensure that you continue to feel sluggish, unmotivated, and overwhelmed. Instead, choose fruits, vegetables, whole grains, and high quality protein to give you the energy you need to face your challenges.

No matter what else you do, make time to exercise. We all need a constructive and healthy way to blow off steam, and the energy and fitness you develop will empower you to tackle your work with more energy and optimism.

PERSONALITY AND HEART DISEASE

If you are a Type A personality, hard-driven, ambitious, quick to anger, and never satisfied, you may have the ambition and competitive drive to get ahead and achieve great things, but the hostility and intolerance that often accompany these personality traits may be toxic.

When Type As get stressed out, their heart rate and blood pressure may climb dangerously. Their personality traits do not necessarily cause atherosclerosis to develop, but rather make plaque that is already there more vulnerable to rupture, increasing the likelihood of a heart attack or stroke. For instance, the risk of a heart attack escalates dramatically, up to nine times normal, in the first hour after an angry rage.

Being a Type A isn't always a bad thing. If she can focus the drive and competitiveness and control the hostility and impatience, a Type A person is more likely than others to achieve healthy goals, such as exercise and weight loss, and to be professionally successful.

Type B personalities are the original beach bums, the lighthearted, worry-free, noncompetitive spirits who prefer to live-and-let-live. Type Bs in general have a lower risk for heart disease than other personality types, but they often don't do as well after a heart attack occurs. This is probably because they frequently fail to take an active role in their recovery, assuming that everything will turn out all right in the end.

Type Cs are the appeasers. They have difficulty expressing any emotions, especially anger, and tend to bottle things up inside, preferring to maintain a neutral outward appearance. They are often lonely and feel a sense of despair and hopelessness that they prefer not to discuss with others. A Type C personality may be at greater risk for cancer, but this personality type hasn't yet been studied much in regards to the risk for heart disease.

Type D is the pessimist. She is often irritable, anxious, and unhappy and frequently suffers from depression. The Type D personality has a more dramatic physical response to stress and is much more likely to do poorly than a non-D after a heart attack, particularly if she is less than 55 years of age. Despite this, she is likely to delay visiting the doctor for serious health issues, waiting until the problem becomes critical.

DEPRESSION AND HEARTBREAK

While we all get the blues from time to time, people who suffer from true depression may be at higher risk for developing heart disease. Depression is characterized by feelings of hopelessness and worthlessness and by an inability to experience pleasure and interest in activities of everyday life. In depression, the brain chemistry is altered, so it is difficult, if not impossible, to "just snap out of it." Nearly 12% of women and 6% of men will experience a major depression at some time in their lives. It can come on without warning and last for months or even years.

Insomnia, low energy, and difficulty concentrating are hallmarks of depression. Studies have found that depression may raise the risk of a heart attack up to twice normal. Depression will dramatically increase the likelihood of a stroke, with a fourfold risk in people under the age of 65. Depression also increases cholesterol buildup and the probability of dying in the years following a heart attack.

People who experience anxiety along with depression may be especially vulnerable. Depressed people are less likely to exercise, more likely to make unhealthy dietary choices, and less likely to take medications.

It is not easy to overcome depression alone. The first step towards recovery is recognition that there is a problem, and the second step is to seek help from your doctor. Psychotherapy and medication, when appropriate, can be lifesaving.

LOOKING ON THE BRIGHT SIDE

Can a positive attitude save your life? While positive thinkers are less likely to develop chronic illnesses, this is probably because they are more apt to exercise, eat well, and cultivate other healthy habits. They may also cope better with stress than habitual pessimists. Once a serious disease develops, however, optimism will not necessarily prolong survival, although it may improve the quality of life.

People who eat healthy foods are more likely to avoid or overcome mild cases of depression. Those who are aerobically fit feel less anxious and stressed, and their blood pressure and heart rate are much less affected by the day-to-day trials and tribulations we all face.

Yoga is a great way to learn how to control the way you respond to stress, allowing you to slow your breathing and to focus your mind. Meditation has a similar effect. Several mainstream medical studies of transcendental meditation, based on ancient Indian tradition, have found important cardiovascular benefits, including a reduction in blood pressure, improved blood glucose levels, and, in people with heart disease, fewer episodes of congestive heart failure. Quality of life and measures of depression also improved. Even listening to slower-tempo music will help calm the mind, reduce the heart rate, and slow down respiration.

Sleep is a necessity, not a luxury. Those of us who get less than six hours of sleep are twice as likely to feel sad, stressed, and angry as those who sleep at least eight hours.

Your attitude is a reflection of how you choose to live your life. Do your best to maintain a healthy optimism but, most importantly, follow through with a forward-thinking approach to your life and your health. Of course, if you need help, do not hesitate to turn to a doctor or other trusted professional who can help you. Allow yourself to experience the joy of a positive attitude.

THE LOW-DOWN ON STRESS, ATTITUDE, AND DEPRESSION

- Stress can raise blood pressure, blood sugar, and heart rate and cause irregular heartbeats. It can also make you fat.
- The unhealthiest stress is stress you cannot control.
- Type A people with irritable and hostile personalities are at higher risk for heart disease. Type A people with a positive outlook are more likely to achieve exercise and healthy diet goals.
- Type B people have a lower heart attack risk but often take a passive approach to health.
- Depression is twice as common in women as in men and can increase the risk of cardiovascular disease, including stroke.
- A healthy diet, exercise, meditation, and sleep can all reduce levels of stress, anxiety, and depression.

SMART WOMEN ARE HIP TO THEIR HORMONES

As women, we are intensely aware of the changing hormonal tides that affect our bodies and minds. Thanks to birth control pills and postmenopausal estrogen replacement, we no longer have to be bound to the whims of our hormones.

While we are fortunate to have these options, taking control of our hormones may have some unintended consequences. Medical science has arrived to the party unfashionably late, and the risks and benefits of birth control pills, hormone replacement therapy, and alternative treatments for menopause symptoms are still being worked out. In the midst of this uncertainty, important information is finally beginning to emerge that will help us make some sense out of the confusion and come to our own informed decisions about hormones and heart health.

17

SMART TALK ABOUT HORMONES

Thanks to good nutrition and high quality health care, women are living longer, healthier, and more productive lives than ever before. Only a hundred years ago, our ancestors did not expect to live past 50, which conveniently dovetailed with the end of their childbearing years. These days, many women pass through menopause and thrive well into their 80s and beyond, with the average life expectancy around 80. For many women, those extra thirty or so years are highly productive and rewarding, particularly when the body and mind are healthy and strong.

MENOPAUSE AND YOUR HEART

Menopause is a perfectly normal and natural stage of life, yet it brings with it challenges that can seriously rock a woman's world, escalating her

299

risk of heart disease, stroke, and other unpleasantness. As the T-shirt says, "Menopause is not for wimps."

While most women will suffer through hot flashes, mood swings, and insomnia as estrogen levels decline, the majority will be rid of these annoyances after about five years, although vaginal dryness often persists. An unlucky 15% will struggle with menopausal symptoms for years. Without a doubt, hormone replacement therapy (HRT) will put the brakes on these troublesome symptoms, and for many women, it is the only effective treatment. At some point, nearly all women will face the dilemma of whether or not to start hormone replacement therapy.

MENOPAUSE

- What it is: the natural decline of estrogen production that usually occurs in women between the ages of 45 and 55, when the ovaries stop functioning. Menstruation will gradually become less frequent and eventually stop. It can also happen suddenly if the ovaries are surgically removed, or after some forms of radiation therapy or chemotherapy.
- How you know: a woman has usually passed menopause when she has not had a period for twelve months in a row. Blood tests can help determine when menopause is beginning.
- The downside: a cornucopia of physical symptoms— hot flashes, night sweats, irregular heart beat, insomnia, irritability, mood swings, loss of libido, vaginal dryness, and fatigue.
- The upside: no more periods—hooray! No worries about getting pregnant. Liberating sex. Aging with grace.

THE HORMONE DEBATE: A DOCTOR'S DILEMMA

The study of estrogen and menopausal hormone replacement therapy is still a work in progress. Although the effect of HRT on the heart is controversial, it is well-established that HRT slows down bone loss caused by low levels of estrogen. However, since there are several other good medications available to protect bone health, HRT is not considered to be the first choice to treat this condition. While we worry about raising the risk for breast cancer, there is a possible small decline in the risk of colorectal cancer in women who take HRT.

There are two basic HRT regimens. If a woman has had a hysterectomy and chooses HRT, she will receive estrogen. However, if she still has her uterus, estrogen replacement puts her at risk for uterine cancer, so another hormone, progesterone, will be added in order to cancel out the risk.

In the past, doctors happily prescribed HRT to help guard against the well-known complications of menopause, with no thought to heart health. Later, numerous retrospective studies, evaluating women who had taken HRT by choice, suggested that heart disease rates were lower in hormone users. This seemed logical, since we know that heart disease risk climbs precipitously after menopause, regardless of the age of onset, and doctors and their patients responded to the news with a flurry of new prescriptions for HRT.

The first HRT, Premarin, was introduced in 1942. By 2001, 42% of women aged 50 to 74 were taking some form of HRT. Beginning in 1998, formal clinical trials began to reveal that hormone therapies, especially those that combined Premarin with the hormone progesterone, posed serious risks and might even increase the danger of heart attack and stroke. In 2002, an estrogen-progesterone study was stopped earlier than planned because the risks to women in the study appeared to be greater than the benefits. These risks included heart disease, breast cancer, stroke, dementia, and blood clots. In women who received Premarin without progesterone, there was an increased risk of stroke and blood clots, but no significant effect on heart disease. Although less than five out of every one thousand women would experience a problem, the risks were substantial, given the number of women taking HRT.

HRT: WHERE DO WE GO FROM HERE?

The recent sea change in our understanding of HRT has shaken some women's faith in medical science. Take Jennifer, a patient who first came to my office in 1995 full of trepidation. At age 50, she was just beginning menopause. She had heard that estrogen might help to prevent heart disease—the scourge of her father's side of the family.

As a cardiologist, I never prescribe hormone replacement therapy myself. This is a decision best made by a woman with her gynecologist or primary physician. However, since Jennifer was interested in keeping her heart healthy, she sought my opinion because she was aware of my great interest in estrogen and its effects on the heart and cardiovascular system.

At that time, the best information available to us, from both observational studies and laboratory experiments, suggested estrogen actually protected the heart. Although it was well-established that HRT could cause harmful side effects, most studies before the mid-1990s indicated that the benefits outweighed the risks.

The problem was that none of those scientific studies was definitive, and the answers Jennifer was searching for that day in my office were still another five to ten years away.

By the next time I saw Jennifer, in 2002, the news on hormone replacement therapy was not good. The latest research suggested that hormone replacement therapy might not protect her heart, and the chance of serious complications, such as cancer, stroke, and blood clots, was higher than we once thought. Furthermore, HRT had been found to increase the likelihood of dementia, urinary incontinence, ovarian cancer, and gallbladder problems. Due primarily to these concerns, prescriptions for HRT fell by a third between 2001 and 2003.

My advice to Jennifer was this: review her case again with her gynecologist or primary physician. As her cardiologist, I advised her that based on the most up-to-date research available I could not recommend estrogen replacement for heart protection. The only clear-cut indication for estrogen replacement was for prevention of intolerable menopausal symptoms.

Fast forward to the present, and we are seeing the pendulum swinging back toward a potentially beneficial effect of estrogen replacement therapy for heart health, but only when started early in menopause. Many have criticized the large HRT studies for the fact that only about 30% of the women studied in both groups began HRT before the age of 60, whereas in practice, HRT therapy is usually prescribed near the beginning of menopause. Proponents of the so-called "timing hypothesis" believe that it is possible that the effects of hormones are very different in women who are just entering menopause, compared to women who have had no estrogen for ten years or more.

However, women who are on combination HRT remain at greater risk for complications than women who take estrogen alone; thus, women who have had a hysterectomy and can forgo progesterone may stand to benefit the most.

This issue remains highly controversial. Just how long estrogen can be safely continued is unknown. Importantly, the risk of harm appears substantial in women over age 60, especially when the drug is first taken more than five years after the onset of menopause. Diabetic women may also be more vulnerable to HRT complications.

Several large scale studies are still in progress, but the picture is becoming clearer. The bottom line (admittedly a moving target) is this: take HRT only if you need it for symptoms of menopause, and take it at the lowest possible dose for the least amount of time necessary. If your problem is primarily vaginal dryness, you have the option of a low dose vaginal estrogen cream, which typically can be used without progesterone, since it will not raise blood levels of estrogen substantially.

Pill, Patch, or Cream—Smart Talk about Tough Choices

If you have decided to take prescription HRT, the next step is to pick your potion and consider the facts.

ESTROGEN PILLS

All forms of HRT pills may raise levels of triglycerides, lower LDL cholesterol, increase HDL, and raise hs-CRP. If you have not had a hysterectomy, you must take progesterone along with estrogen to reduce the risk of uterine cancer. Whether or not you choose to use HRT, you need yearly gynecological checkups and mammograms to screen for cancer and other complications. Most large research studies used the drug Premarin, so less is known about other forms of estrogen. Use the lowest dose necessary to relieve symptoms. If you are on HRT, ask your doctor if you can go lower.

PREMARIN (conjugated equine estrogens)
- The original HRT; formerly the No. 1 selling drug in the country.
- Derived from pregnant horse urine.
- Contains more than a dozen forms of estrogen, unlike our own natural estrogen.
- Probably higher risk of blood clots, heart attacks, and strokes than with other types of estrogen.
- May increase risk of depression more than other forms of HRT.
- Also found in Prempro and Premphase (combined with progesterone).

CENESTIN (synthetic conjugated estrogens)
- Similar to Premarin, but derived from plant sources

ESTERIFIED ESTROGENS
- Estratab and Menest.
- Derived from plant sources.

ESTROPIPATE
- Ogen and Ortho-Est.
- Derived from plant sources.

17-BETA-ESTRADIOL

- Estrace, derived from plant sources.
- Also found in Activella and Ortho-Prefest (combined with progesterone).

ETHINYL ESTRADIOL

- Estinyl.
- Derived from plant sources.
- Also found in Femhrt (combined with progesterone).
- A small study reported fewer side effects with Femhrt than Prempro.

ESTROGEN, PLUS TESTOSTERONE

- Estratest (esterified estrogens plus methyltestosterone).
- Used when estrogen alone does not restore libido.
- May cause acne, hair loss, deepening of voice, breast pain, leg swelling.
- May raise cholesterol levels.

BIOIDENTICAL ESTROGEN

- Various combinations of estrogen, progesterone, DHEA, and testosterone, usually produced by a compounding pharmacy.
- Often sold over the Internet, without a prescription, based on saliva analysis.
- Few studies have been done on these compounds, so no guarantee of safety.
- Generally no FDA oversight.
- Risks probably similar to prescription HRT

ESTROGEN PATCHES, CREAMS, AND VAGINAL PRODUCTS

- Estrogen skin patches, creams, and vaginal rings release estrogen directly into the bloodstream, bypassing the liver. Because of this, there is no increase in triglycerides or CRP and no change in cholesterol levels.

- Some women may be sensitive to the adhesive used on the patch.
- These products should be used along with progesterone, unless you have had a hysterectomy.
- All but Premarin are derived from plants.
- Use the lowest dose necessary to relieve symptoms.
- As with HRT pills, regular gynecological checkups and mammograms are essential.

HOPE IN A BOTTLE: THE SEARCH FOR A NATURAL SOLUTION

"The change of life" is big business, and natural foods stores and neighborhood pharmacies alike stock a variety of products marketed as natural treatments for menopausal misery. But medical researchers, and most of my patients, have found little evidence that these treatments work. Moreover, the risks are largely unknown.

Common supplements include soy, black cohosh, red clover, evening primrose, and Mexican yam. Many of these products claim to provide nonprescription forms of estrogen. This sounds good, but we have no way of knowing if they are any safer than prescription hormone replacement.

Placing blind faith in prescription estrogen replacement can lead to disastrous consequences for many women. There is no reason to believe that other forms of estrogen might not be equally harmful. Furthermore the products are not standardized and are not regulated by the FDA, meaning that you have no guarantee that the product actually contains the ingredients listed, or that it is consistent from one batch to the next.

Mexican yam raises some serious red flags. Its active ingredient, diosgenin, is used to make a synthetic progesterone cream that can be bought over the counter. Women sometimes use this instead of prescription progesterone pills when taking combination HRT. This cream may improve menopause symptoms, but its safety has not been carefully investigated.

Black cohosh may help some women, but although its short-term use may be safe, there are reports of liver toxicity. Studies have not shown either red clover or evening primrose to be useful in improving menopausal symptoms.

The bottom line: if you choose to take one of these products, it's important to have regular checkups so your doctor can watch for harmful side effects.

DHEA—Fountain of Youth or Just a Wash?

As the baby boomers reached their mid-century mark, makers of dietary supplements began aggressively marketing dehydroepiandrosterone, or DHEA, as a way to combat menopause in women and to slow the aging process in both men and women.

While our adrenal glands produce DHEA from cholesterol, these over-the-counter pills are generally made from the same Mexican wild yams that are used to make progesterone cream. The body converts DHEA into estrogen and testosterone, but the process is inexact and may vary from person to person.

The use of DHEA can have unintended consequences. Increased aggressiveness and heart palpitations are potential side effects. Higher levels of testosterone generated by the supplement may cause acne and growth of facial hair and even male-pattern balding in women. There are also reports of serious liver damage with DHEA.

A two-year Mayo Clinic study of men and women over the age of 60 showed no improvement in body composition, physical performance, or quality of life with DHEA.

What to Do Now

If you are postmenopausal or getting close, you no doubt have many questions about what type of therapy, if any, is right for you now. The answers are still far from clear, but we are getting closer all the time. Keep yourself informed. Read the newspaper, talk to your doctor, and realize that the answers are slowly coming. In the meantime, exercise, follow a healthy diet, and get adequate sleep. As simple as it sounds, this will help you through the process.

"The Pill" and Your Heart

Oral contraceptive pills (OCPs) were first introduced in the early 1960s. They were arguably a powerful force in the development of the women's movement, allowing women to control a part of their biology that was previously by definition uncontrollable.

It is important to understand that what we know about HRT for menopause does not apply to oral contraceptive pills. The doses and types of hormones are quite different, although OCPs are typically combinations of estrogen and progestin.

Early versions of oral contraceptives, containing up to five times the estrogen and ten times the progesterone found in today's pills, clearly raised the risk of heart attacks and strokes in women who used them. Thankfully, times have changed, and most recent studies have shown no increase in heart attacks and strokes in women who use modern lower dose OCPs, with three important exceptions.

Risks with Today's Oral Contraceptive Pills

First, women with blood clotting disorders should not take OCPs. Although OCPs do not appear to cause atherosclerosis, they do increase the likelihood of blood clots, particularly in vulnerable people. This is a small minority of women, but unfortunately the clotting disorder is often not identified until a stroke or heart attack occurs while on the pill. Specific blood work can be ordered by your doctor to test for one of these disorders, but it is not standard practice to do so. If you have a family history of unexplained blood clots, it is critical that you let your doctor know this before OCPs are prescribed.

Second, some women will develop high blood pressure or high cholesterol while on OCPs, in which case it may be necessary to discontinue or change the dose or type of pill. When starting OCPs, it's important to get your blood pressure checked within a few weeks after your first dose.

The most important high risk group is smokers. A woman on the pill who smokes, particularly if she is over 35, has a probability of a heart attack that is 40 (yes, forty!) times normal. The risk for stroke is similar. As a cardiologist, I've seen both scenarios more times than I'd like to remember. Since up to 20% of women and nearly 35% of teenage girls smoke at least occasionally, the potential for harm is tremendous.

Taking any form of OCP increases the risk of deep venous thrombosis (DVT), or blood clots in the legs, even in women without a clotting disorder. The risk is low, but it is real. These clots are more common in women who are sedentary, overweight, or can't move their legs due to injury or illness. Women over 40 are more vulnerable than younger women are to DVTs.

If you use the birth control patch, your risk for DVT is twice that of women on the pill. Although the number of women affected is small, about six out of every 10,000 who use the patch, there is a chance that the clots can migrate to the lungs, a potentially fatal condition we call a pulmonary embolus.

Pills containing the specific progestins desogestrel and gestodene are more likely to be associated with this problem, with an estimated 16 to 30 extra DVTs per 100,000 women per year. With other progestins (norethindrone, levonorgestrel, or ethynodiol diacetate), the risk is lower. (If you are taking OCPs, the composition of the pill will be listed on the package.) Of course, having a pre-existing clotting disorder greatly increases the likelihood of this complication.

Oral contraceptives can raise inflammatory C-reactive protein (CRP). Some studies have found a doubling of CRP in pill users. Since our understanding of CRP is still in its early stages, no one really knows yet what to do with this information. Aspirin lowers CRP, so taking an aspirin a day is a reasonable option, if your doctor agrees, but it has not been studied in the context of OCPs. One retrospective study actually found less cholesterol buildup in postmenopausal women who had previously taken OCPs, so the news is not all bad.

We still don't know for certain whether OCPs increase the likelihood of breast cancer, although most studies show little if any risk. Women with a strong family history of breast cancer should be extra careful to have close medical follow-up, since they may be at higher risk than women with no such family history. On the other hand, it is well-known that OCPs cut the risk of ovarian cancer in half.

Contrary to popular belief, the pill will not make you fat although, for some women, it may cause water retention on the order of about 5 pounds. However, if you are overweight, the pill may not be as effective. Researchers at the University of Washington found that overweight women who took their pills faithfully were more than twice as likely to become pregnant as women on the pill whose weight was in the normal range.

HORMONES AND MENOPAUSE:
WHAT A SMART WOMAN NEEDS TO KNOW

- Hormone replacement therapy (HRT) decreases the risk of osteoporosis and helps with menopausal symptoms such as hot flashes and vaginal dryness.
- Don't use HRT to help prevent heart disease, since there is no definitive proof that it does.
- Estrogen without progesterone increases the risk of endometrial cancer in women who have not had a hysterectomy.
- The combination of estrogen and progesterone increases the risk of heart attacks, strokes, dementia, blood clots, and breast cancer, especially in women over 60.
- Estrogen alone increases the risk of strokes, blood clots, and possibly dementia. It may be less likely to cause harm when started within a few years of menopause.

- Natural products sometimes taken for menopausal symptoms include soy supplements, black cohosh, and red clover. Although they may work for some of us, most women will experience no relief with these products, and their long-term safety is unknown.
- Smokers who use birth control pills have a heart attack risk up to forty times that of non-smokers. Bottom line: If you light up, the pill (and the patch) is not for you.
- Birth control pills are less effective in women who are overweight.

AND THAT'S NOT ALL

SMART WOMEN KNOW THE FUTURE IS IN OUR HANDS

A healthy lifestyle, nutritious diet, and regular exercise in childhood lay the foundation for a healthy life. Since heart disease can begin as early as the teen years, it is critical to get a healthy start in life.

Living well is not complicated nor should it be costly. No matter what our limitations, a positive commitment to our health will infuse us with energy and vitality. It will open up an active way of life, brimming with possibilities, for ourselves and for those we love. Believe in yourself and in your power. Now it is up to you to take the next step.

18

KIDS HAVE HEARTS, TOO

The first time I met 16-year-old Katrina, I was charmed by her wide smile and sunny disposition. The teenager, with her mom in tow, came to see me because her blood pressure was dangerously high.

After other causes were ruled out, it became clear that Katrina's obesity and couch-potato lifestyle had put her on the fast track to hypertension. Tipping the scales at nearly 300 pounds, Katrina had spent her summer break sleeping late, eating pizza, playing video games, and watching TV.

Katrina did not have a summer job because she preferred to sleep in. She had tried working at a book store but shrugged that "it just wasn't for me." Her cholesterol was sky-high, and her blood sugar was pushing the upper range of normal. It was clear to me that without serious intervention, Katrina was barreling headfirst towards a lifetime of high blood pressure, diabetes, heart disease, and arthritis. If the statistics were right, she was also destined to face a lifetime of personal hurdles and disappointments in employment and relationships brought on by her weight and her lifestyle choices.

If you think heart health is for mature audiences only, think again. Childhood is the springboard for a lifetime of habits and choices, nurtured and shaped by family, friends, and teachers. During these early years, atherosclerosis often takes a foothold in the arteries throughout the body, including the heart. This slow, insidious process may culminate decades later in a heart attack or stroke. While cholesterol buildup in adults may have many causes, including genetics, in children, atherosclerosis is nearly always a direct result of an unhealthy diet and sedentary lifestyle.

The effects of diet and lifestyle are profound and far-reaching. Kids who eat foods high in saturated fat and cholesterol tend to have lower levels of cognitive and social functioning, regardless of socioeconomic status. The heart size of obese kids is measurably larger, and their arteries respond poorly to physical stress. Many already have fatty deposits in their livers or high blood pressure and up to 40% have the metabolic syndrome, a condition closely linked to diabetes (see chapter 13).

There are more obese kids per capita in the United States than virtually anywhere else on Earth. About 30% of our children are overweight, and nearly one in every six teens is obese. When it comes to gender, obesity is an equal opportunity player, although black girls are at especially high risk. If the rate of obesity continues on its present course, researchers at the University of California, San Francisco, predict that by 2020, a staggering 44% of women and 37% of men ages 35 and up will suffer from obesity and all of its attendant complications.

Where Obesity Starts

Young creatures, human or otherwise, are not naturally inclined to laziness or obesity. The truth is that we have allowed this to happen.

The stage for obesity may be set during pregnancy, as overweight moms (who are more prone to develop gestational diabetes) tend to give birth to larger babies. Obese moms are also up to twice as likely as those of normal weight to give birth to babies with serious birth defects.

The last two decades have seen a nearly 75% increase in markedly overweight infants, and today, more than 20% of children aged 2 to 5 are medically overweight, with more than 10% meeting the criteria for obesity. Since these kiddos are more likely to become obese as they grow older, it is vital that we recognize that good health begins with a healthy mother.

CAREGIVERS COUNT

Moms are important every step of the way. For instance, babies who are breast-fed tend to have fewer chronic health problems, including obesity, high blood pressure, and diabetes.

Young children are absolutely dependent on their parents and caregivers for the food they eat. But in the United States, where fresh food is abundant, nearly one-third of infants and toddlers aged 4 months to 24 months eat no fruits or vegetables; by the age of 18 months, the most common "vegetable" consumed is the french fry.

It is way past time for parents to take responsibility for the lives of their little ones. Let's be honest. It is not the kids pulling up to the drive-through on the way home from work. It is Mom or Dad, choosing the path of least resistance.

WHAT'S GOING ON HERE?

The more often a kid eats fast food, the more likely he or she is to be obese. Eating out also raises blood pressure and lowers good cholesterol in kids, just as it does in adults. And it has been well-established that a kid will tend to eat more food when given larger portions. This is why "super-sizing" is such a harmful practice. Perhaps even more alarming is the recent finding that preschool girls who are regularly fed french fries grow up to have a measurably higher risk of breast cancer, with the risk rising an additional 27% for each weekly serving.

Marketing junk food to kids takes many forms. Don't be fooled by so-called "kid-sized" meals. As of 2008, McDonald's Web site claimed that its food was something you could "feel good about." In fact, the company's "Happy Meals" supply between 370 and 700 calories per meal, with up to 27 grams of fat (for a small cheeseburger, small fries, and low fat chocolate milk), including 9 grams of saturated fat, 1 gram of trans fats, and 50 mg of cholesterol. To put this in perspective, a sedentary child between the ages of 4 and 8 does not require more than 1200 calories daily. And at this rate, a child could easily reach the daily maximum for saturated fat in a single meal.

Research shows that active kids are less likely to overeat, probably because they do more to keep their minds and bodies engaged, and thus have less time for mindless snacking. Not surprisingly, kids whose parents habitually feed them meals from fast-food joints are much more likely to be sedentary than kids who eat home-cooked meals.

THE ROLE OF TELEVISION

American kids watch, on average, three to four hours of television every day and spend nearly two more hours on the computer or playing video games. A child spending this much time in front of the tube is not experiencing his or her own life, but living vicariously through make-believe characters and strangers. Although the American Academy of Pediatrics strongly advises against any TV for very young children, a recent report that found 40% of 2-year-olds watch at least three hours of television a day.

Kids who watch two or more hours of TV daily tend to eat more high caloric snack foods, including chips and caffeinated sodas. They are also more likely to start smoking, to be overly aggressive, and to have difficulty concentrating. One study found that kids who watched TV three or more hours a day were more likely to struggle in school and less likely to pursue higher education. Even an hour of TV every day put kids at a disadvantage when compared to those who watched little to no television.

THE ROLE OF SMOKING

Like poor eating habits, smoking is a behavior that usually begins in childhood or adolescence. About one in four teens smoke, and most believe they can quit whenever they want. Nearly all of my smoking patients started as teenagers, and most would do anything now to have never taken that first drag. Tobacco is highly addictive, perhaps more so than any other drug available. Kids who are exposed to smokers at home or in their community are up to four times more likely to smoke, with smokers' kids as young as three or four years old showing a fascination for cigarettes. Children of smokers are more likely to suffer from asthma and other diseases of the respiratory system.

OTHER FACTORS: LOVE AND MEDICINE

Love really does nourish a healthy heart. Children who are emotionally abused, those who come from families where substance abuse is commonplace, and those who grow up in crime-riddled homes are more likely to develop heart disease later in life.

A small percentage of overweight kids may have medical conditions that predispose to obesity, so it is important to check in with your pediatrician or family doctor. These conditions include genetic abnormalities, diabetes, thyroid problems, polycystic ovary syndrome (see chapter 13), depression, and eating disorders. Doctors can screen for most of these ailments.

Kids with a family history of heart disease or high cholesterol are at higher risk for cholesterol problems and should be screened at least once. Adopted kids should also be tested, since their family history is often unknown. Since high cholesterol in childhood is clearly linked to atherosclerosis in young adulthood, many pediatricians recommend routine screening, on the order of every five years, for all kids. In children, cholesterol can often be lowered with a healthy diet and exercise. However, severely elevated levels may require medical treatment.

HOW TO HELP YOUR CHILD MAKE HEALTHY CHOICES

First, understand, and take to heart, that you are personally responsible for the food your youngster eats. It is not a toddler's decision to eat fries or drink a soda—that choice is made by the parent. If your child is exposed to these foods at school, it is your responsibility to effect change. Enlist other parents and make your voices heard. You cannot just love your child passively; as her mom, you must be her advocate and her protector.

Second, limit snack foods, candy, and sodas to special treats, if you allow them at all. Teach your child to enjoy nature's wide bounty of fruit, even if it does cost a bit more than a bag of chips. Watch out for "liquid sugar" in the form of high fructose corn syrup that is frequently found in so-called "fruit drinks," as well as sodas. Americans, on average, gobble and slurp the equivalent of a whopping half a pound of sugar a day, and children may consume even more, most often in the form of soft drinks and sweetened juice drinks. The average teen drinks nearly a gallon of soft drinks each week. Kids who drink more milk tend to be healthier and leaner.

Third, be sure your child gets plenty of grains, dairy foods, and healthy proteins. Avoid prepared foods filled with food coloring and preservatives, since these have been linked to attention deficit disorders. Stay away from trans fats, which are found in many snack foods and bakery products. Don't be fooled by labels listing "no trans fats," since regulations allow serving size levels of less than half a gram to be considered "zero." Look for the words "partially hydrogenated" in the ingredients list and avoid these products.

Fourth, control portion size. This is so easy to overlook, especially when eating out. Why not share your own restaurant meal with your child? That way you'll reduce your own portion, teach your child how to make smart choices, and save a little money in the process. If you choose to eat most of your meals at home, you not only have more control over how much your child eats, you can also steer clear of the excessive sugar, starch, sodium, and fat found in typical restaurant meals.

Avoid mindless nibbling and snacking. And don't eat meals in front of the television—it is too easy to lose track of how much you've eaten.

Most importantly, teach your child to revel in the joy of good health. Maintaining a healthy weight and exercising cannot happen without motivation and support. Don't forget to take care of your own health, since you are your child's most important role model. Overweight and obese parents tend to raise overweight and obese kids. For a child or teen, it is critical that the whole family be involved in making smart choices and limiting dangerous temptations.

More than ever before, this is the time for tough love. Put your love into action, and stand your ground, even when your kids accuse you of being cruel, out of touch, even uncool. Join a gym together, boycott fast food and high caloric snacks, and shop smart for food at the grocery store. Make a bike ride together a regular outing, or just take a walk or a hike. Enroll your child in a physical activity that she or he enjoys; some kids enjoy competitive team sports, but many do not. There are so many options. Dancing, swimming, even yoga for kids are all possibilities. Limit everyone's TV and video time, your own included, to less than two hours a day (preferably much less), and keep computer time to a minimum. Help your child to know the joy of a strong, healthy body and a well-nourished mind. Resolve to get healthy and stay healthy together.

We all want the best that life can offer our children. It takes more than money and platitudes. A commitment to a heart-healthy lifestyle takes discipline, but for young people, like my patient Katrina, caring enough to make these changes is truly love in action.

KEEPING YOUR KID'S HEART HEALTHY

- Approximately 30% of kids are overweight; one in six teens is obese.
- Obese moms tend to give birth to large babies, who are, in turn, more likely to become obese kids than are babies of normal size.
- Breastfeeding helps reduce a child's risk of obesity, diabetes, and high blood pressure.
- More active kids are less likely to overeat.
- Kids who eat fast food and other foods high in saturated fat and cholesterol are more likely to become obese and tend to have lower levels of cognitive and social functioning.
- The average kid watches three to four hours of television daily and spends two hours on the computer. It's best to limit total screen time to two hours or less.
- Kids who watch two hours or more of TV daily have higher levels of aggressive behavior, are more likely to be obese, eat more junk food, and are more likely to smoke.
- Parents do make the difference. Teach your children well, and lead by example.

19

EMPOWER YOUR HEART AND POWER UP YOUR LIFE

Writing this book for you has been a deeply satisfying experience. Through my research and critical review of the medical literature, I have deepened my understanding of the ways our small and seemingly trivial daily choices can profoundly influence our health and well-being.

Living is all about learning. No matter what your age, weight, or medical conditions, I hope that I have helped to empower you to take control of your health and, in so doing, to create a more satisfying and joyful life for yourself and for those you love. Good health is truly a journey, not a destination, and I hope that this book will serve as a road map to help guide you along your way.

We are fortunate to live in a time of tremendous progress in medical science. As I write, new developments and discoveries are emerging, and I have no doubt that our understanding of heart disease, diet, supplements, and lifestyle will continue to evolve. It is an exciting time to be a cardiologist.

Despite all our advances, we are far from having all the answers. Life is tremendously complex, a rich and spicy gumbo of possibilities and permutations. If we were simply machines, our lives would be predictable, our breakdowns all repairable. But we are not. There are very few straight lines or absolutes for the human organism. A plus B does not always equal C, and that is why we, as a species, survive.

Yet despite the uncertainties, when it comes to diet, exercise, and lifestyle there is no doubt that the choices you make each day will have a tremendous influence on the quality and duration of your life. Choose wisely, and live well. You owe it to yourself and to those you love.

APPENDIX

BODY MASS INDEX (BMI)

The BMI uses height and weight measurements to calculate whether you are at a healthy weight. The way to find your exact BMI is to divide your weight in kilograms by the square of your height in centimeters. This table makes it simple to see where you fall. A BMI below 18.5 is consistent with underweight. If your BMI is 25 or more, you are probably medically overweight, unless you are exceptionally muscular. A BMI of 30 defines medical obesity, and more than 40 is considered morbidly obese.

BMI (kg/m2) Height (in.)	19 Weight (lb.)	20	21	22	23	24	25	26	27	28	29	30	35	40
58	91	96	100	105	110	115	119	124	129	134	138	143	167	191
59	94	99	104	109	114	119	124	128	133	138	143	148	173	198
60	97	102	107	112	118	123	128	133	138	143	148	153	179	204
61	100	106	111	116	122	127	132	137	143	148	153	158	185	211
62	104	109	115	120	126	131	136	142	147	153	158	164	191	218
63	107	113	118	124	130	135	141	146	152	158	163	169	197	225
64	110	116	122	128	134	140	145	151	157	163	169	174	204	232
65	114	120	126	132	138	144	150	156	162	168	174	180	210	240
66	118	124	130	136	142	148	155	161	167	173	179	186	216	247
67	121	127	134	140	146	153	159	166	172	178	185	191	223	255
68	125	131	138	144	151	158	164	171	177	184	190	197	230	262
69	128	135	142	149	155	162	169	176	182	189	196	203	236	270
70	132	139	146	153	160	167	174	181	188	195	202	207	243	278
71	136	143	150	157	165	172	179	186	193	200	208	215	250	286
72	140	147	154	162	169	177	184	191	199	206	213	221	258	294
73	144	151	159	166	174	182	189	197	204	212	219	227	265	302
74	148	155	163	171	179	186	194	202	210	218	225	233	272	311
75	152	160	168	176	184	192	200	208	216	224	232	240	279	319
76	156	164	172	180	189	197	205	213	221	230	238	246	287	328

SARAH SAMAAN, MD, FACC

A Vanderbilt University Medical School graduate, Dr. Sarah Samaan is a board certified cardiologist, with additional board certifications in echocardiography and nuclear cardiology. She is also board certified in internal medicine which allows for key insight into the whole health of her patients.

Dr. Samaan considers heart disease prevention the cornerstone of her medical practice and works passionately to educate women on the message that heart disease prevention should be a life-long pursuit.

For the past three years, Texas Monthly magazine has named Dr. Samaan as a "Texas Super Doctor." She is a fellow of the American College of Cardiology and was listed as one of "America's Top Physicians," by Consumers' Research Council of America. In 2005, she was profiled in Medicine Men, a book celebrating notable Texas physicians. Dr. Samaan practices cardiology at Legacy Heart Center in Plano, Texas, near Dallas and at the Baylor Heart Hospital.

Away from work, Dr. Samaan's passion is horses. She enjoys dressage and cross country jumping, and stays fit with a regimen of running, weight training, and yoga.